# HUMANITY, FREEDOM AND FEMINISM

*For My Family*

# Humanity, Freedom and Feminism

JILL MARSHALL
*Queen Mary University of London, UK*

ASHGATE

Published by
Ashgate Publishing Limited
Gower House
Croft Road
Aldershot
Hants GU11 3HR
England

Ashgate Publishing Company
Suite 420
101 Cherry Street
Burlington, VT 05401-4405
USA

Ashgate website: http://www.ashgate.com

**British Library Cataloguing in Publication Data**
Humanity, freedom and feminism. - (Applied legal
    philosophy)
    1. Feminist theory 2. Women - Legal status, laws, etc.
    3. Human rights - Philosophy 4. Social values 5. Humanity
    6. Globalization - Social aspects
    I. Title
    305.4'2'01

**Library of Congress Cataloging-in-Publication Data**
Marshall, Jill, 1966-
    Humanity, freedom and feminism / by Jill Marshall.
        p. cm. -- (Applied legal philosophy)
    Includes bibliographical references and index.
    ISBN 0-7546-2562-1
    1. Feminist theory. 2. Feminist jurisprudence. 3. Feminism. 4. Women
(International law) I. Title. II. Series.

    HQ1190.M364 2005
    305.42--dc22

                                                                2005011818

ISBN 13: 978 0 7546 2562 9

Reprinted 2007

Printed and bound in Great Britain by MPG Books Ltd, Bodmin, Cornwall.

# Contents

*The fact that we are human beings is infinitely more important than all the peculiarities that distinguish human beings from one another.*
Simone de Beauvoir, *The Second Sex* (London: Jonathan Cape 1953; Vintage 1997) p. 737.

*Feminism has at its heart the demand that women be treated as free human beings.*
Drucilla Cornell, *At the Heart of Freedom: Feminism, Sex and Equality* (Princeton, New Jersey: Princeton University Press 1998) p. 20.

# Foreword

Jill Marshall's book is an important contribution to the revival of a sympathetic feminist engagement with liberal theory. Her argument is that liberalism contains as yet untapped potential for the articulation of an adequate feminist politics. In contrast to some postmodern and critical theories, but in common with the recent work of writers like Drucilla Cornell and Martha Nussbaum, she argues that a properly developed liberalism has two key advantages for the feminist project of realising the full humanity and improving the lives of women: its strong conception of subject-hood and agency; and its commitment to normative thinking as one pre-condition for social change. In the context of globalisation, liberalism's core commitment to common humanity has acquired, she argues, a new significance for the advancement of feminist values.

Drawing on an impressive range of sources, Marshall puts the case for a liberal individualism which places the social construction of personhood and autonomy at its core; for a revised conception of the public-private divide; for a conception of positive freedom, and of such freedom as founded in social as well as internal conditions of existence; and for a recognition of human interdependence. Focusing in particular on liberalism's humanism and universalism, she argues for a vision of human potential, and the freedom to develop this potential, as the core of liberalism, and further argues that such a vision is indispensable to feminism. Hence the incorporation of women as fully human subjects of liberal politics – a project of which much feminist theory over the last 30 years has been deeply sceptical – is in her view the agenda to which feminism needs to return.

In the course of setting out this agenda, Marshall also develops a challenging critique of the slippage in some political (including feminist) theory between empirical and normative arguments. And she maintains a consistent focus on social structures as a pre-condition for human freedom – a claim which is all too often ignored in political theory, feminist or otherwise, and which itself opens up a substantial research agenda. The practical upshot of her arguments is underlined by the final part of the book, in which she uses a case study which is informed by her analysis of the impact of globalisation. Taking recent developments in international human rights, humanitarian and criminal law dealing with sexual violence against women, Marshall argues that these developments are evidence of the continuing ethical and political potential of liberalism for women.

Marshall's cogent synthesis of existing arguments brings a fresh impetus to the important field of feminist legal and political theory. It deserves to find an appreciative audience.

Nicola Lacey FBA
Professor of Criminal Law and Legal Theory, London School of Economics

# Series Editor's Preface

The objective of the Applied Legal Philosophy series is to publish work which adopts a theoretical approach to the study of particular areas or aspects of law or deals with general theories of law in a way which focuses on issues of practical moral and political concern in specific legal contexts.

In recent years there has been an encouraging tendency for legal philosophers to utilize detailed knowledge of the substance and practicalities of law and a noteworthy development in the theoretical sophistication of much legal research. The series seeks to encourage these trends and to make available studies in law which are both genuinely philosophical in approach and at the same time based on appropriate legal knowledge and directed towards issues in the criticism and reform of actual laws and legal systems.

The series will include studies of all the main areas of law, presented in a manner which relates to the concerns of specialist legal academics and practitioners. Each book makes an original contribution to an area of legal study while being comprehensible to those engaged in a wide variety of disciplines. Their legal content is principally Anglo-American, but a wide-ranging comparative approach is encouraged and authors are drawn from a variety of jurisdictions.

Tom D. Campbell
Series Editor
Centre for Applied Philosophy and Public Ethics
Charles Sturt University, Canberra

# Preface and Acknowledgements

This book originated from my thoughts, ideas and research over a three year period at Queen Mary University of London. The use of the facilities and libraries at Queen Mary and various colleges of the University of London was invaluable.

I would like to thank various people for their assistance and support at different times throughout the project including those who have reviewed the book in different guises. Michael Lobban was kind enough to comment on very early drafts of what now forms Chapters 1 and 2. Eric Heinze has always been enthusiastic about the project, and provided many helpful and insightful comments on drafts, as well as help, support and friendship throughout the process. My colleague and friend Roy Gilbar and I spent many good times together debating, amongst other things, the relationship between the community and the individual. Particular thanks go to Katherine O'Donovan for her proactive support and belief in the project from its inception as thoughts and ideas and proposal, right through to the end product. Our meetings, her ongoing constructive comments and inspiration provided a catalyst and integral part of the work. My appreciation also extends to Richard Collier and Nicola Lacey for their thoughtful analysis, comments and examination of my research and their continued supportive and warm attitudes towards this work since its early stages. I would like to additionally thank Nicola Lacey for taking the time to read a near final draft of the book and for her generous foreword. Thanks to Tom Campbell and John Irwin for commissioning the book. Valerie Saunders, Helen Harvey and all the staff at Ashgate involved in the project, including of course, my editor Pam Bertram.

Finally, thanks to all my friends and family for listening to, and discussing with me, my ideas throughout the last four years.

# Introduction

*"What is a human being? Legal Theorists must, perforce, answer this question: jurisprudence, after all, is about human beings."* Robin West.[1]

In 1988, Robin West began her well-known article "Jurisprudence and Gender" by asking WHAT IS A HUMAN BEING?[2] She concluded that women are not human beings insofar as legal theory is concerned. Her question, and the contribution of feminist theory to the answer, forms a central theme to this work.

## Four Contentions

If the definition of a human being is central to jurisprudence, it is vital to uncover whether that definition adequately encompasses *all* human beings. Arguments are presented in this book that traditional Western conceptions of the human being have been inadequate in that they have failed to encompass all human beings. In some instances this is because of the inherent constitution of the definition, while in others, the problem arises from the way theories have been (mis)interpreted. However, it is possible to use these conceptions to form a more inclusive, universal conception of the human being or subject that can then be used to form the basic unit of philosophy, politics and law. As a fuller, more inclusive, conception of the human subject, it will lead to a better, more just, place for all to live on a global scale. With this underlying theme in mind, the book has four organising contentions.

The first relates to normative ethics and human flourishing. Work is investigated and arguments presented involving not just what people actually value now but seeking to address the normative question of what it is right or appropriate to value, and why.[3] Written from a feminist perspective, one of my aims is to make a contribution to the ethical question: what would be of moral importance in a post-patriarchal world; suggesting how traditional conceptions of the human subject need to change if they are to assist as guides in constructing a better place, and

---

[1] R West "Jurisprudence and Gender" (1988) 55 *University of Chicago Law Review* 1 at p 1. It is largely recognised that one of the main issues for law resides in its very conceptions of the human being and the social order which are presented as universal but which are in fact highly contested – see N Naffine and R Owens (eds) *Sexing the Subject of Law* (London: Sweet & Maxwell 1997) at p 29.
[2] R West, 1988. My emphasis.
[3] See E Frazer, J Hornsby and S Lovibond *Ethics: A Feminist Reader* (London: Blackwell 1992) Introduction.

way, to live.[4] Post-patriarchy means a move away from the patriarchal system that exists as a system of hierarchical power, oppressing and devaluing women and the feminine: definitions of the human which actually mean "man" contribute to that system. The ultimate concern is with making women's lives better. Women have been constrained and often oppressed by the hierarchical gender system that pervades all political and legal systems.[5] Ethics and morality must be concerned with all individuals or human beings – men and women – with their identity or subjectivity, including how that identity and consciousness is formed in this unjust and unfair system. For this reason, I concentrate on feminist critiques, insights, contributions and reconstructions of what it is to be a human being, with the aim that this will assist in leading to formulations of a better place to live.

Secondly, the position is taken that feminist theorising cannot evade the question of the normative foundations of theory and the necessity of the minimal criteria of validity. A feminist jurisprudential project should ask in what ways women's theories of being re-map forms of human flourishing.[6] The argument developed is that feminism is a necessarily normative project: creating alternative interpretations, envisioning different futures and possibilities and being concerned with women transforming their own identity and becoming empowered.[7] I therefore question those theorists who criticise any feminists (and others) for producing normative agenda. How such issues have caused problems for feminist legal theory, particularly in recent years, is examined. Feminists are interested in

---

[4] Patriarchy has been defined as "a system of male domination that involves the subordination of women. Patriarchy takes different forms in different societies and different historical periods. It interacts with other forms of oppression, such as class, race and sexuality, in very complex ways". C Johnson "Does Capitalism really need Patriarchy? Some Old Issues Reconsidered" *Women's Studies International Forum* Vol 19 No 3 1996 at 201.

[5] See, for example, United Nations *The World's Women 1995: Trends and Statistics* (New York: United Nations 1995); KD Askin and DM Koenig (eds) *Women and International Human Rights Law* (Ardsley NY: Transnational Publishers Inc) Vol 1 (1999), Vol 2 (2000), Vol 3 (2001), Vol 4 (2004); KD Askin *War Crimes Against Women* (Dordecht: Kluwer Law International 1997); J Gardam and M Jarvis *Women, Armed Conflict and International Law* (The Hague, London, Boston: Kluwer Law International 2001); H Charlesworth and C Chinkin *The Boundaries of International Law: a feminist analysis* (Manchester: Manchester University Press 2000); RJ Cook (ed) *Human Rights of Women* (Philadelphia: Pennsylvania Press 1994); S Fredman *Women and the Law* (Oxford: Clarendon Press 1997); MC Nussbaum "The Sleep of Reason…" *The Times Higher* 2 Feb 1996; Amnesty International's website lists 857 of their own documents alone on the human rights violations of women globally; see web.amnesty.org/library; see generally www.eoc.org.uk; Human Rights Watch *The Human Rights Watch Global Report on Women's Human Rights* (1995).

[6] In this respect see, for example, J E Grbich "The Body in Legal Theory" in M Fineman and N Thomadsen (eds) *At the Boundaries of Law: Feminism and Legal Theory* (New York and London: Routledge 1991).

[7] See A Phillips *Democracy and Difference* (Cambridge: Polity Press 1993) at p 113.

producing more just societies than those which already exist.[8] To produce such societies, it is my contention that the presence of *active* and *intentional* subjects is needed. The analysis in this regard involves examining aspects of the modernity-postmodernity debate. The position taken is that feminism constitutes a critique, as well as a defence, of modernity and has a great stake in this debate which is at heart about the possibility of a *subject* of social theory.[9] Feminists cannot embrace an unreconstructed modern subject or a postmodern rejection of the subject because women as subjects have not been accorded the coherence, autonomy, rationality or agency of the subject which forms the basis of an unreconstructed modernism and which postmodernism has deconstructed out of existence.[10] It is not only argued that normative foundations need to be sustained in feminist legal theory, but also that it is necessary to hold onto, and indeed strengthen, particularly for individual women, the idea of an active and intentional subject to do so.

Thirdly, although certain communitarian critiques have been useful, to some extent, in illuminating certain inconsistencies in liberal theory, it is shown that unless criteria that transcend the local are invoked, it is not possible to distinguish between *progressive* and *regressive* theories. Feminism has been described as a project redefining the relationship between the individual and society; seeking an integration of the individual and the collective in an ongoing process of authentic individualism and genuine connectedness.[11] Making demands for change will inevitably involve an explanation and arguments demonstrating why certain standards are used for judging existing social arrangements. Reliable theories are needed to explain the criteria used for accepting some social, political and legal practices while rejecting others.[12] In this context, the discourse of human rights, so prevalent in the world today, which necessarily flows from ideas of what it means to be human, and who is counted as human, provides an example of the instrumental use that can be made of certain legal concepts to assist human flourishing. In an international legal context particularly, it is essential to retain feminist politics to sustain the rights of women as humans (during war and conflicts, as well as situations in peace time). For legal claims to be made, a rights holder is needed, thus the retention of subjectivity and the sense particularly of women as subjects in their own right is essential. Accordingly, it is part of my argument that the "local" will need to be transcended in favour of ideas of common humanity and international human rights' standards, while being sensitive to the differences between all individual humans, including their cultural heritage, and

---

[8] J Conaghan "Reassessing the Feminist Theoretical Project in Law" 27 *Journal of Law and Society* (2000) Vol 3 351 maps this element within feminism. This is dealt with in Chapter 3.

[9] See B Marshall *Engendering Modernity: Feminism, Social Theory and Social Change* (Cambridge: Polity Press 1994).

[10] B Marshall, 1994, p 148.

[11] B Marshall, 1994, p 158.

[12] See I Barwell "Towards A Defence of Objectivity" in K Lennon and M Whitford (eds) *Knowing the Difference* (New York and London: Routledge 1994).

aiming to prevent the imposition of norms or standards that could be, or could be seen as, exclusionary.

Closely linked to that concept is my fourth. As the world gets smaller with the impact of information technology, global non-governmental organisations, the international economic and political community, world-wide terrorism and general globalisation issues, valuable work is being done to highlight human beings' shared humanity rather than irreconcilable differences in this global "community".[13] Global institutions are contributing to this process, not only by their very existence, but also through the policies and law applied through them. I look at the case law of the International Criminal Tribunal for the Former Yugoslavia (the ICTY) in relation to rape and sexual violence in this context.[14]

## The Importance of Freedom

These four contentions are highlighted throughout this work, showing their development and expansion through the increase of individual freedom and a more consistent expression of the ideals of egalitarian liberalism.

To live freely, women need a strong sense of self or subjectivity to be empowered to plan their own projects. This strong subjectivity is developed through the use of imagination or critical consciousness, then through discourse with others, being listened to and acknowledged, while at the same time changes to external structures are needed. Feminists want to free women to shape their own lives, and form their own self-definitions, rather than simply accepting pre-existing definitions given to them by others.[15] Feminists therefore need a language of freedom with which to express the value underlying this concern. Freedom is the goal of women as it enables them to live more worthwhile lives.

The position is taken that in the formation of human beings' sense of selfhood their environment is crucial and thus it is imperative that a certain type of environment and society be encouraged to thrive. The constitutiveness of the individual in a network of social relations is combined with the value of self-determination. As individual consciousness is created in large part by the social

---

[13] See, for example, R Falk *Law in An Emerging Global Village: A Post-Westphalian Perspective* (Ardsley, New York: Transnational Publishers Inc 1998); B Holden (ed) *Global Democracy: Key Debates* (New York and London: Routledge 2000); N Dower and J Williams (eds) *Global Citizenship: A Critical Reader* (Edinburgh: Edinburgh University Press 2002); T Dunne and NJ Wheeler (eds) *Human Rights in Global Politics* (Cambridge: Cambridge University Press 1999); F Robinson *Globalizing Care: Ethics, Feminist Theory and International Relations* (Colorado and Oxford: Westview Press 1999); T Franck *Fairness in International Law and Institutions* (Oxford: Clarendon Press 1995); TW Pogge (ed) *Global Justice* (Oxford: Blackwell Publishing 2001); R Brownsword (ed) *Global Governance and the Quest for Justice* Vol 4 (Oxford: Hart 2004).

[14] S C Res 827 (25 May 1993) establishing the International Criminal Tribunal for the former Yugoslavia.

[15] See J Nedelsky "Reconceiving Autonomy: Sources, Thoughts and Possibilities" (1989) 1 *Yale Journal of Law and Feminism* 7 at p 8.

conditions in which people find themselves, and when born and growing up most have little or no choice as to these social conditions, it is important that feminist legal theory retains an idea that these social conditions allow for the development of a consciousness that will increase the freedom of every human being. A person's consciousness, in turn the choices made, and its context in surrounding social conditions are therefore fundamentally connected. It is shown that social conditions which encourage such consciousness to develop will be found in a society based on care, love and empathy, interdependency and the mutual recognition of each individual as a fully free subject. External structures, including international law and international institutions and courts, will form a part of those conditions.

Such conditions will lead to ideas of a more inclusive conception of the human subject which involves treating everyone as a free human being. Such treatment will, in turn, lead to a fairer, more just world and a better foundation for human flourishing. Human beings need the freedom to decide on their own plan of life, rather than it being imposed on them, as in doing so, they engage in a uniquely human experience that expresses their moral dignity and worth. The aim is to create social, political and legal structures that assist all individuals in their search for a flourishing life. In this respect, therefore it is possible to say that all human beings share a common potentiality to develop and grow as persons. This potentiality is something that all humanity has in common and which should be encouraged to progressively develop. Such a conception of the human subject does not involve ideas of a "common essence" in that it is not the unified, unchanging subject often presented and critiqued as the subject of Western philosophical, political and legal thought. Instead, it leads to a claim to the possibility of an ever-changing, unfixed personhood, with a corresponding right to be treated as an end and not an instrument of others, not to be categorised according to someone else's imposed view of how one ought to behave or live because as an individual human subject there exists the potentiality to develop and grow and make real choices for oneself. It is argued that gendered identity, as currently existing in hierarchical patriarchal structures, is socially constructed, and restricts the freedom of women by preventing them from living a free existence.

The conception of the human subject presented is one that develops, flourishes and is protected most when the ideals of egalitarian liberalism are embodied in the legal and political system. This is different from existing liberal states which do not currently enshrine these ideals of liberalism. Feminist analyses, critiques and reconstructions of the human being or subject made by "second wave" feminists are examined.[16] Focus is placed on feminist work that critiques the Western philosophical tradition, in particular liberalism, and some time is spent analysing the issues surrounding feminist critiques of the liberal individual. When certain feminists critique liberalism, a common occurrence during the 1980s in

---

[16] The "second wave" is traditionally considered to be from the 1960s onwards. The first wave of feminism is usually considered to run through the 19th century and end in the early 20th century suffrage movement – see J Mitchell and A Oakley *What is Feminism?* (Oxford: Basil Blackwell 1986).

particular, they often produce a "straw man" of liberalism, highlighting the worst qualities within it, and ignoring other aspects of the rich and varied liberal tradition, particularly the positive, social welfare liberal tradition of, for example, LT Hobhouse and TH Green.[17] In feminist critiques of liberalism, classic liberalism has been the main focus. Further, often the critiques fail to convince that they are arguing for anything other than a *fuller expression* of the liberal tradition, usually retaining concepts of freedom and equality of the individual human being. This aspect of such critiques is explored.

The focus on the feminist critiques of liberalism further highlights how many of these critiques centre around the allegation that liberals say all individuals are equal and should be treated normatively as free and equal. Yet, at the same time, many feminists argue that this is what feminism is all about. Liberalism began as an emancipatory project which expressed the radical moral belief in the equal and intrinsic worth of each individual. Further, the freedom of the individual is the most important liberal value.[18] As freedom is the most important liberal value and liberalism's central belief rests on the intrinsic dignity and equal worth of each individual, inevitably the interaction between individuals will be fundamental. If each individual in liberal theory is an end in themselves, it is an important question how limitations can be put or imposed on what people can do in society without impinging on others' freedom and thus potentially using some people as means to others' own ends rather than as ends in themselves.[19]

The relationship between feminism and liberalism has been described as close but complex.[20] The roots of both lie in the emergence of individualism as a general theory of social life – both need some conception of individuals as free and equal beings, emancipated from the ascribed, hierarchical bonds of traditional society. Feminism has sometimes been presented as the completion of the liberal revolution – an extension of liberal principles and rights to women as well as men.[21] However, according to many feminists, such attempts to universalise liberalism have far-reaching consequences because in the end, they challenge liberalism itself.[22] It is argued here that there is still much to be gained from liberal theory, particularly at the international level, and that feminism is an expression of

---

[17] See LT Hobhouse *Liberalisms* (New York and Oxford: Oxford University Press 1964); TH Green *Lectures on the Principles of Political Obligation* (London: Longmans, Green 1895).

[18] See M Ramsay *What's Wrong with Liberalism?* (London: Leicester University Press 1987) at p. 7 and p. 17.

[19] A Kantian notion: see I Kant *Fundamental Principles of the Metaphysic of Morals* (New York: Prometheus Books 1988).

[20] C Pateman "Feminist Critiques of the Public/Private Dichotomy" in A Phillips (ed) *Feminism and Equality* (Oxford: Basil Blackwell 1987) at p. 103.

[21] C Pateman, 1987.

[22] C Pateman, 1987; Z Eisenstein *The Radical Future of Liberal Feminism* (NY: Longman 1981); E Frazer and N Lacey *The Politics of the Community: A Feminist Critique of the Liberal-communitarian debate* (Hemel Hempstead: Harvester 1993); N Lacey *Unspeakable Subjects: Feminist Essays in Legal and Social Theory* (Oxford: Hart Publishing 1998).

the basic tenets of liberalism – that every human being should be treated as free and equal.[23]

The issue is also raised that liberal theory underpins Western political and legal structures in contemporary society, and has increasingly spread throughout the world following the fall of communism in Eastern Europe and the former Soviet Union. This is particularly noticeable in the field of international law, the work of the United Nations and the forces of globalisation.[24]

## The Structure of *Humanity, Freedom and Feminism*

The book has three parts. Part I, consisting of an Introduction and the following three chapters, presents a thematic intellectual history of how second wave feminist legal theory critiqued existing conceptions of the human subject, finding them based on male experiences while being presented as the "human" norm. It examines how some feminists then looked for an inclusive human subject while others argue for a separate woman-centred subject and still others argue for the deconstruction of the subject. Part I sets out the theorists' arguments, objections to arguments and then my counter-arguments, often aiming to use the arguments of those theorists critiqued to realise their own ideas more fully.

In Chapter 1, I show how feminists critiqued existing conceptions of the human subject to see if these conceptions included women; asking who the individual is at the heart of Western philosophy. I show how they uncovered the paradigm of the human to be male. Included within this Chapter are feminist critiques of the nature of what it means to be human, the "man" of reason, transcendence and reason as achievement.

While some feminists sought to include women in the definition of the universal human being or subject, I also examine those feminists who began to question the standards by which moral subjectivity is judged. The debate between this type of feminism and the type which tried to include women within the universal subject is often described as the "sameness/difference" debate. In Chapter 2, the universal and abstract reasoning method of liberalism, often using social contract theory, is examined from the perspective of critiques by communitarians and ethic of care theorists. In this context, claims of the presentation of the liberal individual as radically possessive, atomistic and aprioristic, seemingly exclusionary of the dependency of human beings on social context, is critiqued. In particular, the work of Carol Gilligan and Robin West is

---

[23] In the same way as it has been argued that socialism is an extension of liberalism but is obviously not liberalism, so feminism can be seen as an extension of liberalism. However, some have difficulty incorporating it into the definition of liberalism as currently understood.

[24] Indeed, I argue that international law is largely governed by liberal philosophy. This is perhaps seen most obviously in the United Nations, international law and liberal globalisation. This is one of the reasons why I have concentrated on the individual and the human being that comes from this tradition.

analysed, showing how there are a range of problems, particularly relating to charges of "essentialism", and critiques around the idealised female or feminine subject of some types of feminist legal theory. Time is then spent looking at how feminists turned elements of the alternative "woman-centred" subject into aspects of a more inclusive humanist "relational" subject, a point developed later in Part II.

The influence of certain strains of postmodern theory on feminist legal thought is then analysed in Chapter 3. Focus rests on the postmodern deconstruction of the universal subject. The postmodern deconstruction of the subject *on its own* is argued to be destructive to feminist normative agenda and feminist politics. What is needed instead is a retention of normativity which is linked to the idea of humans as active and intentional subjects.

This examination, analysis and critique in Part I of these aspects of feminist theory from my perspective of their impact on the human being, is developed in Part II which begins with an Introduction, followed by Chapters 4 and 5. Here, my own arguments are set out on individual subjectivity and freedom.

Retaining normativity and active intentional subjects and their connection with individuals' freedom is dealt with in Chapters 4 and 5. Instead of women's subjectivity simply being deconstructed, it needs to be reconstructed to increase individual freedom, strengthening a woman's sense of her own subjectivity and thus her ability to freely choose and determine for herself her own life plan.

The idea of positive freedom is presented, allowing for freely determined choices and preferences in a caring reciprocal environment with such an environment creating, developing and sustaining a new, more inclusive, conception of the human being which will assist in global improvements and reconnecting feminist legal theory to a normative agenda. I concentrate on a mixture of Hegelian ethics, freedom and critical theory, arguing that a conception of the human being which takes on board many of the "relational" feminist insights about existing conceptions of the human being, combined with Hegelian intersubjectivity and a search for positive freedom, will lead to a fairer, more just, ethical (feminist) world. This involves an analysis of freedom, a brief overview of the negative/positive freedom debate; the shaping of desires and preferences and internal obstacles to freedom.

In Part III, these ideas are placed in a global context showing how they can lead to a fairer, more just, world where human rights violations would be minimised as individual well-being is increased in a new global order. In Chapter 6, links are made between the failure of the concept of the human being to encompass women and the male-based features of the human on which international human rights and international humanitarian law are based. In Chapter 7, analysis is given of some existing aspects of these "external structures", particularly the jurisprudence of the ICTY on rape and sexual violence. This external structure of law is shown to be able to assist in increasing human freedom by empowering humans as rights holders so that women, just as much as men, will be able to claim that their individual rights have been violated and know that their claims will be taken just as seriously as men's.

The retention of an active and intentional subject is of particular importance in the field of international human rights and humanitarian law where the concept of women as subjects who are rights holders is necessary. Deconstructing that concept out of existence precludes any idea of meaningful women's rights as human rights. There is a need also to retain a sense of wrongness and rightness and violation by a wrongdoer. In this context, provisions of international humanitarian law relating to rape and sexual violence victims are examined. This examination shows how the laws fail to protect women as individual subjects in their own right, concentrating as they do on women's relationships with others and the protection of their (and their families') honour. The argument is that as conceptions of the human being at a philosophical level have inadequately included women, so the conception of the human in international human rights and humanitarian law fails to treat women as ends in themselves, as subjects in their own right. Instead, these laws have viewed women as objects or property or in need of special protection as deficient human beings. Treating women instead as full human subjects and human rights violations to women as human rights violations will assist in developing a fuller more inclusive conception of the human. At an international level in particular, this should assist women by making their lives better.

In the ICTY case study, analysis involves looking at rape and sexual violence as war crimes, grave breaches of international law and as crimes against humanity. This jurisprudence shows that attitudes are changing. The case study shows how an international court has interpreted its statutory provisions and customary international law in a way that ensures that sexual crimes against women are not marginalised but are dealt with to include women as full human subjects, as individuals in their own right, to be accorded rights as human beings who should not be tortured and inhumanely treated. The Chapter ends with a positive hope that the new International Criminal Court will continue to develop the jurisprudence in this way. The book ends with a concluding hope.

# PART I
# FEMINIST ANALYSIS OF
# THE HUMAN

# Introduction to Part I

*"Feminists are centrally concerned with freeing women to shape our own lives, to define who we (each) are, rather than accepting the definition given to us by others (men and male-dominated society, in particular)."* Jennifer Nedelsky[1]

A thematic analysis is presented in Part I of second wave feminist critiques of the human being that certain feminists saw presented by classic Western philosophers and, in particular, presented by liberal theorists, upon which the individual of legal and political thought was built.[2] My interpretation of those feminist critiques is that they seek to show if, and if so how, and why, certain Western philosophers had excluded women from their definitions or conceptions of the human being.[3] My purpose here is to highlight the main and recurring themes identified in such critiques which include characteristics said by classic Western philosophy to be vital to inclusion within the definition of "human". Analysis of these characteristics shows that often such a definition represents a certain type of male experience and is therefore exclusionary. The question then arises as to whether there is something inherently within the concept of human subjectivity itself which is exclusionary or whether it can be reconceptualised to be inclusive of women and all humanity so that the word "human" and expressions "human subject" and "human nature" can

---

[1] J Nedelsky, 1989, p 8.

[2] Reference is made to various Western philosophical writings in such critiques, including Plato *The Republic* (Harmondsworth: Penguin Books Ltd 1987); *The Laws* (Loeb Classical Library 1968); Aristotle *The Nichomachean Ethics* (New York and Oxford: Oxford University Press 1986); T Hobbes *Leviathan* (1651: M Oakeshott edn Oxford: Basil Blackwell 1960); JJ Rousseau *Emile* and *The Social Contract* see *The Essential Rousseau* (L Bair trans. New York and Scarborough Ontario: The New American Library Inc 1974); J Locke *Two Treatises of Government* (Cambridge: Cambridge University Press 1988); I Kant, 1988; GW Hegel *Phenomenology of Spirit* (AV Miller trans. Oxford: Oxford University Press 1977). See the following footnote for references to the main feminist critiques.

[3] The most comprehensive and one of the earliest contributions in this area is SM Okin *Women in Western Political Thought* (Princeton, New Jersey: Princeton University Press 1979): Okin examines in turn, and in detail, certain works by Plato, Aristotle, Rousseau and Mill. See also G Lloyd *The Man of Reason: Male and Female in Western Philosophy* (London: Methuen 1984); C Pateman *The Sexual Contract* (Cambridge: Polity Press 1988); A Jaggar *Feminist Politics and Human Nature* (Totowa NJ: Rowman and Allanheld 1983) and C Pateman and E Gross (eds) *Feminist Challenges: Social and political theory* (London: Allen and Unwin 1986); SM Okin *Justice, Gender and the Family* (New York: Basic Books 1989); LM Antony and CE Witt (eds) *A Mind of One's Own: Feminist Essays on Reason and Objectivity* (2nd Edn) (Boulder, Colorado and Oxford: Westview Press 2002).

mean something of value to women. In particular, can a deeper conception of the human being be reconceived to provide for a fuller, more flourishing, ethically better, life; an improved, and more plausible, feminist legal theory, and a retention of a shared universal common humanity?

Analysis in this Part identifies and deals with the overarching themes of the capacity for reason, transcendence and universality which Western philosophers emphasised as the essential component of human "nature". Although there is a certain degree of overlap, these elements show how women have arguably been excluded from certain philosophers' conceptions of the human being. Many feminist critiques succeed in showing how this "nature" contains constituents and characteristics based on particular types of human being but yet was then universalised and presented as the human norm or standard, purportedly representative of the whole of the human species to which all should live, thereby being biased against women.[4] This "particular type" had a "male nature".[5] Second wave feminist scholars reveal much misogyny and sexism in many classic writings, often arising from a lack of imaginative input by those authors to follow through often enlightened theories to their rationally logical conclusions.

Sometimes, women's characteristics (as seen by the classic theorists), often described as "women's nature", explicitly excluded women from membership (as a social group) of the category or definition of human being. Indeed, some feminists argue that the definition of a human being or man presented by the Western tradition *depends on* the lesser definition of woman or the feminine as *the other*. Part I therefore also examines what were seen to be the components of women's "nature" and her "proper place", and how these often precluded her inclusion in the definition of the human being in the classic texts as analysed by second wave feminists.

As part of my analysis of those feminists who critiqued Western philosophers for doing this, I also examine the contribution of the feminist ethic of care theorists and cultural feminists who seek to acknowledge and to valorise a different moral voice many see as belonging to women.[6] This work has been influential in feminist legal theory in seeking to celebrate women's differences from men and often arguing for a "different voice" identified as correlating to the female gender, to be heard, recognised and used, alongside the "male voice" which it is argued is already present and dominant within social, political and legal systems. This is analysed in the context of the themes I have identified as essential to human "nature" according to Western philosophical thought.

---

[4] This is not to say that it was not biased against certain types of men. However, this point is beyond the scope of this book.

[5] One response was to declare that the whole tainted heritage must be rejected and that feminist theorists must make a new start. But like C Pateman and E Gross (1986), I think it is impossible to completely turn our backs on classics – all modes of discourse reflect and are implicated in the past.

[6] As particularly represented in the work of C Gilligan *In a Different Voice: psychological theory and women's development* (London: Harvard University Press 1982).

Some classic theorists analysed by second wave feminists had presented conceptions of the human being which did not explicitly exclude women from its membership *in theory*. However, *in practical terms*, when the social role of women was taken into account, it was clear that it was harder, and perhaps virtually impossible, for women to be included. The analysis here thus highlights the dichotomy between the aspiration for transcendence and universalisation in the Western philosophical tradition's "ideal person" and the concrete, real, empirical experiences of men and women, and how that led to the privileging of a particular type of (empirical) person being representative of all humankind in the "ideal" version.

In many of the feminist works examined, the importance of retaining the idea of the human subject is asserted, with women's emancipation being sought through access to participation in the existing world and in its transformation to fully realise human equality.[7] The emphasis lies on highlighting "woman's" exclusion but seeking her inclusion as a universal subject.

At the same time, the ability of the existing tradition of political philosophy to sustain the inclusion of women in its subject matter is questioned.[8] For example, it is queried whether the philosophers' arguments about the nature of women and their proper place in the social and political order will help in understanding why the formal political enfranchisement of women has not led to substantial equality between the sexes.[9] When aiming to attain justice, it is relevant and important to ask *who is being included* in the debate or distribution. If women are *excluded* from the definition of the human being – a prerequisite to being a party to the debate or a distribution of resources amongst persons – this will obviously cause severe problems for women's liberation.

However, while much of these feminist critiques prove invaluable, certain elements presented by various Western philosophers are shown to have been glossed over by these critiques, with liberalism in particular often being presented in its least attractive and unrepresentative, "straw man" way. Increasingly, such critiques lead to unconvincing and unhelpful conclusions, arguably taking feminist theory in a direction destructive to feminist agenda for change.

This is evident in movements away from including women within a conception of a universal human subject. Such movements are in the direction of presenting a separate "woman-centred" subject and then away from both a universal or "woman-centred" subject to a fragmented, un-unified, non-existent subject by certain postmodern feminists. The latter query the "essentialism" in the other two approaches and the exclusionary potential of presenting as a standard or norm one type of subjectivity. Their deconstruction can lead to an increasing reluctance to form any normative agenda for change, inertia and often threatens feminist political progress.

---

[7] See I Whelehan *Modern Feminist Thought* (Englewood Cliffs NJ: Edinburgh Hall 1995) at p 104, 120, 138.
[8] SM Okin 1979.
[9] SM Okin 1979, p 4 and 6. Okin points out that in Kant's writings, for example, even the words "persons" "human" and "rational" do not necessarily include women.

The elements are dealt with sequentially in Chapters 1 to 3. Firstly, the "man" of reason and ideas of transcendence are contrasted with the "natural" role of women as reproducers, said to have a specific role within the family, and the idea of women having a separate nature. This analysis looks at feminist critiques of (male) Western thought, and feminists who argue for the inclusion of women as capable of reason, with the hindrance to women's advancement of that capacity being lack of opportunities and possibilities for the achievement of projects. In this context, the feminist critique of the division between public and private spheres is also explored. Then feminist analysis of universality and views that men and women do have different "separate natures" is examined.

Secondly, the methodology of many liberal philosophers using ideas of a "state of nature" and "social contract" is analysed. Based on the idea of the primacy of the individual as moral agent, many feminist and communitarian thinkers critique what they see as liberalism's presentation of humans as possessive individuals.

Thirdly and finally, questioning any idea of the human subject having an essential nature, either as universal of all humanity or as idealising women's "nature", postmodern feminism deconstructs the human subject, offering some interesting insights but which are ultimately self-destructive to feminist politics.

# Chapter 1

# Reason and Humanity

*"The principle which regulates the existing social relations between the two sexes – the legal subordination of one sex to the other – is wrong in itself, and now one of the chief hindrances to human improvement; ...it ought to be replaced by a principle of perfect equality, admitting no power or privilege on the one side, nor disability on the other".* John Stuart Mill[1]

## Denying Women Opportunities to Develop their Reason

Throughout the history of Western philosophy, one of the most important components to possess in order to be considered a human is the capacity for reason.

Second wave feminists had much to say about "reason" as the necessary component of human nature or subjectivity and how it impacted on women.[2] Although philosophers and theories throughout history are analysed, and often re-interpreted, by second wave feminists, those concentrated on include Plato and Aristotle, Descartes, Hobbes and Kant and the general tenets of liberalism. The assumption that all individuals have an equal capacity for reason has been described as the basis of liberalism's central moral belief: the intrinsic and ultimate value of the human individual. This conception of human nature therefore sets the terms of liberal political theory.[3]

The capacity for reason was incorporated into the Western understanding of what it is to be a human being, with the common *essence* that all are equally said to have being the capacity for moral agency. The idea of reason has been described as founding (in Western philosophical thought) the basis for character ideals when working out the priorities of the good, well-lived life.[4]

In terms of the Western philosophers critiqued, feminists accurately highlight that Plato, writing circa 400 BC regards elite men and women as having the *same nature*.[5] Setting out his theory of an ideal utopian society in *The Republic*, Plato states that the male and female guardians chosen to rule the ideal society

---

[1] JS Mill *The Subjection of Women* in *On Liberty and Other Essays* (New York and Oxford: Oxford University Press 1991) at p 471.
[2] See references listed in note 3, Introduction to Part I.
[3] A Jaggar, 1983, at ch 3.
[4] A Jaggar, 1983.
[5] SM Okin 1979 and LM Antony and CE Witt (eds), 2002.

have the same nature.[6] Plato considered women as potentially individual citizens, as persons without a preordained and all encompassing "function" in life.[7] But in this work, the family and private property do not exist and those men and women live in a utopian ideal society.

Plato's writings reveal ambiguities and inconsistencies as to his views on women but it is clear that he sees no reason why qualities regarded as "natural" cannot be altered because it is only convention and the social environment that makes these appear "natural". There is no such fixed quality as "female nature", it is what different societies have made it. The only "natural" difference in the guardian class is their roles in procreation. The guardian women may be able and allowed to become pregnant but once their babies are born, these are removed from their biological mother and father and brought up in communal nurseries, never knowing the identity of their biological parents.[8]

However, in Plato's *The Laws*, a treatise on how to reform the existing state rather than set out an idealised state, the family and private property are reintroduced.[9] Correspondingly, "woman" is seen as a privately owned appendage of a man: family, and its needs, define her function.[10] Her socialisation must ensure that she is formed and preserved in accordance with this role and it is then *seen as* natural.[11]

Second wave feminist critiques which highlight this aspect of Plato, particularly that made by Susan Moller Okin, illustrate how Plato fails to follow through his own ideas to their logical conclusion. Plato could have stressed his own original idea expressed in *The Republic* of all human beings' (men's and women's) "human nature" being formed by convention and social environment rather than something intrinsically different between the two and unchanging within them. This would have allowed women to be free through aiming for different social environments coming into existence rather than a version of the family where women are men's property. So although Plato's views on women as human beings are inadequate, it is simply because they are illogically developed. Using his own argument, Plato could and should have argued for the freedom of

---

[6] Plato *The Republic* , 1987.

[7] Plato *The Republic* Book V, and SM Okin 1979, p 233. Okin cites this, in a sympathetic reading of Plato, as one of the very few instances in the history of thought when the biological implications of femaleness have been clearly separated out from all the conventional institutional and emotional baggage that has usually been identified with them at p 41 and 65.

[8] Plato, 1987.

[9] Plato *The Laws*, 1968.

[10] The tension between reforms in existing worlds and idealising a future one that can be seen in these works is a central feature of feminist legal theory. Some reviews of the problem can be seen in R Sandland "Seeing Double? Or why 'To be or not to be' is (not) the question for feminist legal studies" (1998) 7 *Social and Legal Studies* 307; N Lacey, (1998) and N Lacey "Violence, Ethics and Law: Feminist Reflections on a Familiar Dilemma" in S James and S Palmer (eds) *Visible Women* (Oxford and Portland Oregon: Hart Publishing 2002) at p 117ff.

[11] See SM Okin 1979, p 67–70.

women to be developed to allow them to be full human beings by recommending changes to the structure of the family and social environment in existence.

Plato's student, Aristotle, the standard-bearer for, and foundation of, much present-day philosophical, political and legal thought, is presented by some feminists critiques as one of the worst culprits for emphasising the "natural" role of women.[12] His view of human nature rests on biology. In his philosophy, the essential character of a thing is derived from its function and women's primary function according to him is reproduction. This aspect of Aristotle's thought shows that he classifies the female as a deformity: the first deviation in nature is *"when a female is formed instead of a male"*.[13]

Criticisms have been made of Aristotle's use of circular reasoning. He perceives woman as an instrument; he then assigns her an entirely separate scale of values and measures her against the scale of male values and, not surprisingly, finds her inferior.[14] The legacy of this aspect of Aristotelian thought pervades discussions of the subject of women through to contemporary society. Women's nature and their proper position and rights in society have been described as predominantly *functionalist* meaning that women are seen as performing functions in relation to men (in other words are means to men's ends or are instrumental to men's lives).[15] It is assumed that the male-headed nuclear family and women's traditional role within it are not only needed but are *natural*.

Unlike Plato's views, Aristotle's presentation of the different, meaning deviant, nature of women, make it extremely difficult to argue that changes in existing social structures will lead to equality. If most people think that the subordinate role assigned to women is "natural" as a consequence of their reproductive capacities, then there will be a reluctance to change, or be seen to be little point in changing, such social structures. Feminist critiques accurately pinpoint crucial aspects to perceptions of women's "nature" that adversely impact on the lives of women.[16] The ill-founded and dangerous elements of what is seen as "natural" in the role of women reappear at various points throughout this book.

---

[12] Okin 1979, p 79–83. Although also critical of Aristotle's biologically based sexism, for a more sympathetic reading of him see ML Homiak "Feminism and Aristotle's Rational Ideal" in LM Antony and CE Witt, 2002, p 3–20; see also J Richardson *Selves, Persons, Individuals: Philosophical Perspectives on Women and Legal Obligations* (Aldershot: Ashgate 2004) at p 38.

[13] Okin 1979, citing and quoting Aristotle at p 82. See also G Lloyd, 1984, p 36 in the context of Aquinas's interpretation of Aristotle.

[14] Okin 1979. A similar point is made by CA MacKinnon in relation to current liberal society and liberal legalism – based on Aristotelian concepts of equality: CA MacKinnon *Toward a Feminist Theory of the State* (Cambridge, Mass. and London: Harvard University Press 1989). Analysis of certain aspects of MacKinnon's work is presented in Chapter 5. Okin shows that Rousseau viewed women in a similarly functional way, again because their "nature" was more attuned to natural life, the senses and reproduction.

[15] Okin 1979.

[16] Okin 1979; Lloyd, 1984.

Moving on to the early modern period, things might be expected to improve, given that the emphasis moves to viewing the human being as a separate individual entity.

The emergence of the importance of the individual and the emphasis on individual human subjects as the prime units of Western political and legal thought is, historically speaking, a modern phenomenon. A shift from a hierarchical society based on customary status to an equal society based on personally chosen contracts is described as having taken place from the medieval to the modern period.[17] This is shown in the loosening of family ties and the gradual emergence of the autonomous modern individual or person, exemplified in the theories of one of the founders of modernity, Thomas Hobbes.

The idea presented in Hobbes's social contract theory is that human beings are first solitary, but equal and free, in a state of nature. Because they are equal and free, they will conflict with each other and the state of nature thus equates to a state of war. Hobbesian human beings only form together in a contractual way because of the benefits they obtain in return, ultimately to ensure their own self-preservation.[18]

Although the truth of this shift from hierarchical to contractual society as a factual progression is doubted by many, and has been described instead as a fiction, it still contains the overarching ideal of *liberation*: of a social movement and of aiming to *attain human freedom* and dignity. It is therefore undoubtedly normative, if perhaps only loosely descriptive.[19] It is in the context of this historical progression of the emergent individual human being seeking freedom and dignity that many Western philosophers were writing, who were then subsequently critiqued by second wave feminists.

Here is a philosophy that starts with an abstract individual view of human nature: all are born free and equal in the state of nature. The idea of a pre-social, atomised, unsituated or decontextualised individual is introduced.[20] Thomas

---

[17] See N Naffine "The Legal Structure of Self-Ownership: Or the Self-Possessed Man and the Woman Possessed" (1998) 25 *Journal of Law and Society* 193 at p 195, citing Sir Henry Maine.

[18] T Hobbes, 1651. The greatest benefit is self-preservation, security and order, all of which are missing in the state of nature where "man" is constantly under threat from other hostile individuals and where life is *"solitary, poor, nasty, brutish and short."*

[19] N Naffine, 1998, p 196. The historical truth or not of this progression is not examined further here as my concern lies with its symbolic impact and normative force. However, when talking about the autonomous modern "person", it should be borne in mind that it was not until 1929 that the Privy Council finally admitted that women were "persons" in the eyes of the law: see A Sachs and J Hoff Wilson *Sexism and the Law: A Study of Male Beliefs in Britain and the United States* (Oxford: Martin Robertson 1978) at p 38 and 40. For a more sympathetic reading of this lack of personhood see S Wolfram "Husband and Wife are one person: the husband (Nineteenth century English aphorism)" in A J Arnaud and E Kingdom (eds) *Women's Rights and the Rights of Man* (Aberdeen: Aberdeen University Press 1990).

[20] See generally B Redhead (ed) *Plato to Nato: Studies in Political Thought* (London: Penguin Books 1995); M Forsyth and M Keens-Soper *The Political Classics: A Guide to the Essential Texts from Plato to Rousseau* (Oxford: Oxford University Press 1988). See

Hobbes therefore claims original equality between all in the state of nature. A revolutionary idea in the 1600s, this claims such equality not just for all men regardless of class or colour, but for all men and women.[21] However, this does not translate into freedom and equality in the social contract that is then formed between all members of society to ensure self-preservation.[22] It is claimed that, like most liberal thinkers since, Hobbes justified women's exclusion from political life and their inequality in society by substituting the male-headed family for the individual as his primary subject matter.[23] He presents the view that once formed into society, women are somehow "naturally" inclined to reproduce and look after children and household, nurturing their family.[24]

Similarly, another classic theorist, John Locke presents men and women as equals for some purposes but then, inconsistently, appeals to "nature" to legitimise women's subordination to men.[25] The fundamental subject matter of Locke's political philosophy is again the male-headed family, failing to follow through his critique of state patriarchy to its logical conclusion.[26]

---

critiques by C Taylor "Atomism" in S Avineri and A de-Shalit (eds) *Communitarianism and Individualism* (Oxford: Oxford University Press 1992); M Sandel *Liberalism and the Limits of Justice* (2nd Edn: Cambridge: Cambridge University Press 1982, 1998); A Jaggar, 1983; N Lacey, 1998. I expand on this aspect of human "nature" in Chapter 2.

[21] T Hobbes, 1651. Jonathan Wolff describes how the mother is given rights of dominion over her child in the state of nature. See J Wolff *An Introduction to Political Philosophy* (Oxford: Oxford University Press 1996) at p 216. See J Pietarinen "Early Liberalism and Women's Liberty" in A-J Arnaud and E Kingdom, 1990, at Chapter 12; C Pateman "God Hath Ordained to Man a Helper: Hobbes, Patriarchy and Conjugal Rights" in ML Shanley and C Pateman *Feminist Interpretations and Political Theory* (Cambridge: Polity Press 1991) at p 59; C Pateman , 1988; SM Okin 1979.

[22] See C Pateman, 1988, for a critique of social contract theory from a feminist perspective: see in particular p 44–50 on Hobbes. See also analysis of Pateman in J Richardson, 2004, at chapter 5; K Hutchings *Hegel and Feminist Philosophy* (Cambridge: Polity Press 2003) at chapter 6.

[23] SM Okin 1979. While it may be contested that Hobbes is a liberal, whether or not he is, he certainly is the precursor of liberal individualism with his starting point of individual freedom and equality in the state of nature. For example, CB Macpherson *The Political Theory of Possessive Individualism*: *Hobbes to Locke* (1962) recognises that Hobbes's theory of monarchy is not liberal but argues individualism that influenced subsequent theory starts with Hobbes.

[24] Okin 1979, p 99. Okin thinks this is paradoxical since the tradition of which Hobbes is the founder is supposedly defined by its founding of politics on the characteristics and rights of individual atomistic human beings, renunciation of natural hierarchies or groups as the fundamental entities with which politics has to deal – at p 199.

[25] J Locke, 1988.

[26] Okin 1979, p 200–1. See also Melissa Butler "Early Liberal Roots of Feminism: John Locke and the Attack on Patriarchy" in ML Shanley and C Pateman (eds), 1991: M Butler's analysis shows a sympathetic reading of Locke. In her view, although his feminist sympathies certainly did not approach the later feminism of JS Mill, in view of the intense patriarchalism of 17th century England, she believes it would be surprising to find such views expressed at all.

Although the individualist rhetoric of early modernity held out hope for women, it therefore ended up transferring women to the private "natural" sphere of the family by using the male-headed family, and not each adult individual, as the basic political unit of society. An inconsistency can therefore be seen in the work of these early modernists between their individualistic rhetoric and the social, particularly gender-divided, inequalities that resulted.[27] This inconsistency is notable in the contrast between free and equal human beings in a state of nature and unfree and unequal gendered individuals in the social contract.[28] This is an unnecessary inconsistency and fails to take seriously the individual subjectivity of women as human beings in their own right. The methodology used by the male theorists allows them to read their own patriarchal beliefs and views back into their theories. As there is no such thing as a state of nature and a social contract, the views of human nature they rest on depends on the person expounding the theory (for example compare Hobbes' and Rousseau's view of human nature which have vital bearing on the social contract and State that result).[29] Such theorists make important points regarding the common humanity of all in the state of nature but fail to see the gender egalitarian consequences of their own logic, a point further developed in Chapter 2. One important thing that second wave feminists show is that, at the very least, exponents of contract-type arguments must be aware of the gender dimensions of the contract tradition and make explicit efforts to counteract it.[30]

Another early modernist thinker, Descartes, divides the soul (the mind) and the body (the non-rational), but represents his method as accessible to all. In Descartes' theory, *everyone* – men and women – has the capacity for reason, and can potentially exercise it, but the problem lies in the realities of the lives of women.[31] Practically speaking, women's *experiences and activities* prevented them from any major contributions to rational thinking. *Theoretically*, there was nothing to stop women exercising their capacity for reason but *practically* there were major impediments to their doing so. According to this view, there is nothing intrinsic to women or women's "nature" to stop them from developing the capacity for reason. It is "simply" the social structures and context in which men and women live that

---

[27] For a good analysis of social contract theory see D Boucher and P Kelly (eds) *The Social Contract from Hobbes to Rawls* (New York and London: Routledge 1994). This leads to citizens with a twofold identity: in the public sphere and as heads of private households – see my discussion of public and private spheres below. The tradition is analysed further in Chapter 2.

[28] See C Pateman, 1988, and SM Okin 1979 and 1989.

[29] See, W Morrison *Jurisprudence: from the Greeks to post-modernism* (London: Cavendish Publishing Ltd 1997) at p 75ff; P Riley *Will and Political Legitimacy: A Critical Exposition of Social Contract Theory in Hobbes, Locke, Rousseau, Kant and Hegel* (London: Harvard University Press 1982); D Boucher and P Kelly (eds), 1994; L Strauss and J Cropsey (ed) *History of Political Philosophy* (3rd Edn Chicago and London: University of Chicago Press 1987.

[30] See C Pateman, 1988; E Frazer and N Lacey, 1993, p 72.

[31] See G Lloyd, 1984; see also analysis by M Atherton "Cartesian Reason and Gendered Reason" in LM Antony and CE Witt, 2002, note 3 at p 21–37.

prevent this from happening: if these are changed, women could also exercise their capacity for reason.

The distraction of social contingencies attaching to being female, preventing women from developing the capacity for reason is highlighted in Mary Wollstonecraft's writing in the late eighteenth century.[32] In her view, the problem was a lack of opportunities given to girls and women for them to develop their capacity for reason.[33] She wants women to be included within the category of human being with the same capacities as men: to be allowed to be autonomous individuals who can make rational choices. Women lacked the capacity to engage actively in political processes only because they had been denied opportunities to develop their intellectual faculties.

Feminists of the early second wave, like Betty Friedan, then Susan Moller Okin and Martha Nussbaum, use a similar language of liberalism to show how women have not been given the opportunities to develop their capacities and abilities but that these have been thwarted and stunted by women's seclusion in the family.[34] Such views are used further in Part II.

In comparison to those philosophers already mentioned, John Stuart Mill writes specifically about the emancipation of women.[35] As a utilitarian and liberal thinker, he writes, together with collaborator Harriet Taylor Mill, of his concern for women's freedom and equality. He wants women to attain the same levels as men, seeing this as leading both to an improvement of humankind and to the added happiness of women themselves. Mill is aware of the extent to which "nature" has been used to legitimise convention "*so true is it that unnatural generally means only uncustomary and that everything which is usual appears natural.*"[36] Mill attempts to show that the reasons considered for treating women differently from men – they are naturally inferior, less rational, more emotional – were not founded on good evidence and were probably all fake. He points out that conceptions of the "natural" woman often differ entirely from one culture to another. He says: "*I deny that anyone knows or can know, the nature of the two sexes, as long as they have only been seen in their present relation to one another*".[37] No-one could presume to know the nature of women until women are free to develop it themselves.

Like Wollstonecraft, the basis of Mill's and Taylor Mill's arguments rests on the assumption that women and men have the same capacity for reason which could and should be developed in women and so they campaigned for equal opportunities for women. But even Mill, for all his talk of women's freedom, falls

---

[32] M Wollstonecraft *The Vindication of the Rights of Women* (London: Dent 1970, 1st published 1792).
[33] M Wollstonecraft, 1970. See also P Ward Scaltsas "Women as Ends – Women as Means in the Enlightenment" A J Arnaud and E Kingdom 1990, p 138.
[34] B Friedan *The Feminine Mystique* (London: Penguin 1963); SM Okin, 1979, 1989; MC Nussbaum *Sex and Social Justice* (Oxford: Oxford University Press 1999) and *Women and Human Development* (Cambridge: Cambridge University Press 2000) and 1996.
[35] JS Mill, 1991.
[36] JS Mill, 1991, quoted in SM Okin 1979, p 215.
[37] JS Mill, 1991 – see SM Okin, 1979, p 215–6.

short of advocating true equality and freedom for all women. The reason for doing so is, like Plato, Hobbes and Locke, the family. Mill assumes that this unit is natural and somehow naturally provides men and women with distinctive traditional roles.[38]

Like many still in today's contemporary societies, Mill believes that women should have a real choice of a career or marriage and children, but once married, he is in favour of the traditional division of labour within the family. Having said that what is seen as natural is generally decided by convention and custom, Mill fails to consider whether the qualities of motherhood and gender roles within the family structure, seen as "natural", might be, even at least, partly due to convention, custom and environmental social factors.[39]

Mill, like other theorists before him, fails to see through his own thoughts to their logical conclusion. Some feminists, like Okin and Nussbaum, attempt to rectify the faults they see in this aspect of the liberal tradition arising from the division of women who choose to work outside the home and women who choose to marry and/or have children who are then somehow seen as more "naturally" suited to life within the private, domestic sphere.

The divisions of viewing single women and married women, and women with children differently are still strong. They are evident in the current division between employed work and home life and within the structure of the employed working environment. The distinction is arguably even more evident in certain countries where a strict demarcation of women's family role exists. This division hinders the developmental capacities of women who wish to exist meaningfully through their work and their private home life. There is no logical reason why women should have to "choose" between the two. As Juliet Mitchell says, in a manner reminiscent of Mill, *"like woman herself the family appears as a natural object, but is actually a cultural creation"*.[40] As is shown in Part II, members of the two sexes have to be able to develop in the absence of detrimental differential treatment during the socialisation process and throughout their lives to ensure their potentiality is not hindered.

Additionally, Mill's views seem to support the view that an "essential nature" of the two sexes exists, presumably somewhere beneath the layers of social convention. How "essentialism" has impacted on feminist thought is developed in Chapter 3 and ideas of potentiality are presented in Part II particularly to show that

---

[38] Mill's feminist writings are implicitly concerned with the middle-class and upper-class woman. The middle-class family is therefore his model: women who marry do not work outside the home but devote themselves fully to their husbands and family. This fails to consider those women who have always had to work outside the home (whether having a family or not) because of their economic circumstances.

[39] This failure in Mill to examine the existing family structure and its repercussions for the lives of women is a gap in his feminist thought which SM Okin viewed in 1979 as something the feminist movement was attempting to remedy: SM Okin 1979, p 227–8. JS Mill also stresses the separation between the state and the individual, causing an aversion to state power but at the same time seeing it as a site for social progression – a point highlighted by E Frazer and N Lacey, 1993.

[40] Okin 1979, p 296 quoting J Mitchell's *Women's Estate* (New York 1973 at p 99–100.

retaining such an idea of essence is not necessary if "potentiality" is used as the basis of ideas of common humanity. Using potentiality rather than essence removes any unchanging, fixed restrictions on individual freedom and restrictive norms: these ideas are developed in Chapter 5.

Those philosophers who consider the capacity for reason to be a quality of all human beings hold promise for some feminists. The philosophers had failed to see that women did have the same capacity for reason as men or they saw this but then refused to allow the capacity to develop because of a lack of opportunities in the empirical world within which individuals then had to live. Either way, the philosophers had failed to follow through their ideas to their logical conclusion. This was usually because the philosophers held views and assumptions that women are reproducers and nurturers in the family and, correspondingly, women's place or role in the family is "natural". Such views are inconsistent with the recognition of women as individuals equal to men.[41]

Critiques which reveal certain male Western philosophers' views on the conception of the human being to be gendered are not confined to historical figures. The excuse that such Western philosophers were simply men of their times, reflecting views of people existing at their point in history fails to convince, especially given Plato's ahistorical views.

One of the most influential contemporary theories to be critiqued is that of John Rawls whose work will be investigated now and in Chapter 2 in the context of abstract reasoning.[42] His theory sets out an updated social contract theory where imaginary individuals debate in the "Original Position" behind a "veil of ignorance" with the aim of agreeing on principles of justice to govern them in society. These individuals do not know their place in society, their sex, their race and colour, their age and in which part of the world they will live.

Rawls has been criticised for, amongst other things, substituting the male head of the household for the individual in the Original Position.[43] Further, Rawls is criticised for failing to consider justice and injustice *within* families.

Certain feminist critiques of Rawls can be interpreted to show how the justness of the institution of the family is relevant to ideas of the nature of what it

---

[41] The best examples of such feminist critiques are Okin 1979 and 1989. This overlaps with the discussion of "immanence" and "transcendence" which follows.

[42] John Rawls *A Theory of Justice* (Oxford: Oxford University Press 1971). See also T Pogge *Realizing Rawls* (Ithaca and London: Cornell University Press 1989); R Plant *Modern Political Thought* (Oxford: Blackwell 1991); D Boucher and P Kelly, 1994.

[43] J Rawls, 1971: see my more detailed analysis of his theory in Chapter 2. See critiques by SM Okin 1989, in particular p 91 ff and J Rawls 1971 at p 128, 146; MC Nussbaum 1999; A Baier "The Need for More than Justice" in *Canadian Journal of Philosophy Supplementary Vol 13 Science, Morality and Feminist Theory* 1987, all on this point. There have been many other feminist critiques of J Rawls, particularly on his methodology. As I show in Chapter 2, SM Okin argues that, although his methodology is sound and his principles of justice can be used to challenge the gender system and a produce a just, genderless society, Rawls fails to do this. He shows little indication that "*the modern liberal society to which the principles of justice are to be applied is deeply and pervasively gender-structured*": SM Okin 1989, at p 89.

is to be human, as it is largely within that family structure that human identity is usually developed.[44] What gender roles developing children see in that structure will be fundamental to their resulting moral outlook and beliefs in justice. Although Rawls's theory includes families as part of the subject matter of a theory of justice and requires that families are just, he appears to simply assume that families are just.[45] Although sex is not specifically mentioned in *A Theory of Justice*, Rawls later clarified (in an article written subsequently) that sex is one of the morally irrelevant contingencies that are hidden by the veil of ignorance.[46] As parties in the Original Position know the general facts about human society, it has been noted that they presumably know that it is gender-structured.[47]

Feminists point to the importance of examining the justice of the social institution of the family in any discussions about theories of justice because the family can be a breeding ground for an unjust society in its patriarchal, gendered form, upholding the existing power imbalance in favour of men. Although Rawls does not apply his principles of justice to this realm of human nurturance which is essential to the achievement and maintenance of justice, the feminist potential of his methodology, and the principles of justice that emerge, have been viewed in a sympathetic manner as considerable.[48] From this perspective, although Rawls's liberalism fails to go far enough to deal with justice within the family structure, there is no logical reason why it cannot, and indeed to be truer to its liberal principles, it should. As can be seen, the theorist's own arguments can be more fully realised by highlighting their own illogicality, with the male theorists failing to follow through the sexually egalitarian insights in their own work.

Such feminist critiques of traditional views of the human being show how the family, at least as it is structured in patriarchal society, constrains rather than enhances women's, and often men's, opportunities as human beings to live free, creative and fulfilling lives. They also show how many philosophers, while purporting to stress the importance of the freedom of the individual human, have in mind the male head of household and not every adult individual. This has been described as a fundamental ambiguity pervading most liberal thought: the tendency has been to make allegedly general statements (as if the human race were not divided into two sexes) and then either to ignore the female sex or proceed to discuss women in terms not at all consistent with the assertions that have been made about man and, accordingly, humanity.[49]

---

[44] Okin, 1979; N Chodorow *The Reproduction of Mothering: psychoanalysis and the sociology of gender* (Berkeley: University of California Press 1978).
[45] Okin 1989, p 92–3, 97 discussing Rawls, 1971, 462–3.
[46] There is some debate about this point amongst liberal egalitarian theorists given further comments Rawls has made in his developing theory resulting in J Rawls *Political Liberalism* (New York: Columbia University Press 1993). See also J Rawls "Fairness to Goodness" *Philosophical Review* 84 (1975) 537. For examples of such debate, see GA Cohen "Where the Action is: On the Site of Distributive Justice" (1997) 3 *Philosophy and Public Affairs* 26; MC Nussbaum 2000, p 270ff.
[47] SM Okin 1989, p 91, J Rawls 1971, p 137.
[48] See Okin, 1979 and 1989.
[49] SM Okin 1979, p 202 and 282.

While this analysis seeks to show how philosophers had emphasised women's "natural" role within the family, supplementing men's lives, making women less able to fit within the definition of human, analysis also carried out by feminists in the second wave into the public-private division highlighted how these "natural" qualities impacted on the wider world. One legacy of the past for feminism and the construction of the common capacity for reason is the division of the social and political world into public and private spheres.[50]

Much feminist analysis has been carried out showing a division between the public sphere of the economy, politics, law, employed work, and the private sphere of the family and domestic relations.[51] As has been shown, the family and domestic relations were (and often still are) treated as the "natural" foundation of civil life that requires little critical theoretical scrutiny.

Second wave feminist analysis of the public and private spheres brought to the fore the asymmetrical hierarchical nature of the different public and the private spheres, with the public (male) being shown as dominant and more valued. It also highlighted how women have been prevented from, or at least greatly hindered from, participating in the public sphere and, by extension, excluded from the definition of the human being to the extent that that definition is based on the experiences of men in the public sphere; and how this dichotomised system prevents all human beings from realising their full potential.

This analysis can be interpreted as showing how women were excluded from the public, more dominant and more valued, sphere in two ways. First, *physically*, by not actually, materially and socially being in the arena of the public in many ways and being excluded from it by formal political and legal impediments.[52] Secondly, *abstractly* by the definition of the public individual of philosophical, political and legal thought being cast from the particular, male, experiences operating in the public sphere.

In many ways, the public figure depends on a corresponding private sphere where men recoup their energy after a hard day's work in public life.[53] The history of this division shows women excluded from the world of the "marketplace" and encouraged to be caring, concerned with sustaining relationships and looking after others, particularly the men who work and live daily in the public sphere. This role is seen as more important than women's own individual autonomy: the assumption

---

[50] The dichotomy between the public and the private has been described as ultimately what the feminist movement is about – see C Pateman in A Phillips 1987, p 103.

[51] See for example C Pateman, 1987; K O'Donovan *Sexual Divisions in the Law* (London: Weidenfeld & Nicholson 1985). Nicola Lacey sees the separate sphere divide as self-defeating for liberals. In her opinion, the limits of the scope of justice and politics asserted by Rawls etc are inconsistent with the realisation of the general values they claim to espouse. Saying that the private ought to be within the scope of political critique is not the same as saying that it should be regulated but this has not always been observed. For Lacey, the problem with the public/private critique is that feminists can remain within a framework they are trying to transcend. See discussion in N Lacey, 1998, p 78–84.

[52] For example, see the "persons" cases analysed by A Sachs and J Hoff Wilson, 1978.

[53] C Pateman, 1987; K O'Donovan, 1985; W Brown *States of Injury: Power and Freedom in Late Modernity* (Princeton: Princeton University Press 1995).

being that the two roles are mutually exclusive. In particular, socialist feminist critiques of the family represent it as part of the private sphere where men can relax and be compensated for the failure of the marketplace, with its lack of meaning and failure to fulfil men's needs.[54]

Because the two areas have historically been divided, some feminists argue that they compartmentalise human experience in a way that prevents human beings from realising the range of choices that should be available to all.[55] It has been asked how it is possible to *"radically [increase] the options available to each individual...allowing the human personality to break out of the present dichotomized system".*[56] The argument is that because individuals are faced with a sense of powerlessness, in both the market and the family, male and female genders need to be deconstructed to regain this power so that they no longer have *"warped and impoverished notions of freedom".*[57] This view sees human qualities as having been separately projected onto males and females, making each the object of the other. The relationship between the sexes becomes a means by which members of each gender can reclaim their own projected nature: in becoming acquainted with the other, they become acquainted with themselves.[58] The division into two genders has been viewed as a useful device for enabling all to become conscious of the wide range of human possibilities.[59] However, in transcending the male/female dichotomy, individuals would be reaching the final reclamation of the whole self, the last stage in this historical process.[60]

This representation of the human subject or self shows how many feminist theorists at that time had been advocating a reclamation of freedom which had been buried somewhere within the subject or self: the classic liberal or socialist essential element of the self, which needed to be uncovered and emancipated.[61] This essentialism is unnecessary if a view of the subject as self-actualising is accepted. Instead, it is possible to retain a strong and active intentional subject but without the fixed rigidities of a non-changing subject which can exclude certain people and restrict individual growth: an idea developed in Chapter 3 and Part II.

---

[54] A point highlighted in F Olsen "The Family and the Marketplace" in F Olsen (ed) *Feminist Legal Theory* (London: Dartmouth 1995). See analysis in chapter two of women's alleged more caring "nature".

[55] The best example of this can be seen in F Olsen, 1995.

[56] F Olsen, 1995. The dichotomized system being the market and the family, translating to the two genders.

[57] F Olsen, 1995.

[58] F Olsen, 1995, p 1569, 1578.

[59] F Olsen compares the gendered system to religion in this respect, giving it its historical place presenting it as somehow now to be transcended.

[60] F Olsen, 1995.

[61] A clear example is Ruth Colker "Feminism Sexuality and Authenticity" in M Fineman and N Thomadsen, 1991. Colker describes the discovery and understanding of authentic female sexuality as part of women's authentic self, aiming to peel away the social influences that limit women's freedom or authenticity, leaving the authentic self. This "essentialist" view of the self fell out of favour in later years and I discuss this development and its consequences for feminist legal theory in Chapter 3.

Feminists also seek to show that the private sphere is at the heart of civil society rather than apart or separate from it.[62] Others point out that in a sense there is no private sphere in twentieth-century liberal states, with the free market and family law both being heavily regulated.[63]

From a feminist perspective, it is important to dismantle any division there may be to aim to make the two spheres more compatible, with favourable consequences for women's, as well as men's, employed work-other life balance while retaining a space for individual thought, development and privacy.

If women are or have been traditionally allocated to the private sphere, and the individual of the public sphere is the norm of the human being, then this conception of the human being takes little account of women's actual real life experiences.[64] Such a division between the sexes means that often classic theorists explicitly exclude women from the public realm because they are said to lack the capacities required of the free and equal individuals who inhabit it and make important decisions in it.[65] The reason for this is, according to the classic theorists, purportedly because of women's "nature", yet often this argument is shown to be illogical because, often at the same time, these theorists state that convention creates the so-called "natural". Thus it is really as a result of a lack of opportunities being given to women to form and develop these capacities that they are not free and equal individuals. Following on from this, the masculine public world, the universal world of individualism, rights, contracts, reason, freedom, equality, impartial law and citizenship, is taken to be the proper concern of social and political theory, while the domestic sphere of motherhood and family life is not. This is why one of the earliest rallying cries of second wave feminism was "the personal is political".

Allowing women access to become human beings when the definition has already been based on qualities and characteristics seen in the public sphere, inhabited by particular types of human (originally white middle-class males), will inadequately take into account how the freely choosing individual depicted by such theories may have their choices limited by family and responsibility to others.[66] Not only is this individual constrained by "external" forces and the fact that she may be a parent, but her own conception of the good is also shaped by her moral beliefs in the rightness of her conduct in that role.[67]

Through feminist critiques of these different spheres and the presuppositions of the philosophers as to women's natural functions and capacities, the apparently universal categories of the "individual" were shown to be often sexually particular, constructed on the basis of male attributes, capacities and modes of activity. If what is defined as human nature is actually applicable only to certain men in a gender structured society where they dominate women and do not

---

[62] C Pateman, 1987, p 119.
[63] E Frazer and N Lacey, 1993, p 72–3.
[64] See also K O'Donovan, 1985.
[65] See G Lloyd, 1984.
[66] See K O'Donovan, 1985.
[67] K O'Donovan, 1985.

share the responsibilities of domestic life, then clearly human "nature" has to be rethought.[68] However, a strict division of the two spheres is unnecessary.

Those who argue for a reinterpretation of public and private along less gender exploitative lines (because women have suffered from the lack of any real "private" space to pursue their own concerns) highlight an important point for feminism.[69] There is a need to see the reconstruction of the private as political but this does not imply any general prescriptive position on the aptness of state intervention as a response. Instead, if a caring, interconnected environment exists in society and is acknowledged as existing rather than a world of isolated, separate "atoms" of individuals, then the division would be less obtrusive and have less detrimental consequences for women.[70]

These critiques of Western philosophy's conceptions of the human being lead many feminists to advocate the need for the recognition of the existence of women *as individuals in their own right*, showing the role of women in the family, relegated to the private sphere, for what it is: a social construction, not "natural". Therefore one of the main complaints is that these philosophers are *not being individualistic enough* when talking about the human subject of political and legal theory: a complaint reiterated recently in a revival of liberal feminism advocated by Martha Nussbaum.[71] Taking this perspective has been described as rebelling against a supposedly "female" nature and the associated subordination of women to men. Such feminists demand public space, away from traditional women's roles in the family.[72]

While it is important that feminists demand the space for women to be individuals, that includes women who freely choose to live the role of wife and mother in the family. Such women should be treated as individuals in their own right just as much as those who freely choose not to live in such roles: a point developed in Part II. The feminist critique of the failure by many liberal thinkers, including feminists like JS Mill and Harriet Taylor Mill, to see the role of wife or mother (amongst many roles of women) not as a "natural" role but as a construction formed in a hierarchical way, is well-founded.

There is generally acknowledged to have been a movement within feminist legal theory, certainly here in the UK, away from liberal feminism in that it is seen as having less to contribute to feminist legal theory than "difference" feminists (with the two "groups" being seen as somehow opposed). This may, however, be

---

[68] See SM Okin's Afterword to SM Okin 1979.

[69] See E Frazer and N Lacey, 1993, p 74.

[70] The word "atoms" is based on Charles Taylor's critique of liberal rights theory. These ideas are discussed further in Part II.

[71] MC Nussbaum 1999 and 2000. I develop this later in the context of international ethics in Part III.

[72] Thus making it easy for feminism to be associated with political citizenship ideals of freedom, equality, redistribution, autonomy and individualism. See S Sevenhuijsen *Citizenship and the Ethics of Care: Feminist Considerations on Justice, Morality and Politics* (New York and London: Routledge 1998) at p 5. A similar point is made by N Lacey – liberal feminists had a very direct inference from theory or analysis to policy or strategy – see N Lacey, 1998.

changing.[73] In my analysis, the view that philosophers, and liberalism in particular, have not been individualistic enough with regards to the social construction of women and the family, in representing as "natural" what is socially constructed, still has transformative potential for feminist jurisprudence, and particularly as translated into the international sphere in the area of globalism and international humanitarian law as explained in Part III.

There is potential for all human beings to become more and more specifically human, achieving the fullness of their human potentiality. Included in this vision is freeing women from the internal and external obstacles which hinder this development. One aspect of this is the social construction of the family and correspondingly women's role within it in patriarchal society. Such construction is then presented as "natural". While it is self-evident that only women (but not all women) can become pregnant and bear children, this should not lead to the inevitability of women rearing children.[74] Most feminists aim for a future when child-rearing will be equally shared between the sexes, for flexibility of work for all and for early second wave feminists the ideal "subject" was often an androgynous one.[75] Opportunities being given in all of the ways mentioned in this section, through the reconciliation of the public-private, fair employment and childcare practices, will enable women to exercise their capacity for reason with less hindrances to their potentiality.

The feminist work analysed in this section concentrates on increasing women's opportunities, freeing them to use and develop their capacity for reason. A difference in emphasis is placed by other feminist critiques which are dealt with in the next section, concentrating on projects and achievements, transcending what may be seen as the predictable.

## Achieving Reason: A Project

Reason has not only been seen as a distinguishing feature of human nature, it is often classified as an *achievement* – a skill to be learned. This distinctively methodical way of thinking, sharply differentiated from other kinds of thought and living, means rational knowledge is construed as transcending, transforming or controlling natural forces while the feminine has been associated with what that

---

[73] See analysis of this shift in N Lacey, 1998. However, also see E Jackson and N Lacey "Introducing Feminist Legal Theory" in J Penner, D Schiff and R Nobles (eds) *Jurisprudence and Legal Theory: Commentary and Materials* (London: Butterworths LexisNexis 2002). This shift is dealt with at various times throughout this book.

[74] A point also made by C Pateman, 1987; also SM Okin 1979, amongst others.

[75] SM Okin 1979, p 297–302. This androgynous ideal is perhaps more in favour by those who agree with J Butler's views – see Chapter 3 below. Criticising such a view, Jean Bethke Elshtain, in A Phillips 1987, argues that human bodies disappear to androgyny. If one agrees that sex distinction is ineliminable and important does this mean one simply acquiesces in recognised notions of masculinity and femininity? Clearly not says Elshtain. For her, maleness/femaleness/individuals' corporeal sexual selves are the ways individuals experience the world.

rational knowledge transcends.[76] On this view, an exclusion or transcendence of the feminine is built into past ideals of reason as the sovereign human character trait. And correlatively, the content of femininity has been partly formed by such processes of exclusion.[77] Historically, women were seen in reality as, in some way, closer to nature and grounded in everyday activities: the very areas Cartesian man had to "transcend" to have true knowledge.[78] With the rise of science in Europe, there was a shift in the understanding of the human relationship to nature. It was now a force to be controlled. Translated into gender terms, maleness came to be seen in itself as an achievement, attained by breaking away from the more "natural" condition of women.[79]

Criticisms have been made of the Western philosophical human being on the basis that embodied identity was denied by its abstraction from social and economic "contingencies" and biological "contingencies" that make up sexual difference. This means not only that the individual has embraced a masculine experience, but also that *of its very nature* it remains bound to only one sex. When a disembodied degendered abstraction is introduced only one sex will be the norm.[80] Correspondingly, some feminists say transcending to achieve a form of abstraction, in relation to which all are equal, cannot be achieved because doing so will always impose a part as a norm.[81]

A philosophical split between the mind and the body is shown to exist by various feminist writers, as exemplified by this statement:

> It is the male body, and its historically and culturally determined powers and capacities that is taken as the norm or the standard of the liberal "individual".[82]

Discussions of sexual equality are said to silently privilege the male body – when men and women are treated the same, women are treated as if they were men. When men and women are treated differently, the man remains the norm against

---

[76] G Lloyd, 1984, p 2, 5 and 104. Plato said that "matter", with its overtones of femaleness, is seen as something to be transcended in the search for rational knowledge (although it was the relation of master to slave that provided the metaphors of dominance for the Greeks). See also M Gatens *Feminism and Philosophy: perspectives on difference and equality* (Cambridge: Polity Press 1991) who says that conceptions of women are formed and reformed depending on the dominant conception of male subjectivity and its needs, with a history of women being defined only in terms relative to men who are taken as the norm, the standard or primary term.

[77] G Lloyd, 1984, p 37.

[78] See G Lloyd's analysis, 1984.

[79] M Evans, *Introducing Contemporary Feminist Thought* (Cambridge: Polity Press 1997).

[80] See C Pateman, 1987.

[81] See A Phillips' (1993) analysis of this point, p 48–49, where she discusses Pateman's view that human identity is sexually differentiated and exists in a bodily form. Those who seek to abstract will be writing in one sex alone as their standard.

[82] M Gatens "Powers, Bodies and Difference" in M Barrett and A Phillips (eds) *Destabilising Theory* (Cambridge: Polity Press 1992) at p 125.

which the woman is peculiar, lacking, different.[83] If women have historically been seen as closer to nature, naturally within the realm of the "sensuous", emotions and the body, and men have been associated with the rational and the mind, any definition of a human based on the capacity for reason will inevitably suit men more than women.[84]

For some, the major feminist arguments since the seventeenth century advocating that women possess the same capacities and abilities as men, and if only educated properly can do everything men can, is a strategic approach but such an approach glosses over the so called "*womanly capacity*" that men do not possess. This implicitly denies that birth, women's bodies, "*feminine passions inseparable from their bodies*", and bodily processes, have any political relevance.[85] On this interpretation, Western philosophy, and liberalism in particular, is criticised for presenting a disembodied view of the human subject. For the transcendence of reason to be attained, the attributes of the human are implicitly abstracted from, and transcend, the body.[86] Humankind attempts to transcend a merely natural existence so that nature is always seen as of a lower order than culture, and if the feminine is seen as closer to nature, it is this that has to be transcended.[87] If fulfilment consists in primarily exercising the individual human mind, rather than developing mental and physical capabilities in co-operation with others, some feminists describe it as a condition to which relatively few may aspire, leading some feminists to criticise liberalism and liberal feminism as being incapable of guaranteeing a fulfilling life for all.[88]

---

[83] See A Phillips 1993, p 45.

[84] Some have commented that this is also reinforced by the sexual division of labour – A Jaggar, 1983, and W Brown, 1995.

[85] C Pateman and E Gross, 1986, at ch 7.

[86] C Pateman and E Gross believe that it is important for feminist theory to begin with the recognition that individuals are feminine and masculine, that individuality is not a unitary abstraction but an embodied and sexually differentiated expression of the unity of humankind. To develop a theory in which women and femininity have an autonomous place means that the private and the public, the social and political also have to be completely reconceptualised, bringing to an end a sexually particular theory that masquerades as universalism.

[87] For example, Aristotle repudiated the divided soul but presented reason as controlling or subduing by its own force the emotional part of human nature. Notable exceptions to the prevailing division between the mind/rationality and the body/emotions include Spinoza who rejected the distinction between will and understanding – reason was an active, emotional force, able to engage with passions in its own right: see M Gatens "The Politics of "Presence" and "Difference": Working Through Spinoza and Eliot" in S James and S Palmer (eds), 2002. David Hume believed that reason has of itself no power to control passions or to deliberate about ends. Its motivating force lies outside itself in the driving force of passions. For Hume, reason must rest on and conform to individuals' "natural" propensities – see G Lloyd, 1984, p 51. See also A Baier's work: she reinterprets Hume from a feminist perspective. For example, A Baier "Hume, the Women's Moral Theorist?" in G Lloyd (ed) *Feminism and History of Philosophy* (Oxford: Oxford University Press 2002).

[88] See M Gatens, 1991; A Jaggar, 1983.

Some therefore contend that if the Western philosophical and liberal emphasis on the neutrality of the mind is accepted, sexual discrimination will continue to be justified by bodily difference.[89] In these arguments, liberal theory is seen as offering a situation of equality on the basis of women being entitled to be treated like (meaning "the same as") men, and the founding principle of liberal theory – the right and freedom to use one's bodily capacities as one sees fit – is denied to women with regard to the specific character of their bodies.[90] This point illustrates how feminists have highlighted inconsistencies within liberal views of the person but do not thereby succeed in showing that liberal theory is redundant. Instead, it shows that liberal theory is not being followed through to its logical conclusion, being inconsistent to its founding principles. Further, this criticism fails to acknowledge that individual human minds can be exercised, and will only be able to do so, having developed psychologically in a relational social context, necessitating co-operation with others: these points are elaborated in Chapters 2 and 4.

It has been argued that the only way to explain why the value universally assigned to women and their activities is lower than that assigned to men and their pursuits is that women are a symbol of all *"that every culture defines as being of a lower order of existence than itself."*[91] However, biology, of itself, is neither oppressive nor liberating, it can become a source of subordination or liberation and creativity for women only because it has meaning within specific social relationships.[92]

Some feminists who focus on reason as transcendence view femininity as socially constructed, most famously espoused by existentialist Simone de Beauvoir in the expression that *"one is not born, but rather becomes a woman."*[93] Woman is the other to man who is the universal subject. This existentialist theory takes to an extreme the liberal aspiration to autonomy and self-willed choice, but it is acknowledged that a completely autonomous life is impossible because, as individuals, all are constrained by social and moral norms and bodily needs: this is the human condition. However, it is believed that individuals can constantly and deliberately take responsibility for their obedience and disobedience to authority and to their bodies. On this view, for individuals to be truly ethical subjects, exercising their powers of "authentic choice", they must aim to transcend the social and the physical. If women are not out there engaging in their own projects and

---

[89] See M Gatens, 1991.

[90] M Gatens, 1991.

[91] S B Ortner "Is Female to Male as Nature to Culture" in M Z Rosaldo and L Lamphere (eds) *Women, Culture and Society* (Stanford: Stanford University Press 1974) at p 72.

[92] C Pateman, 1987, p 111. See A Rich *Of Woman Born* (London: Virago 1976) discussed below.

[93] S de Beauvoir, *The Second Sex* (London: Jonathan Cape 1953: Vintage 1997). Although not strictly speaking a second wave feminist, but a precursor to that stage in the feminist movement, de Beauvoir's work is fundamental to a great deal of second wave feminism and must be examined, having particular relevance to the topic of the human subject and freedom.

exploits, they are reduced to mere "immanence" or immersion in life with no middle ground existing between transcendence and immanence. Female biology is represented as a conflict between being an inalienable free subject reaching out to transcendence and being a body which drags this subject back to a merely "natural" existence: it is as if the female body is an intrinsic obstacle to transcendence. However, it could be that the experience of a female body that is described is the experience of a body that has been culturally objectified by exposure to the male look, rather than the female body in, and of, itself. Humanity values the *reasons for living* above *mere life* so man assumes mastery confronting woman. Women achieve transcendence only at the expense of alienation from their bodily being.[94]

The idea is that gender is constructed but there is an "essential" human subject or self who somehow takes on that gender. It could therefore take on some other gender and it is only the feminine gender that is "marked".[95] The universal person and masculine gender are conflated, but women are defined in terms of their sex. Men are the bearers of a body-transcendent universal personhood. The identity of women with sex is a conflation of the category of women with the ostensibly sexualised features of their bodies and a refusal to grant freedom and autonomy to women. What is proposed instead is a new order in which woman becomes part of the world of the *active other*: woman becomes like man in order to escape the debilitating and endlessly disempowering impact of femininity as the condition of otherness. Refusing this condition is the process of becoming the definitive feminist project.[96]

Similarly, other feminists argue that women have the same capacity for judgement and valuation as men and that to be consistent with this, women must discover independently of their "biological nature" what principles best encapsulate and protect the worth of persons.[97] The most extreme example of this view is Shulamith Firestone's work, written in the 1970s, arguing that women's biology has to be controlled if women's liberation is to be achieved.[98] Advocating that culture should overcome nature, the position is taken that humanity has begun to outgrow nature. People can no longer justify the maintenance of a so-called *"discriminatory sex class system"* on grounds of its origin in "nature". Women's biology and their natural reproductive difference from men is presented as leading to the first division of labour as the origins of sex-class. The solution presented is

---

[94] G Lloyd, 1984, p 101, quoting de Beauvoir p 97.
[95] As expressed by J Butler *Gender Trouble: Feminism and the subversion of identity* (New York and London: Routledge 1990) at p 9. Butler's work is examined in detail in Chapter 3 with its possibility for the reconstruction of identity which may allow both sexes to construct new forms of relationships with themselves and others.
[96] M Evans, 1997, p 45.
[97] J Radcliffe Richards *The Sceptical Feminist: a philosophical enquiry* (Harmondsworth: Penguin Books Ltd 1982).
[98] S Firestone *The Dialectic of Sex: the case for feminist revolution* (New York: Bantam Books 1971).

the necessity of *"freeing...women from the tyranny of their reproductive biology".*[99]

Such a view has been criticised for, amongst other things, failing to take account of what the experience of biological pregnancy and birth might be in a wholly different political and emotional context.[100] Critics point out that the social, political structures, and particularly the *institution* of motherhood in a patriarchical system are responsible for the injustice and the alienation of women from the experience of biological pregnancy and childbirth, not women's reproductive capacities per se.[101] The potential pleasure and power, both emotional and social, of motherhood is stunted by such social structures.[102]

Seeking to transcend women's biology has been described as working so long as the devaluation of the private sphere is acceptable to women and so long as women view their "problem" as restriction or confinement which can be overcome by entering the public realm on the same terms as men.[103] It has been claimed that such attempts at objectivity result in isolation and estrangement from the real lived conditions which contribute to moral consciousness in the first place and it is an awareness and sensitivity to these which could provide the grounds for social and political change: these points are developed in Part II.[104]

This devaluation of the "feminine" involves a rejection of the traditional female experiences of the household and motherhood and embracing wholeheartedly the cause of rationality and intellectual life: what has been called *"reconstructing femininity in more masculine terms".*[105] Men, it has been said, are able to try to achieve such transcendence, thanks to women's work in the home but women have not traditionally been able to do so.[106]

While criticisms of transcending the feminine have validity, feminist arguments approving of some type of transcendence have value in thinking about

---

[99] S Firestone, 1971, p 206.

[100] De Beauvoir and Firestone have been criticised for failing to question how the female body is socially constructed and its possibilities socially limited: see M Gatens, 1997, and C Mackenzie "Simone de Beauvoir: philosophy and/or the female body" in C Pateman and E Gross, 1986.

[101] See A Rich, 1976; N Chodorow, 1978; M O'Brien *The Politics of Reproduction* (London: Routledge 1981); A Dally *Inventing Motherhood: the consequences of an ideal* (London: Burnett Books Ltd 1982).

[102] A Rich, 1976 – see in particular p 174. Rich believes that the free exercise by all women of sexual and procreative choice will bring about enormous social changes but in conjunction with other claims which women and certain men have been denied for centuries, what she sees as *"the claim to personhood; the claim to share justly in the products of our labor, not to be used merely as an instrument, a role, a womb, a pair of hands or a back or a set of fingers; to participate fully in the decisions of our workplace, our community; to speak for ourselves, in our own right."* Rich, p xxi–xxii sounding reminiscent of Kant (1988).

[103] S Parsons "Feminism and the Logic of Morality: A Conclusion of Alternatives" in E Frazer et al (eds),1992, p 380ff.

[104] S Parsons, 1992.

[105] M Evans, 1997, p 46.

[106] See E Frazer et al, 1992, at ch 11.

conceptions of the free human being which are developed in Part II. Indeed, it is queried why embracing reason, intellectual life and transcendence have to be seen as somehow intrinsically masculine. Whilst it is acknowledged that often these have been presented in ways which better fit male experiences, this is not inevitable.

The criticisms made by many second wave feminists as to the "maleness" of reason and transcendence could be met by re-shaping what it means to be a man and a woman as a human subject. There is no need for subjectivity (male) and its other (female).

The aspiration to transcend contingent historical circumstances which differentiate human beings from each other, to a quality common to all, lies at the heart of this philosophical heritage and is one that has provided inspiration for many oppressed groups. Care needs to be taken to ensure that such an idea of transcendence is not unduly discarded as irredeemably "male". The idea that who or what you are should not matter: that all are different but yet those differences should not be allowed to count; that all should be seen as individuals, independently of their class and social status, race, colour, sex, is, as Anne Phillips has noted, a powerful and attractive idea for women.[107] This idea is progressed in Chapter 2 in the context of the ideal of a pre-social, aprioristic "person".

Much of the personal impetus towards a feminist politics is to do with claiming the space to choose who and what you are – not to be defined, contained and dictated by notions of what society means by "woman".[108] The idea that it should not matter who or what you are has been an inspiration to generations of women as has the associated notion that women should be regarded as individuals, as persons in their own right, as independent of contingencies of sex. Liberals abstract the essential "man" from the accident of history or biology and, as Phillips so neatly puts it, while the emphasis on man is a bit of a blow, the basic structure seems to fit: everyone is different but those differences should not be allowed to count.[109] Equality despite difference has been described as the point of greatest contact between liberalism and feminism.[110] If transcendence means ignoring difference it can confirm inequalities that socially exist. The pretence that sexual difference is irrelevant has been shown to deny women the chance of equal jobs and political involvement.[111]

Analysis in Chapter 2 seeks to show how transcendence does not have to be always, only, inevitably a male ideal and that it is possible to reconstruct the ideal of transcendence in terms of abstract thought so that it is something to which more women could and would want to aspire because it enables a distancing and detachment from one's own particular situation to allow for a re-evaluation of present circumstances. Linked to this idea is an analysis of the work of those feminists who argue that reason and universalism exclude the feminine.

---

[107] See A Phillips 1993.
[108] A Phillips 1993, p 43.
[109] A Phillips, 1993, p 38–43.
[110] A Phillips, 1993; C Pateman, 1987.
[111] A Phillips, 1993.

## Conclusion

Those who have often been categorised as liberal feminists in second wave and contemporary feminism use similar arguments to those of Wollstonecraft, Taylor and Mill, stating that women have the same capacity for reason as men and ought to be allowed to develop it. In the work of liberal feminists, this view is central. They seek to follow it to its logical conclusion by emphasising the injustice in excluding women from the definition of the human being, using liberalism's foundational tenets of reason, freedom and equality and turning them back on those writers to show how they failed to live up to their own standards.[112]

It is widely acknowledged that primarily through the efforts of liberal feminism, the legal status of women in most industrialised nations has improved considerably.[113] However, as feminist theory has developed, particularly here in the UK, what is left is a largely nodding acknowledgement of the debt to liberalism but its perceived shortcomings appear to many to have exhausted its usefulness to the feminist project.[114] Despite this, as will be seen in Parts II and III, most feminists still use the language of liberalism and make strong claims for women to their very liberal right to self-determination and personal autonomy which still remain to be fulfilled world-wide.

The work of feminist theorists critiquing representations of the so-called "human" through reason and lack of opportunities and development of projects for themselves is invaluable. Such representations show views of human nature, the "subject" at the heart of their theories, as seemingly representing the whole of humankind. It has been shown how the first manifestations of second wave feminism drew on liberal values, arguing that they should be applied more consistently to women. However, there soon emerged a critique of the norm of equality and a reorientation of women's voice in politics and culture. This theme will now be explained in detail in my next chapter.

---

[112] See Okin 1979; MC Nussbaum, 1999; C Pateman, 1988; G Lloyd, 1984; JR Richards, 1982; D Kirp and L Yudof *Gender Justiice* (Chicago: University of Chicago Press 1985), A Gutmann *Liberal Equality* (Cambridge: Cambridge University Press 1980); W Kymlicka *Contemporary Political Philosophy* (Oxford: Oxford University Press 1990); C Littleton "Reconstructing Sexual Equality" (1987) 75 *California Law Review* 1279; J Nedelsky, 1989. See analysis of liberal feminism (in the context of the liberal/communitarian debate) in E Frazer and N Lacey, 1993, and N Lacey, 1998.

[113] Acknowledged by many, including A Jaggar, 1983, and A Phillips, 1993, p 103.

[114] See E Frazer and N Lacey, 1993, p 100; E Jackson and N Lacey, 2002.

Chapter 2

# Universalism and the Exclusion of the Feminine

*"Women are actually or potentially materially connected to other human life. Men aren't."* Robin West.[1]

**The Pre-Social Person**

While some feminists presented the view that women have been denied opportunities to develop the capacity for reason, others that femininity is the other to be overcome and transcended, others still argue that women have a *different kind of character* which may complement, but is different to the man of reason.[2]

As has been shown, the capacity for reason often points to a core essence of personhood, represented as a metaphysical essence that all human beings have regardless of history, environment, age etc and all contingencies. In the work of many Western philosophers critiqued by second wave feminists, finding the essence of moral agency largely involves purely rational non-empirical ideas, not derived from human psychology and actual lived experiences. Feminist critiques seek to highlight the contrast between the search for abstract universality, finding a common characteristic of humans, and their specific experienced empirical circumstances in a gendered world.

This common characteristic of humans or essence is often described as a *pre-social* aspect of persons. This essence is particularly evident in the social contract tradition which certain second wave feminists argue lead to solipsistic views of humanity.[3]

The social contract tradition forms one of the most widely argued bases for State and government legitimacy, and accordingly, the laws existing in various countries.[4] The idea is that individuals are originally in a state of nature but form together with each other in the interests of self-preservation and enter into a social pact or contract either with each other or between themselves and the state. There

---

[1] R West, 1988, p 6.
[2] See G Lloyd, 1984, p 50.
[3] See A Jaggar, 1983; V Held *Feminist Morality* (Chicago: University of Chicago Press 1993); but see J Hampton "Feminist Contractarianism" in LM Antony and CE Witt, 2002, p 337–368.
[4] See P Riley, 1982.

are various versions, including those of Hobbes, Locke and Rousseau, with the most eminent modern day theorist being John Rawls.[5]

This Chapter investigates the pre-social, abstract individual which forms the basis of this tradition and which communitarian and many second wave feminist critiques see as the liberal individual. An investigation is made as to whether the ideal of the abstract universal individual has any merit. Many feminist criticisms investigated in this Chapter focus on the fact, as they see it, that the individual human being is presented as too individualistic, contrasting with the views (mentioned in the previous chapter) of Okin and Nussbaum who say it has not been individualistic enough. Ultimately, the conclusion is reached that the abstraction of the individual can be interpreted as a heuristic device which can allow for common humanity and still have force for women's liberation, particularly as translated into legal globalism and human rights under international humanitarian law all of which are investigated in Part III. Although it is argued that the idea of a social contract is unnecessary, the idea of the abstract individual still retains force. Not precluded by this conclusion however is the importance of social context in identity formation and the inherent interconnection of humans. The argument presented is that these are two different aspects of what it means to be human. The first is an imaginary device, the second is a psychological account of identity formation.

In the social contract tradition, the individual is presented as innocent, independent and alone, solitary and prior to society, in what is known as the "state of nature". He is generally fearful of what others will do to him and his aim is self-preservation. He is also free and on an equal footing with others. No-one is entitled to more than the other, each is entitled to all in common.[6] Traditionally, in a state of nature, the starting point is that everyone is a separate individual who is free and equal. However, these pre-social individuals then come together by voluntary consent and agree to form a society and then a state, institutionalising social and political arrangements. As was shown in Chapter 1, when such views were presented for the first time, they were revolutionary: if all individuals are free and equal, and any social realities and contingencies of actual people are "simply" the result of living under the social contract (and could therefore be rearranged), this idea can form the foundation for many oppressed people seeking liberation. Such a theory allows for a shared characteristic which constitutes basic or formal humanity: that all are free and equal.

The social contract which emerges takes on different forms in different theories. In what is generally considered to be the classic liberal view, the society which emerges would allow each individual the maximum freedom from interference by others, and the state would seek to protect individual rights to fair shares of resources and maximise opportunity for individual autonomy and self-fulfilment. Given humans' essential capacity for reason, all are capable of making choices, entering agreements with each other and are often represented as being somehow able to separate themselves from feelings, emotions, passions, personal interests and motives, socio-economic and political factors, the past, their

---

[5] See T Hobbes, 1960; J Locke, 1988; and JJ Rousseau, 1974; J Rawls, 1971.
[6] Mainly a paraphrase of Hobbes's position.

aspirations for the future etc., and are not dependent on socially particular circumstances. These humans are capable of achieving distance from known objects and therefore are able to reflect on them. This has been described as human beings having minds unlocated in space, time or constitutive interrelations with others.[7]

In Immanuel Kant's work, the notion that moral worth cannot depend on contingencies is starkly presented.[8] In addition, it emphasises the idea of respect which is owed to each "man" as a rational moral agent – "men" are equally such agents and therefore respect is owed equally to all.[9]

This is clearly seen in Kant's theory of the Kingdom of Ends, where men must be regarded as ends and not the means of other men. The Kantian capacity for moral freedom or unconditioned reason as the determining ground of the will provides all rational beings with a particular kind of identity: one that establishes all such beings as ends in themselves and defines what it is to be human. Such free and rational beings choose to govern their associations with each other.[10]

Four claims and assumptions have been identified as forming the essence of Kantian liberalism:

(i)     all individuals share a common identity as free and equal moral actors (at least within their political community);

(ii)    the common identity of humans is discerned by *abstracting* from social and natural contingencies;

(iii)   just political principles and institutions are those that would be selected if individuals reason primarily from the common ground provided by their identity as free and equal moral actors (taking a neutral standpoint which is assumed to exist);

(iv)    proper reasoning from this common ground will lead to approval of certain liberal practices.[11]

One would have thought that surely such noble, universal ideals could form the foundation for a universal conception of humanity to include women. However, Kant's theory has been critiqued by feminists for its masculine bias. Such critiques have drawn attention to the fact that, for Kant, women do not possess the most important human quality of reason which forms the basis of all moral agency in his

---

[7] E Gross "What is Feminist Theory?" in C Pateman and E Gross (eds), 1986, p 190.

[8] I Kant, 1988. See a good analysis of this aspect of Immanuel Kant's work by B Yack "The Problem with Kantian Liberalism" in R Beiner and WJ Booth (eds) *Kant and Political Philosophy: The Contemporary Legacy* (New Haven and London: Yale University Press 1993).

[9] B Williams "The Idea of Equality" in H Bedau (ed) *Jurisprudence and Equality* (Englewood Cliffs, NJ: Prentice-Hall 1971) in particular at p 121–124.

[10] See G Lloyd's discussion of Kant, 1984, p 64–70.

[11] B Yack, 1993, p 225.

theory.[12] According to this theory, each person has fundamentally the capacity to form and act upon intelligent conceptions of how his or her life should be lived (that is, choose their life plans) and the law's purpose has been described as being to capture and give effect to the rights that people in fact have and respecting the rational choices they make.[13]

In John Rawls's contemporary social contract theory, Rawls relies on a claim about individuals' shared identity as moral actors that is very similar to Kant's.[14] The view of the human being presented by him has been described as an abstracted capacity to choose, unencumbered by any particular loyalties, values, tastes, commitments, history or identity.[15] As already mentioned in Chapter 1, in *A Theory of Justice*, Rawls uses the heuristic device of a hypothetical discussion taking place between hypothetical individuals. This is the "Original Position" similar to the state of nature in traditional social contract theories and leads to a hypothetical contract being agreed upon, where the moral actors involved produce principles of justice.[16]

This "discussion" takes place behind a "veil of ignorance", Rawls's device to abstract individuals from their "contingencies" such as status, environment, age, sex. Assuming, as Rawls does, that all individuals would be self-interested and therefore biased, this device is used to ensure that the individuals will not be biased in trying to obtain the best for themselves because, not knowing where they will end up, they cannot take into account their own place in existing society when trying to agree on the principles. The hope is that this will lead to a fairer set of principles being agreed.

This inherent self-interest which Rawls assumes all human beings to have in the Original Position is the motivating factor of human nature and has been described as, "universal egoism".[17] Because of "natural" selfish human motivation, the notion of impartiality and a striving for objectivity to stop people placing their own selfish interests before the interests of others is needed. This view represents

---

[12] See N Naffine *Female Crime: The Construction of Women in Criminology* (London: Allen and Unwin 1987) at p 107–8; A Barron "Illusions of the I: Citizenship and the Politics of Identity" in A Norrie (ed) *Closure or Critique: New Directions in Legal Theory* (Edinburgh: Edinburgh University Press 1993) at p 80–100; B Herman "Could it be worth thinking About Kant on Sex and Marriage?" in L Anthony and C Witt, 2002.

[13] See A Barron, 1993, p 80–81 where this supposedly universal citizen is criticised as a mechanism of exclusion.

[14] J Rawls, 1971.

[15] J Penner, D Schiff and R Nobles, 2002, p 764.

[16] J Rawls, 1971: Rawls argues that in this "Original Position" individuals would all agree on the following set of principles:

(1) each person is to have an equal right to the most extensive total system of equal basic liberties compatible with a similar system of liberty for all;

(2) Social and economic inequalities are to be arranged so that they are both:

   (a) attached to offices and positions open to all under conditions of fair equality of opportunity and

   (b) to the greatest benefit of the least advantaged – at p 206–7.

[17] A Jaggar, 1983.

human beings motivated by a concern for themselves before others, and with no necessary connection with each other. The respect owed to others is because of the common characteristic of a free and rational will.

It has been argued that this cannot provide solid foundations for equality and respect for all, as concepts allied to it, like responsibility, are based on empirical fact.[18] The universalising moral duty owed to all persons through their rational nature which Kant takes to give each person dignity and to make each of absolute value, and therefore irreplaceable, has been described as no more than an abstract rational nature in virtue of which all are alike, and if all are alike in this respect, it has been queried why individuals would be irreplaceable.[19] Such a common rational nature would seem to make individuals indistinguishable and therefore mutually interchangeable with specific identity being a matter of indifference. Instead, it has been proposed that everyone should try to respect and understand the other's consciousness of his or her own activities and not suppress or destroy that consciousness, involving a mixture of empirical fact and universalisation. So it could be said that much of past "reason" can be seen as a failure to acknowledge the differences between male and female minds produced and played out in a social context of real inequalities. There is therefore a division between the ideal, imaginary, what "should be" and the actual, empirical "what is". The conviction that minds, insofar as they are rational, are fundamentally alike, underlies many moral and political ideals and provides a basis for ideas of universality and common human equality.[20]

Further, this pre-social essence neglects the reality of childhood, and the necessity of early dependency on others in identity formation. Attacks have been made of this view of the individual and society and the representation of the "moral actors" in the Original Position, particularly in the last few decades by certain communitarian and feminist thinkers.[21] In particular, focus rests on the liberal tradition exemplified in Rawls's theory which reduces individuals to the "essence" of their personhood by detaching "contingencies". But in tandem with these critiques is a view that universalism holds promise for feminists. Therefore the task of feminism has been described as making good this promise and incorporating women into existing institutions as equals.[22] But feminism is often seen as fitting women into a framework that assumes that there is only one universal (non)sex or that insists sexual difference is irrelevant but then leaves intact the sexually particular characterisation of the public world, that is, based on masculine traits or

---

[18] See B Williams, 1971.

[19] B Williams, 1971.

[20] G Lloyd, 1984 at (ix).

[21] A Jaggar, 1983; E Frazer and N Lacey, 1993; N Lacey, 1998; M Sandel, 1982/1998; A MacIntyre *After Virtue* (London: Duckworth 1981); A MacIntyre *Whose Justice? Which Rationality?* (London: Duckworth 1988); C Taylor, 1992; also *Sources of the Self* (Cambridge: Cambridge University Press 1989); S Mulhall and A Swift *Liberals and Communitarians* (2nd Edn Oxford: Blackwells 1992, 1996); S Avineri and A de-Shalit (eds), 1992.

[22] See C Pateman and E Gross (eds), 1986, Introduction.

one to which men – given their life experiences and the different socialisation processes that boys and men and girls and women go through – are more suited. So, it has rightly been pointed out that often the universal standing that will be won by equality is that of a being with masculine characteristics engaging in masculine activities.[23]

The feminist critiques show that what is abstracted as universal is usually based on what men have empirically experienced and therefore hinders women's attainment to this universal standard of humanity.

A search for abstraction or universalisation has been criticised by many in the feminist movement as a male or masculine way of thinking. The work of Carol Gilligan and ethic of care theorists analysed later in this chapter, and the work of postmodern feminists analysed in the next, emphasise this aspect of universal thought. Many believe that focusing on particular women's experiences and concentrating on the particular in contextual situations, rather than generalising and trying not to universalise is of more use to changing people's actual lives. In the following sections, I analyse communitarian critiques of the pre-social before investigating Gilligan and the ethic of care critiques.

## A Feminist Take on the Communitarian Critique Revisited

Many communitarians are critical of abstraction, which they see exemplified in Rawls's conception of the person in the Original Position precisely because that person's contingencies are extracted. This turn presents a defective conception of the self, failing to recognise the self as embedded in, and partly constituted by, communal attachments, commitments and values.[24] An example of a particularly clear, but ultimately unconvincing, critique of this kind is that presented by Michael Sandel.[25] Sandel argues that if abstraction from contingencies takes place, including from the individual's place in society or, in particular, their "community", there will be no individual left. Instead, there will be one "person" in the Original Position who is in effect a personification of Kantian autonomous free will. There is, on this interpretation, no "meeting of minds" or "debate" or "discussion" between different people – for all are the same, meaning one.

The Rawlsian original chooser is presented in ghostly form – the unencumbered, disembodied self. In distinguishing the self from its ends, the Kantian, Rawlsian deontological self has produced a radically disembodied subject; that is, one wholly without character, incapable of self-knowledge, dispossessed. As Sandel sees it, such a person cannot and does not exist. Ends are constitutive of self: communal aims and values are not just affirmed by the members of the community, they define the identity of those members. The shared

---

[23] A point made by many feminists, see, for example, C Dalton "Where We Stand" (1988) 3 *Berkeley Women's Law Journal* 1; M Gatens, 1991.

[24] A Buchanan "Assessing the Communitarian Critique of Liberalism" (1989) 99 *Ethics*: 852–882 at p 853.

[25] M Sandel, 1982/1998.

pursuit of a communal goal is not a chosen relationship but a constituent of identity and discovered attachments. Community becomes an idea of normative significance to be valued in and of itself.

The good society for communitarians is one of settled traditions and established identities. The process Rawls uses of identifying with others is seen as a one-sided approach to identifying with others, in that it merely allows people to *imagine* themselves requiring the treatment they see others receiving. For example, imaginary discussions with imaginary people have been claimed to raise problems about empathetic judgement, in that Rawls seems to assume that a single individual can get inside the experiences of others, imagine what their lives might be, *without ever having actually listened to anyone else.*[26] Instead, it is claimed that if an interpretation of Rawlsian people in the Original Position is to be seen as one where individuals adopt the positions of others and really engage in empathetic judgement, it will only work if the Original Position turns into a conversation between real, socially situated people.[27] In order to see the world from the other's perspective, it is argued that the most salient differences between different, often opposite, perspectives on ways of looking at the world will need to be identified, proceeding to examine one's individual conceptions from the other's perspective.[28] If imagination and not real discussions take place, it is argued that there is a considerable risk that individuals will impose their identity on others by suggesting that they know others better than the others know themselves. Determinations are made about the identity of the other without considering their opinions about their own identities.

The liberal/communitarian debate (at its height in the 1980s and 1990s) has been subject to feminist critique.[29] The liberal counter-argument to communitarians is that the latter's conception of the self is determined and leaves little scope for agency and will as subjectivity, which is central to liberal politics and to feminists. The two groups' starting points for reflection differ. Liberals' ultimate value is the life of self-determination; the communitarian view is that the social structure. The collective is therefore the most appropriate starting point or at least equally important because the individual and community are linked intimately.[30]

Criticisms have been made that the liberal ideal sees persons living autonomous choosing lives pursuing their conceptions of the good but this carries with it a conception of political society and a public culture which must have more priority in political theory than most liberals have been willing to give it and that a greater emphasis must be put on the importance of social context in influencing judgement.[31] Some feminists acknowledge that there has been a significant move in liberal political theory towards a recognition of the social from the 1980s onwards with the political importance of the social, cultural and "other-regarding"

---

[26] N Lacey, 1998.
[27] E Frazer and N Lacey, 1993, p 57 and N Lacey, 1998, p 65–7.
[28] B Yack, 1993, p 236.
[29] E Frazer and N Lacey, 1993; N Lacey, 1998, at ch 3; SM Okin 1989.
[30] N Lacey, 1998, p 56–60.
[31] C Taylor's point from "Atomism", 1992; see N Lacey, 1998, p 67–69.

values beginning to appear on the liberal agenda.[32] However, it is claimed that the very conceptual framework of liberal theory would hamper its development of the insights offered by the movement towards a recognition of the social.[33]

As has been shown, liberalism stresses the rational capacity of individuals to choose as a necessary component of a human being. One disadvantageous consequence of this for women can be a justification of inequalities (including gender-specific ones) on the basis of women's "free" choices.[34] The pre-social self underplays the extent to which social and political institutions shape individuals' preferences, attitudes and dispositions.[35] The focus on interests, rights and entitlements of individuals is claimed to obscure systematic patterns of exclusion of women. Differently patterned outcomes can therefore be explained away as the product of autonomous individual choices and thus be seen as legitimate. Accordingly, it is argued that liberal theory removes from its ambit factors which structure women's choices, for example, their disproportionate responsibilities in the private sphere. That is, liberals have often taken insufficient account of the social and background constraints which are vitally important to the life choices people make. A focus instead on the way identities are developed in concrete social and historical situations, and in relation to social context and other persons, is represented as being at odds with the abstract individualism and "essentialism" of the liberal individual.[36] This point is developed in detail in Chapter 5 in the context of preference formation.

While advocating a full recognition of the embodied and socially situated nature of human life, it has been recognised that an important question for feminism is how to prevent the slide from a radically disembodied subject to a radically embodied subject who is a victim of her circumstances.[37] This is where it

---

[32] E Frazer and N Lacey, 1993, p 68.

[33] See also Z Eisenstein 1981, and *Feminism and Sexual Equality* (New York: Monthly Review Press 1984) discussed below.

[34] E Frazer and N Lacey say that the factors which structure women's choices (for example their disproportionate responsibilities in the private sphere) are removed by liberal theory from the ambit of the political. For them, the liberal individualist discourse contains tools for explaining away, as a political problem, substantive sex inequality. Like many feminist critics of liberal individualism, Frazer and Lacey see it as being ill-equipped to focus constructively and critically on social institutions and relations like gender, class and race: on how social groups and communities function and on how individuals do not choose life decisions independently from the society and community they live in.

[35] See E Jackson and N Lacey, 2002, p 779, a point developed fully in Part II below.

[36] The idea is that with differences in men's and women's experience, differences in conceptualising reality, different standpoints will occur. So many proponents of women's standpoint argue that women's position in society provides the basis for an autonomous epistemological standpoint. Some argue, like Marx, that there is no epistemological standpoint outside social reality with all knowledge being shaped by its social origins. In some versions of standpoint theory, women's subordinate status means they do not have an interest in mystifying reality and will provide clearer and more trustworthy understandings of the world that will therefore be more objective and unbiased than that of men.

[37] E Frazer and N Lacey, 1993, p 58–60.

is necessary to make a distinction between conceptual notions of normative ideals and visions of what *should be* – and descriptions of existing experiences and psychological development – a point developed later in this chapter.

Many feminists argue that recognition needs to be given to the social location of the individual and how community affects who individuals are but their sense of themselves as distinct and autonomous is still important.[38] Advocates of a "relational" theory of the self want a political theory that starts from a *relational* and *situated* conception of the self and a differentiated view of society but yet retain ideas of women's individual subjectivity as autonomous beings. This is not the same as the communitarian self because of the need for individual women in their community or society to be able to *critically reflect* on their circumstances to evaluate whether they are good, fair and just for them as persons and whether enabling conditions to lead flourishing lives exist.

It has been accurately argued that a metaphysical view that all human selves are constituted by their social and communal relationships does not itself entail a critique of highly individualistic selves or yield any indication of what degree of psychological attachment to others is desirable, for both the relational, sociable self and the autonomous, individualistic and separate self would be equivalently socially constituted at a metaphysical level.[39] On this analysis, the communitarian thesis appears to be of little assistance to feminist theorists seeking a normative account of what might be wrong about self-seeking behaviour and the other problems many critics see in possessive individualism.

Using insights about the contribution of community and social relationship to self-identity, yet opening up for critical reflection the moral norms of those communities and identifying the sorts of communities which will provide non-oppressive and enriched lives for women is key. It will be necessary and important to obtain and retain the ability to choose which morals and norms to accept or reject.[40] Thus the modern self or human being may seek new communities whose norms and relationships stimulate and develop his or her identity and self-understanding more adequately than their unchosen community of origin. Some people do not comply or identify with the norms which unify their original communities, including those foundational social norms which ground the most basic social roles and relationships upon which those communities rest. Indeed, the feminist challenge to sex and gender arrangements is that sort of challenge.[41]

---

[38] See N Lacey, 1998; C MacKenzie and N Stoljar (eds) *Relational Autonomy: Feminist Perspectives on Autonomy, Agency and the Social Self* (Oxford: Oxford University Press 2000); S Benhabib *Situating the Self* (Cambridge: Polity Press 1992) ; D Meyers *Subjection and Subjectivity* (New York and London: Routledge 1994). See further analysis in Part II.

[39] M Friedman "Beyond Caring: the De-Moralization of Gender" in *Canadian Journal of Philosophy Supplementary Volume 13 Science, Morality and Feminist Theory* (1987) 87 at p 105–6.

[40] M Friedman uses the example of modern friendship and urban community which she says will help give us insights into the social nature of the modern self, (1987, p 113).

[41] M Friedman, 1987, at 118.

In the context of a capacity to critically revise one's own views and see things from others' perspectives, the veil of ignorance has been described favourably as a demanding stipulation that converts what would without it be self-interest into equal concern for others, including others who are very different from oneself.[42] On Okin's interpretation, those in the Original Position cannot think from the position of nobody, as is suggested by those critics like Sandel who then conclude that Rawls's theory depends on a "disembodied" concept of the self.[43] Instead, they must think from the perspective of everybody in the sense of each in turn. To do this requires both strong empathy and a preparedness to listen carefully to the very different points of view of others.[44] Rawls' Original Position is described as a *"central brilliant idea"* in that it *"forces one to question and consider traditions, customs and institutions from all points of view"*.[45] The importance of adopting the position of others, especially positions you could never be in, has been stressed by some, and individuals thinking in such a way might well conclude that more than formal legal equality of the sexes is required if justice is to be done. On this interpretation, the Original Position – in hiding from its participants their sex, as well as other particular characteristics – is a powerful concept for challenging the gender structure.[46]

By requiring individuals to abstract from particular but not shared interests, the Original Position avoids reliance on existing preferences and allows individuals to stand back to critically evaluate the communities, societies and structures that exist, permitting ideas of the possible which may be better than those already in existence, with the emphasis resting on the fact that all individuals value the freedom to choose a good life for themselves. The Original Position is *a device* to allow individuals to stand back from their own partial situatedness to construct principles fair for all – that is its power, not its weakness. Individual "selves" are perceived prior to their ends in that persons can always envisage themselves without their present ends.

If communitarians only mean that individuals are embedded in their community but that this is not incompatible with rejecting their attachments, then the contrast between their view and that of liberalism is a deception. Communitarians view moral theory as a process of self-discovery, liberals as a process of judgement and choice but if individuals are embedded yet able to critique and change, there seems no difference between the two.[47] If communitarianism means that individuals neither choose nor reject the attachments they simply find themselves in them; if their goals are decided by some sort of self-discovery; if the meaning of the social roles and practices in which a person finds him or herself cannot be rejected as worthless since these are constitutive of the

---

[42] SM Okin 1989.
[43] In particular M Sandel, 1982.
[44] SM Okin 1989, p 100–1.
[45] SM Okin 1989, p 101.
[46] SM Okin 1989, p 108–9. However, Okin is critical of Rawls for using the "male-headed household" as his moral actor in the Original Position as discussed in Chapter 1.
[47] See W Kymlicka, 1990.

person themselves, then communitarianism is a mistaken position because individuals do, and indeed *ought* to be able to, question the value of their attachments and traditions. Structures should enable and allow traditions and practices to be rejected if they come to be regarded as degrading or oppressive.

Often people do consider themselves to be "trapped" by their present attachments, that is precisely why it is necessary to live in a society which enables such individuals to change their situation. Some do not always like what they find when they analyse their various relationships. No matter how deeply implicated individuals may be in a social practice, the capacity ought to be available to, at least, question whether that practice is a valuable one. Sometimes individuals have become so embedded in the community's practices that it is virtually impossible for them to question the fairness of the situation. This is why it is important to ensure that the conditions appropriate to re-examine ways of life and individual ends are readily available: in Chapter 5 ways to enhance this freedom for individual women are presented.

Sometimes, communitarians admit that boundaries of the self, although constituted by its ends, are flexible and can be redrawn in which case the human subject can make choices about which possible purposes and ends it will pursue and which it will not.[48] As has been noted, as long as a person can re-examine his or her ends, then communitarianism has not been justified because there is a failure to show why individuals should not be given the conditions appropriate to that re-examining, as an indispensible part of leading the best possible life. If individuals reject their attachments and redraw the boundaries, then communitarians fail to show why the liberal view of the self is wrong and why liberal morality is wrong.[49]

Ultimately, the presentation of the human as an agent who views all their goals and attachments as subject in principle to critical revision is radically detachable. This is not a view of the *psychological* identity of the individual human, it is a capacity within each person that allows for *imaginative critical evaluation* of their plans of life, allowing for the revision of possible goals.

It is the possession of a sense of being and potential to change and develop which ought to be fostered in humans. However, the assumption that such a presentation of the human is incompatible with making and sustaining commitments in community is mistaken. A liberal society can offer one of the most feasible frameworks for making autonomy and commitment compatible.[50] If the individual's ability to choose and revise their own ends diminishes and the critical distance between them and possible courses of action shrinks, their very status as a moral agent becomes precarious. This is because a moral agent is one whose actual behaviour and potentiality in some basic sense is their own. It is this fundamental characteristic that is common to all human beings but for it to be effective and flourishing it needs to be nurtured in a caring, interdependent environment as will be explained fully in Part II.

---

[48] See M Sandel, 1982, p 152.
[49] See W Kymlicka, 1990, at chapter 6.
[50] See A Buchanan, 1989, p 867.

**The Group, Not the Individual**

Similar in many ways to the communitarian critique of the atomistic liberal individual is the critique that focuses on women as members of collectives or groups rather than individuals. Emphasising the capacity humans have for reason stresses the importance of individuality, rather than on the group and arguably to a view of humans as abstract and atomised individuals rather than situated contextual persons, all of which has been said to favour men's lives more than women's. Certain feminists argue that a representation of humans as radically individualistic is of no use to women because women need to be recognised as a collective or class.[51] However, this is ultimately not the logical conclusion to such arguments. Instead their conclusions highlight how women and others in oppressed groups fail to be treated as human beings in their own right by being used and dominated in an instrumental way. At the same time as arguing that women needed to group together for political purposes, they ultimately seem to want women to be recognised as *human beings* in their own right. The arguments are based on liberal assumptions that the basic equality in life situations for all persons is a moral value; that there are deep injustices in societies that can only be rectified by basic institutional changes; that certain groups are oppressed and that structures of domination wrongfully pervade societies.

   Some feminists argue that the liberal feminist view of the inclusion of women in the universal subject contains the seeds of its own destruction.[52] According to this analysis the radical potential in liberal feminism arises from the contradiction between liberalism as patriarchal and individualist in structure and ideology, and feminism as sexually egalitarian and collectivist requiring a recognition of the sexual class identification of women as women, showing the tension between the individual and the collective. If the feminist demand for real equality of women with men is taken to its logical conclusion, so the argument goes, the patriarchal structure, in tandem with liberal society, would be dislodged. A view of the liberal individual is presented as denying the connectedness and relatedness of individuals which liberal feminists need because its feminist priorities reflect an understanding of the *social nature* of women's oppression, yet a theory of individuality is needed within Western feminism to recognise the necessity of independence and autonomy within and between men's and women's lives. So Eisenstein writes:

---

[51] An interesting analysis of this aspect of the feminist contribution to the concept of the human being is provided in the work of Zillah Eisenstein whose work is largely focused on in this section – see Z Eisenstein, 1981; see also I M Young's work, particularly *Justice and the Politics of Difference* (Princeton: Princeton University Press 1990).

[52] The idea is Eisenstein's: 1981. Lacey says liberal feminism contains the seeds of its own destruction: the examples given being the public-private division and the unattractiveness of the assimilation of women to a standard set by men. Instead of leading to a substantive reconsideration of the way in which the world was organised, the public standards in place were assumed to be valid: N Lacey, 1998, at Chapter 7.

However else one's feminism comes to be defined, its starting point is the notion of the separateness, distinctness, and independence of woman from man. This notion is as liberal as it is feminist.[53]

On this basis, the philosophy of individualism stresses the importance of autonomy and independence as a universal claim and therefore can be used to justify women's independence from men and lay the foundation for recognising women's economic, sexual and political independence from men. However, this must be distinguished from the isolated and competitive liberal individual. Yet, at the same time, feminist politics requires a social collectivity that recognises the interconnectedness of women and a theory of individualism must recognise, as Eisenstein puts it, the *individual character* of social nature and *social nature* of individuality and must also understand the interconnection of power relations and the relatedness of human beings to the other: a theory she sees lacking in liberalism. So feminism is potentially subversive to liberalism and the "*capitalist patriarchal state*" because women will become conscious of themselves as a sexual class as demands for reforms continue and then they realise that liberal reforms will not be enough.[54]

Explicit criticisms of liberalism are mistaken in these analyses. Liberalism does not lack a theory of the social nature of the individual and of individuals' relatedness to each other. It does not need the "*patriarchal state*", in fact patriarchy is at odds with the full realisation of liberal principles of equality, freedom and justice for all humans. Further, feminist politics only requires some sense of social collectivity and the interconnectedness of women because women are not accorded full human rights as full human beings.

Such arguments express the liberal principle of individual freedom of choice but take the analysis further back to more basic levels of power structures, rather than the level of distribution of resources. It is true that often liberals overlook the social significance of relations of power and thus fail to see that gender neutrality results (in existing power structures) in disadvantages.[55]

Failure of liberals to follow through their own ideas to their logical conclusion is to be criticised. However, many liberals advocate different treatment to provide for equality. This can most notably be seen in the work of Ronald

---

[53] Z Eisenstein "Elizabeth Cady Stanton: Radical-Feminist Analysis and Liberal Feminist Strategy" in A Phillips (ed), 1987, p 98.

[54] To be free and equal individuals, women cannot be defined in terms of their difference from men but they need the freedom and sexual equality to explore their particular and universal qualities. This freedom is highly dependent on but not determined by the social relations of society, the degree of sexual, economic racial equality and freedom of sexual preference. So long as work and home do not have the same value in society, the choice of motherhood will be a choice of inferior status. Women cannot be equal to men if the institutional structures of their lives are not of equal value and importance to society. Real egalitarianism requires the destruction of the separateness of family and work and of public and private: Eisenstein, 1984, at Chapter 8.

[55] E Frazer and N Lacey, 1993, p 76–77.

Dworkin.[56] His theory of equality rests on the fundamental equal rights of all individuals to be treated as equals. This will not entail equal treatment, it may involve affirmative action programmes and treating people differently to then treat them as equals.[57] How his work has been used by Drucilla Cornell is examined in Chapter 3.

However, are women somehow excluded from universal ideas of abstraction for more fundamental reasons than those already presented? Can it be shown that women's ways of being and thinking have been excluded from those universally abstracted?

**The Ethic of Care Critique**

The feminist ethic of care critique of universal abstract reasoning came to the fore in the early 1980s following the publication of psychologist Carol Gilligan's work into gendered patterns of reasoning.[58] Gilligan's starting point for her research is a critique of other psychological research that had been carried out by Lawrence Kohlberg.[59]

Kohlberg's research had categorised moral development into six different levels and he concluded that women have a lesser moral sense than men. His claim is that people at the highest stage of moral development (his sixth stage) answer moral dilemmas in moral words like duty or morally right. These words are used by such individuals in a way implying universality, ideals and impersonality.[60] Using this analysis, females were commonly thought to be in some way deficient compared to males and this was reflected in the tendency of females to score lower on Kohlberg's stage achievement allocations. His (developmentally incomplete) stage three – where individuals concentrated on resolving moral conflicts and dilemmas by reference to their interrelationships – was seen as the characteristic mode of women's moral judgement. On this basis, women are not particularly encouraged to develop to the "higher" stages into autonomous and abstract

---

[56] See, for example, R Dworkin *Taking Rights Seriously* (London: Duckworth 1977); R Dworkin *A Matter of Principle* (Cambridge Mass: Harvard University Press 1985); R Dworkin *Life's Dominion: An argument about abortion, euthanasia and individual freedom* (New York: Vintage Books 1994); R Dworkin *Sovereign Virtue* (London: Harvard University Press 2000). See also S Guest *Ronald Dworkin* (2nd Edn Edinburgh: Edinburgh University Press 1997).

[57] R Dworkin 1977. Dworkin is not without his feminists critics too of course: see, for example, A Phillips *Which Equalities Matter?* (Cambridge: Polity Press 1999), V Kerruish "Dworkin's Dutiful Daughter" in A Hunt (ed) *Reading Dworkin Critically* (New York: Oxford, Berg 1992), R Langton "Whose Right? Ronald Dworkin, Women and Pornographers" (1990) 19 *Philosophy and Public Affairs* 311.

[58] C Gilligan, 1982.

[59] L Kohlberg *The Philosophy of Moral Development* (San Francisco: Harper and Row 1981). Gilligan actually helped research some of Kohlberg's work.

[60] See O Flanagan and K Jackson's analysis in "Justice, Care and Gender" (1987) 97 *Ethics* 622–37.

thinking that had been more closely associated with masculinity and are therefore treated as childlike or as lesser forms of the human.[61] For moral agency, like Kant's, reason and rationality are at the centre of the conception of the good or moral person.[62]

In a way reminiscent of the isolated individual of liberal thought, the perception is that the process of increasing differentiation of self from others with a corresponding progression from particular situations to generalisations is of higher moral worth than a way of thinking which concentrates on individuals' relationships with each other and particular contexts. Thus the morally mature individual comes to conceive of self as *separate from*, instead of *connected to*, others, and to favour autonomous life over interdependence. Kohlberg's position has been interpreted as the morally good person being one who reasons with, and acts on, the basis of principles of justice such as those advocated by Kant and John Rawls.[63]

Gilligan's much documented research initially involved psychological tests in girls and boys and men and women. That research centred on posing dilemmas to a total sample of 144 males and females, matched by age, intelligence, education, occupation and social class, at nine different points across the life cycle.[64] From these tests, Gilligan concluded that there are two distinct moral voices that correlate with gender. The feminine moral mode is based on caring, the maintenance of relationships, a web of communications and networks. The particular needs of others are seen in the context of particular relationships and situations. The masculine moral mode is objective and impartial, impersonal, unemotional, and related to obligations, justice and fairness and rules – in short, the generally idealised form of a legal system. One speaks about equality, reciprocity, fairness, rights; the other speaks about connection, not hurting, care and response. Gilligan's results draw attention to the fact that it is the "masculine" mode that coincides with cultural expectations of justice which constitute the idealised form of legal systems. For example, impartiality is seen as vital to adjudication – rules ought to be applied universally; using objective standards irrespective of individuals' particular situations. As to the cause (whether biological, social or other) of the allegedly real differences based on gender, Gilligan remained neutral.

Ethic of care work emanating from the results of this research sets out to re-evaluate the repressed and undervalued "feminine" mode and argues that the different voice of women's experience and judgement needs to be heard alongside

---

[61] See M Drakopoulou "The Ethic of Care, Female Subjectivity and Feminist Legal Scholarship" (2000) 8 *Feminist Legal Studies* 199–226. This correlates with Schopenhauer's view that "woman..is a kind of middle step between the child and the man, who is the true human being".

[62] See L Blum "Gilligan and Kohlberg: Implications for Moral Theory" (1988) 98 *Ethics* 472.

[63] See I Kant, 1988; Rawls, 1974. This interpretation is however open to debate. For example, see B Barry *Justice As Impartiality* (Oxford: Clarendon Press 1995), discussed further below.

[64] Gilligan, 1982, p 3.

the already prevalent male voice. Viewed as a mode of moral reasoning and as a source of moral insight, this different voice is represented as rational and potentially public in scope and is, at least, a necessary complement to impartial thought which men apparently employ in public. It is claimed that these voices are in tension with each other and a transformation in thinking is needed to include the two voices in moral discourse, in thinking about conflicts and in making choices. It is no longer either simply about justice or simply about caring, it is about bringing them together to transform and change the domain.

The idea is that the expression of a *different* rather than *inferior* social and moral understanding of the moral domain of women can be understood as characteristically contextual, connected and narrative. Women's moral dilemmas could be seen as arising from conflicting responsibilities rather than competing rights, their resolution requiring a mode of thinking that depends on an awareness of the connection between people.

This transformation in thinking can be seen as part of the process to transform the conception of the human being and to stop the equation of human with male. No longer can human development be known by studying men. Definitions of identity, morality, power and health etc that have been derived from studies of men's lives have to be questioned. On this account there are social deformations of both equality and attachment: the deformation of equality appears in the equation of human with male and the deformation of attachment in the equation of care with self-sacrifice. Both justice and care have to be reconstructed in different ways.[65]

Gilligan's position seems ambiguous: sometimes she seems to be talking about women being "connected" and caring, but yet she admits that both orientations are present in most people and anyone can speak in both ways.[66] The problem is if only one voice is celebrated, the girl or woman is going to let go of the other one, at least as an articulated public voice. The girl or woman will learn to speak in the voice that everybody hears and understands. In her 1986 work, Gilligan characterises the two ethics as different ways of viewing the world that organise both thinking and feeling and she returns continually to imagery. Justice orientations organise moral perception by highlighting issues of fairness, right and obligation. Care orientations focus on the interconnections among the parties involved.[67] If the two moral voices are *symbolic* of the perception people have of the moral concerns attributed to women and men, rather than empirically accurate: if actual men and women do not fit the traits and dispositions expected of them, this does not necessarily undermine the myths and symbols.[68] Some advocate increasing the options available to each individual – both male and female – allowing the human personality to break out of the present dichotomised system and express the view that the best moral theory is a co-operative product of women

---

[65] Gilligan, 1982, p 58.
[66] Gilligan, 1982, p 15.
[67] See O Flanagan and K Jackson, 1987, p 70.
[68] M Friedman, 1987.

and men, harmonising justice and care.[69] On this view, once there is this union of so-called male and female moral wisdom, each gender might be able to teach the other the moral skills each gender currently lacks, so that the gender difference in moral outlook will slowly become less marked.[70]

In what follows, three strands of ethic of care work are identified and explored. My purpose in doing so is to lay the foundation of its scope for use in conjunction with positive freedom as set out in Chapter 4. The first is the abstract universal reasoning process, as contrasted with particular contextual reasoning; the second is the account of the supposed inherent selfishness and separateness of the individual presented by liberals as opposed to interconnection and relational living; the third is the creative ways of thinking involved in much ethic of care work.

## The Reasoning Process

While the interconnected "nature" of women is examined in the next subsection, I want to concentrate now on the contrast between the universal, just, supposedly male, way of reasoning and the particular, caring, supposedly female way of reasoning.

The ethic of care has been described as...

> the stereotypic moral norm for women in the domestic role of sustaining a family in the face of the harsh realities of a competitive marketplace and an indifferent polis.[71]

The ascription to women of well-developed powers of empathy has been seen as closely connected with the traditional view that women have baser natures because they are closer to the passions.[72] So, in effect, it can be interpreted as the valorisation, not of the human being of the Western philosophical tradition but of the vision of "women" which is produced or created by the placing of women in the private sphere, of their living out their roles as mothers and nurturers in the family and of their being less "rational" than men: these issues were explored in the previous chapter. As it is argued that the Kantian autonomous individual is based on the exclusion of women, with autonomy not being for them (only for "first class" really rational persons), some feminists are of the opinion that a woman-centred subject might be the better option for feminism.[73] It is expressed as ironic that Gilligan's original findings in a way confirm Kant's views, as the woman-centred subject, arising out of the ethic of care analysis, indicates that autonomy really may not be for women.[74]

---

[69] F Olsen, 1995; A Baier, 1987.

[70] A Baier, 1987, p 56.

[71] M Friedman, 1987, p 106.

[72] See G Lloyd, 1984, p 106.

[73] See analysis in M Drakopoulou, 2000.

[74] See A Baier, 1987, p 50 quoting Kant. See also M Drakopoulou's analysis of the ethic of care in the context of the crisis in subjectivity (2000). As Drakopoulou sees it, the opening

However, perhaps there need be no conflict at all between the two moral voices of justice and caring.[75] The universal versus particular presentation of different types of reasoning seen as correlating to gender has been described as the contrast between thin and thick theories of the good.[76] Seeing others "thinly" uses the justice mode: this means that others are seen as worthy of respect purely by virtue of their common humanity. Seeing others "thickly" uses the caring perspective, seeing others as constituted by their particular human face, their particular psychological and social self which is, apparently, illustrated by women's sensitivity, their responsiveness to others' emotional state and others' specific uniqueness.

It has been argued that both men and women use the two orientations of the universal and particular reasoning process some of the time, and the choice of which to use in any given situation depends, at least in part, on the type of problem posed. For example, it has been argued that Kohlberg's sixth stage in moral development should not be adhered to by anyone.[77] This sixth stage appears to provide universal rules of justice as impartiality as a maxim of behaviour in everyday life. This way of looking at justice is what has been called "first order" impartiality which is claimed not to work, and is not what proponents of justice as fairness, like Rawls, are talking about when they talk of justice.[78] Instead, justice as fairness is a matter of having principles and rules that are compatible with "second order" impartiality which governs relationships in the political sphere as a society when forming judgements on social institutions. On such an interpretation, the "Heinz dilemma"[79] – where a husband was forced to decide whether to steal a drug he could not afford because his wife was dying (a dilemma posed by both Kohlberg and Gilligan to their research samples) – arises as a by-product of radically defective institutions, and so the examples used are too extreme. The dilemma would not arise in a society governed by rules of justice as fairness. While the incorporation of Gilligan's different voices should validly occur within any satisfactory account of morality, entailing a rejection of Kohlberg's notion of justice, it does not involve rejecting Rawlsian (or others') "justice as fairness" theories.[80] As such, the ethic of care and empathetic moral reasoning is already arguably an element within justice as fairness theories.

This is a more convincing way of looking at the two ethics. On this basis, the care and justice dichotomy is rationally implausible, the two concepts are conceptually compatible and there is an empirical possibility that the two moral

---

shot in the crisis of subjectivity was fired at liberal individualism and principles of equality and rights. Previously regarded as the animating force of modern feminism, these were now under attack. She cites Juliet Mitchell's and Ngaire Naffine's work as some of the most prominent of these attacks.

[75] See B Barry, 1995.
[76] See O Flanagan and K Jackson, 1987.
[77] B Barry, 1995.
[78] B Barry, 1995.
[79] C Gilligan, 1982, p 25.
[80] B Barry, 1995.

concerns will be intermingled in practice. For example, personal relationships of caring involve justice. It has been argued convincingly that there is a need to advance beyond mere caring dissociated from a concern for justice to an ultimate goal of a non-gendered, non-dichotomised, moral framework in which all moral concerns could be expressed.[81]

The point that needs to be addressed is that individuals do deserve equal respect by virtue of their common humanity but they are also more than abstractly and equivalently human. The ethic of care provides an added dimension of concentrating on the particular face of the individual person to whom justice needs to be applied in a caring way.[82] But by only concentrating on particularity, there will be a lack of the characteristic which some modern moral philosophers take to be the essential characteristic of human selfhood – the capacity to detach oneself from any particular standpoint, to step back and judge that standpoint or point of view from the outside. If identity and difference is stressed to the extent where no commonality can be found, feminists are in danger of giving up on the ideal of equality.

Anne Phillips rightly makes the point that there has been too much confusion of equality with identity or uniformity and that being equal never meant all people had to be regarded as the same.[83] Although the tension of feminists who seek to aspire to equality and those who seek to celebrate women's different "nature" to that of men has always existed within feminism, in legal theory this has led to a tension and resulting dilemma of which policy routes to travel. Two distinct arguments for women's emancipation have arguably been present since the eighteenth century.[84] One has been described as egalitarian-feminism, premising women's emancipation on the belief that men and women basically have the same human character and that the denial to women of their common humanity with men has kept them out of various privileges and resources monopolised by men. The other has been described variously as domestic, cultural or difference feminism which argues for elevating women, not on the basis of their common humanity with men but on the basis of what distinguishes them from men.[85] On this basis, women need rights because they were different from men.[86]

Feminism has moved recurrently between the emphasis on equality and the focus on difference with the irrelevance of sex or their sexual difference offering seemingly opposite starting points. This roared into a sometimes unhelpful and distracting debate known as difference and sameness in the 1980s.[87] Although

---

[81] M Friedman, 1987, p 105.

[82] M Friedman, 1987; S Benhabib, 1992.

[83] A Phillips, 1993, p 62.

[84] See E du Bois in E du Bois et al "Feminist Discourse, Moral Values, and the Law – A Conversation" (The 1984 James McCormick Mitchell Lecture) (1985) 34 *Buffalo Law Review* 11.

[85] By du Bois, 1985; N Lacey, 1998, and R West, 1988, respectively amongst others.

[86] For example, du Bois, 1985, p 66.

[87] See J Sohrab "Avoiding the Exquisite Trap: A Critical Look at the Equal Treatment/Special Treatment Debate in Law" (1993) 1 *Feminist Legal Studies* 141; see

women had made gains through liberal reforms based on equality arguments, formal equality, with its rhetoric of likeness, was seen to be based on the assumption of a much greater degree of sameness between the sexes than actually existed. Anne Phillips describes this as "*a perennial see-saw between the universalising aspirations of equality (my sex does not matter, for I am human, just like you) and the assertion of sexual difference (I am a woman, and that does not make me less equal)*" but feminists are at their most persuasive in emphasising the interplay between universal and particular.[88]

In discussing the particular, situated vision of the female self as a member of a family etc, problems occur precisely because to be a biological female has always been interpreted in gendered terms as dictating a certain psychosexual and cultural identity. The individual woman has always been situated in a world of roles, expectations and social fantasies. Her individuality has been sacrificed to the constitutive definitions of her identity as a member of a family or particular community. The individual subjectivity of the woman has disappeared behind her social and communal persona. So it has been expressed that if unencumbered males supposedly have difficulties in recognising those social relations constitutive of their ego identity, situated females often find it impossible to recognise their individual subjectivity amidst the constitutive roles that attach to their persons.[89]

One of the points made about care is that it applies in a contextual way, applied to particular others with "care" reasoners concentrating on persons in their particularity.[90] The awareness of particularising and setting things in a context which ethic of care theorists have mentioned has been described as possibly obscuring the sometimes damaging ways in which legal subjects are already contextualised.[91] In certain areas, it may be that legal reasoning is already relational but that it privileges certain kinds of relationships (for example proprietary ones). So feminists rightly view the re-negotiation of their psychosexual identities and their autonomous reconstitution as individuals as essential to women's and human liberation.[92] The self is not defined exhaustively by the roles that constitute its identity and social roles should not be accepted uncritically.

The critique of the universal "abstract" individual engages with the issue of providing the space for universal concepts and abstract thought. The liberal distinction between an essential "man" and contingent person gives standards of impartiality without which equality is hard to conceive.[93] How is it possible to

---

particularly the MacKinnon/Gilligan exchange in du Bois et al, 1985; D Rhode (ed) *Theoretical Perspectives on Sexual Difference* (New Haven and London: Yale University Press 1990).

[88] A Phillips, 1993, p 69.

[89] See S Benhabib and D Cornell *Feminism as Critique* (Oxford: Polity Press 1987) at p 13.

[90] M Friedman, 1987, p 108–9; S Benhabib, 1992.

[91] N Lacey, 1998, and "Normative Reconstruction in Socio-Legal Theory" (1996) 5 *Social and Legal Studies* 131.

[92] The language is that of S Benhabib and D Cornell, 1987.

[93] A Phillips, 1993.

stand back from individual prejudices to perceive that those who are different nonetheless deserve respect? The abstract disembodied individual has been credited with giving feminists a weapon they could use in their bid for equality: they could insist that *they were human too*.[94] It has been argued that feminists cannot afford to situate themselves for differences and against universality. The impulse that takes individuals beyond their immediate and specific difference is needed for any radical transformation.[95]

It has been asked, what, if anything, would take the place of abstract humanity if it were abandoned?[96] The very notion of impartial justice, of the "generalised other"[97] implies being able to put oneself in another's shoes and acknowledge his or her entitlement to those rights claimed for oneself. How can feminists root their insights in the uniqueness of female experience and still challenge the dictates of the generalised subject?[98] Dealing with this dilemma involves reconstruction of ideas of moral and political universalism.[99]

The standpoint of the concrete other needs to be taken, knowing the individual's concrete and specific history before it can be said that the situation is or is not dissimilar from another. Both the abstract and the concrete are needed and although understandings of equality need to deal with multiple difference, this is necessary because of an underlying notion of the *human condition* which disregards differences of sex, race, religion or class. It has been argued that this notion may have no substantial content in that there may be nothing there if what makes individuals different or unique is stripped away. However, without such a notion the mass of complicated variations would not even begin to enter the debate.[100]

Defences are presented by some feminists of an interactive universalism, meaning moving to a *discursive*, communicative concept of rationality and a recognition that subjects of reason are finite and embodied.[101] A view of the self as a concrete other in reasoning is advocated. This requires that all view each rational being as an individual with a concrete history etc. The norms of equity and complementary reciprocity ought to be employed. Universality is the concrete process in politics and morals of the struggle of concrete embodied selves striving for autonomy.[102] There are three elements of such a *"post-metaphysical interactive universalism"*. Firstly, the universal pragmatic reformation of the basis of the validity of truth claims in terms of a discourse theory of justification. Secondly, the vision of an embodied and embedded human self whose identity is constituted

---

[94] See A Phillips, 1993.

[95] A Phillips, 1993.

[96] A Phillips cites R Rorty whose answer is literature which increases sensitivity to those different from oneself but A Phillips wonders if this is too parochial.

[97] S Benhabib, 1992.

[98] S Benhabib and D Cornell, 1987.

[99] S Benhabib, 1992.

[100] A Phillips, 1993, p 51 – citing R Norman.

[101] S Benhabib, 1992, p 3.

[102] S Benhabib, 1992, p 153 and 159.

narratively. Thirdly, it involves the reformulation of the moral point of view as the contingent achievement of an interactive form of rationality rather than as a timeless standpoint of legislative reason.[103]

It is true that social criticism of the kind required for women's struggles is not possible without positing the legal, moral and political norms of autonomy, choice and self-determination in that:

> You cannot respect the otherness of the other if you deny the other the right to enter into a conversation with you, if you do not discard the objective indifference of an ethnologist and engage with the other as an equal.[104]

This idea of "dynamic autonomy", stressing the relatedness to, while at the same time the differentiation from, others, has been described as promoting a sense of agency in a world of interacting and interpersonal agents and a sense of others...

> as subjects with whom one shares enough to allow for a recognition of their independent interests and feelings – that is, for a recognition of them as other subjects.[105]

It is vital that individuals develop and retain the ability to reflect and change in response to that reflection.

Warnings that feminists, in critiquing gender neutrality, may give up on any notion of universal humanity and therefore lose what gives equality its power are well-founded.[106] I argue that this has, to a large extent, happened and is one of the reasons why feminist theory and feminist politics seem to have little in common at times and is detrimental to aiming for human flourishing through the use of, amongst other things, the enforcement of women's rights as human rights at an international level: in times of peace and war.

## Interconnection and Relational Ways of Being

At the same time as focusing on the particular other, ethic of care work can be interpreted as showing that women are caring, nurturant, more relational and interconnected than men and that these values are good and to be celebrated. These ways of thinking may, empirically, be true of some women, and it can even be accepted that more women than men demonstrate such characteristics. However, it can be argued that this is only the case because of the way women have been encouraged to behave in the socialisation process. It is not an inherent part of

---

[103] S Benhabib, 1992, p 6.

[104] S Benhabib "Epistemologies of Postmodernism; A Rejoinder to Jean-Francois Lyotard" in L Nicholson (ed) *Feminism?Postmodernism* (New York and London: Routledge 1990) at p 119.

[105] Evelyn Fox Keller *Reflections on Gender and Science* (1985) quoted in C Mackenzie and N Stoljar (eds), 2000, p 10, note 22.

[106] Arguments presented by A Phillips, 1993.

women's "nature". Nevertheless the values in themselves can have inherent worth and ought therefore to be encouraged to flourish in societies world-wide as they will in turn assist in creating better places to live.

However, before arguments against relational interconnection being part of woman's way of being are set out, I want to examine an early piece by Robin West as a clear and influential work on interconnection as contrasted with inadequate conceptions of human beings. While critiquing this work as seemingly biological and therefore (largely) deterministic, the worth of retrieving its interconnection potential is proposed. It can be used to take seriously the morality and consciousness of lives and experiences of women living in patriarchal societies, emphasising positive and important attributes too easily dismissed by classic liberal theory. These attributes can then be applied to all human potential, rather than only to women. Acknowledgement of humans' interconnection will assist a fuller realisation of the human and common standard of humanity that West's work so clearly demonstrates.[107]

Concern is placed on investigating women's lives and experiences to provide a blueprint for feminist jurisprudence. The claim is made that if existing laws are examined, the values characterising women's lives are not reflected in legal doctrine. A presentation is made of a feminist jurisprudence based on a woman-centred subject with the failure of modern legal theory resting on its inadequate understanding of what it is to be a human being.[108]

In West's analysis, both liberal legalism and radical feminism present a male view of the human because both assume that individuals are essentially separate from one another (what she calls the separation thesis). She argues that women are connected to other human beings, especially through the biologically based activities of pregnancy, breast feeding and heterosexual intercourse, contrasting with the standard liberal legalist view of emphasising autonomy. An argument is made proposing a feminist jurisprudence that reconstructs legal concepts to take account of the realities of women's experiences (represented in what she calls "cultural feminism"). Not only is the separation thesis an obstacle to the development of feminist legal theory, but it constitutes a barrier to the demolition of patriarchy.

The general cultural feminist explanation for the sense of connection to other human life which women and not men have is that women are the primary caretakers of young children. Based on Nancy Chodorow's research into the development of children, it is explained that as a female child grows, she develops

---

[107] This is most clearly seen in West's more recent work. See R West "Revitalizing Rights" in R West (ed) *Rights: 2nd Series the International Library of Essays in Law and Legal Theory* (Hants: Dartmouth 2001); R West *Re-Imagining Justice* (Aldershot: Ashgate: 2003); R West *Caring for Justice* (NY and London: New York University Press 1997).

[108] R West, 1988, 1997, 2001, 2003; R West "The Difference in Women's Hedonic lives: A Phenomenological Critique of Feminist Legal Theory" (1987) 3 *Wisconsin Women's Law Journal* 81–145; R West "Love, Rage and Legal Theory" (1989) 1 *Yale Journal of Law and Feminism* 101; R West *Law, Narrative and Authority* (Ann Arbor: University of Michigan Press 1993).

her sense of identity as continuous with her caretaker's, usually the mother, while a young boy develops a sense of identity that is distinguished from his caretaker's. The reason for this is that as the child grows older, he or she identifies with the same-sex parent, and parents reinforce this identification. This is the cause of the gender alignment.[109] In what has been called the "unofficial story" of legal theory, as presented by cultural feminism, women are connected to others, materially and existentially.

What is valued in the "official story" is an autonomous individual, free, meaning separate from others, left alone to choose their own lifestyles, and to exercise voluntary choices in as many spheres as possible through the satisfaction of subjective desires and preferences. Even if maximisation of self-welfare as the motivation for actions is true of men, cultural feminism questions it being true for women. On this account, because of the sense of connection felt by women, women's lives are not autonomous in a way which may be true of men. Because of this, the legal system and legal language fails women, in that it fails to represent women's sense of connection, fear of separation, fear of lack of intimacy, women's experiences and what is viewed by them as harms are all absent from the legal language and system.

West clearly defends the need to root feminist theory in a theory of female nature.[110] In her analysis, although women are different from each other, they share a common biological structure which in turn affects women's psychic identity. On this view, shared experience is possible because of a female nature.[111]

In deciding whether to accept or reject certain differences between women and men, West proposes using a vocabulary to articulate and evaluate them, and power to reject or affirm them, so adopting a critical legal method aiming directly for women's subjective well-being, increasing women's happiness and lessening women's suffering. As she sees it, women's inner reality simply does not fit the Kantian conception of human nature that underlies much of liberal and radical legal theory. In West's view, women are other-regarding – they are giving selves much of the time rather than liberal selves, assuming a difference between the two.

Much ethic of care analysis proceeds on an oversimplification of the liberal individual. Often the economic preference-satisfaction selfish version of the liberal individual, which is not the only one, is presented.[112] For some, liberal

---

[109] N Chodorow, 1978.

[110] R West, 1988, p 3–4. Her search is for "a jurisprudence built upon feminist insights into women's true nature": see D Cornell's interpretation in D Cornell "The Doubly Prized World: Myth, Allegory and the Feminine" (1990) 75 *Cornell Law Review* 644, for the view that she is possibly not biologically determinist.

[111] As Cornell sees it, the feminine is mapped onto femaleness – naturalist or essentialist. This is rejected by many as being inconsistent with postmodernism. West collapses women's essence into her nature. An essentialist theory of women would have to reveal woman for what she truly is, beyond the trappings of culture and the false consciousness of patriarchy. This demands that we purify language so that it is only a medium which would allow the true form of woman to at last be self-evident, D Cornell, 1990, p 650–3.

[112] See M Nussbaum's analysis of the liberal individual in chapter 2 of M Nussbaum 1999, although she does not consider the work of Robin West.

individualism does not entail egoism or normative self-sufficiency. It has recently been argued that making the individual the basic unit of society means that each person has a course of life that is not precisely the same as another, each person is one and not more than one, each feels pain: thus the separateness of persons is a basic fact of life.[113] West and many others would not agree. It is valid to question the separateness of persons, and right to point out that humans are interconnected.[114] However, in my view, this involves a conflation of the empirical and normative. Each person starts life having been physically connected to another while inside their mother and at birth. Many are of the view that spiritually and psychically all are interconnected throughout their lives, but, irrespective of this interconnection, *everyone ought to be treated as persons in their own right* and respected as ends in themselves, not objects or instruments for others. The two ideas are not incompatible.

The contention that women's harms are not as seriously considered as men's harms is accurate. Emphasising connection with others rather than separation from others is extremely useful but it is not female, although I acknowledge that more women empirically may feel this way at present. These ideas can be more fruitfully advanced if this connection with others is seen as a *human* characteristic that ought to be encouraged and emphasised. Men and women both can and do feel connected to other human beings.[115] The insights West brings, together with that of the ethic of care in general, lead to a revaluation of what it means to be human and to reconsider the conceptions valued most in society. These points are developed in Part II, and in a global context in Part III. The point is that any biological differences between the sexes should not lead to treating people as fundamentally different but to treating all people as equal human beings despite different biological make-up and the (socially constructed) differences between people.

Ethic of care work has been described as promising to incorporate a vision of women's reality premised upon the valorisation of a female nature.[116] The attempted transformation of those values and qualities traditionally despised as signs of weakness and inferiority into sources of moral strength is welcomed by

---

[113] M Nussbaum 1999, p 62.

[114] This is particularly so for some – see VE Munro "Square Pegs in Round Holes: The Dilemma of Conjoined Twins and Individual Rights" (2001) 10 *Social and Legal Studies* 459–482.

[115] See for example J Williams' critique of R West in J Williams "Deconstructing Gender" (1987) 87 *Michigan Law Review* 797. Williams rightly queries whether only women are connected and asks whether men are not connected too by the umbilical cord, during sexual intercourse and she queries West's contention that menstruation is connecting. According to Williams, West is dealing with metaphor (though she doesn't realise it). Williams sees the woman-centred critique as part of two influential critiques of contemporary Western culture – epistemology and possessive individualism. The new epistemology is really talking about a new kind of rationality – a broadening of traditional intellectual life. The traditional caricature of women as emotional and irrational represents a formal marginalisation of those characteristics of human personality that the Western tradition has devalued – at p 805.

[116] M Drakopoulou, 2000.

many.[117] The care perspective has been called both feminine and feminist in that the former points to the relational world of women as it appears within a patriarchal order grounded upon notions of abstract justice and contractual obligations, and the moment the otherwise unspoken or dismissed voices of women are listened to, a space opens into which the latter emerges, calling for the displacement of the *patriarchal construction* of relationships.[118]

If women are seen to value care more than men even when they may be treated badly for doing so, does that mean that such care should automatically be valued without question or does that mean investigations need to be made to uncover why and then question the value of such care? Many see the debate between treating women as different or the same as men as an issue of dominance.[119] On this view, terming gender a "difference" systematically relegates women as a group to a condition of *inferiority* within power-based society. Seeing gender as dominance, rather than as difference, changes gender from a presumptively valid distinction to a detrimental one. The "incorporation" of the caring voice with the justice voice has been criticised as repressing contradictions; usurping women's language and continuing to define the world in the male image.[120]

Feminists need to avoid holding as a special sort of feminine or female moral wisdom or outlook that voice which is the product of the socially enforced restriction of women to domestic roles. Saying this way of thinking is somehow intrinsic to women or part of women's essential nature reinforces stereotypes, is self-defeating and makes the aim of women's liberation harder to attain. This is often acknowledged when refusing to associate different voices with males and females. Yet usually men are associated with one voice and women with the other. Such determinism in fixing female identity, binding women to some prescribed quality that is unchanging, is damaging in that it presents women who do not fit this identity as in some way deviant and not up to standard. It makes it even more difficult in a patriarchal structure to allow girls and women to behave in ways they want to which do not conform to such stereotypes and gives recognition and status to aspects of lives that women wish to change because they damage their interests (even though at any particular time women may be happy with that aspect of their lives). Often presenting views in a biologically determinist way is highly dangerous in the existing male-dominated society. Such arguments can lead to

---

[117] Drakopoulou, 2000.

[118] M Drakopoulou, 2000.

[119] See, in particular, CA MacKinnon, 1989; D Rhode (ed), *Theoretical Perspectives on Sexual Difference* (New Haven and London: Yale University Press 1990) and critiques: JW Scott "Deconstructing Equality-versus-Difference: Or the uses of Poststructural Theory for feminism" in F Olsen (ed), 1995; D Cornell "Sexual Difference, the Feminine, and Equivalency: A Critique of MacKinnon's Toward a Feminist Theory of the State" (1991) 100 *Yale Law Journal* 2247.

[120] A Scales "The Emergence of Feminist Jurisprudence: An Essay" (1986) 95 *Yale Law Journal* 1373. Scales, like MacKinnon, looks to a feminist jurisprudence which will focus on domination, disadvantage and disempowerment rather than one which examines differences between women and men.

overgeneralisations about women.[121] By extending the view of a description of some women who experience certain types of maternal feelings to a theory of how women reason morally, theorists can assign all womankind to an essentially biologically determined fate, that no structural changes in society can ever help alleviate.[122]

Ethic of care work says little about power and structures which continually devalue ways of being that are associated with girls and women per se. Even if women care more than men and think more in relational ways, it does not mean that the cause is some inherent female nature or wisdom, that women are closer to nature or naturally more empathetic. It is because of the social construction of gender and the oppression of the hierarchical gender structure.[123] Some have even described the ethic of care as a "slave morality".[124] Such criticisms are valid to the extent that if preferences have been formed under oppression, they need to be queried rather than simply accepted, a point developed in Chapter 5.[125]

So, one of the major problems with the ethic of care being seen as a *woman's way* of thinking is its potential, within existing power relationships and structures in society, of keeping women out of public life. It is precisely these sorts of views held by eighteenth century society which Wollstonecraft argued against in 1792. Mapping reality and describing the existing situation is an important exercise, and any inherently valuable attributes existing should not be devalued. At the same time however, awareness is needed to dangers in accepting and applauding all aspects of care and simply attributing them to the way women think, particularly when societies have frameworks of hierarchical gender divisions. At the root of the problem as regards gender relations is the disparity of power in society's existing structures, as embodied by law and social institutions. Traditional male values are embodied in the main institutions of societies; these are set up in such a way as to reward those who succeed through such techniques and those in power aspire to these values. For example, values like competition, dominance and ruthlessness, material wealth and physical strength are all rewarded either explicitly or implicitly. Thus it is usually men who are advantaged and

---

[121] In this context, some have criticised R West and CA MacKinnon for relying on a concept of "woman" that is abstracted from the experiences of white women – see analysis in Chapter 5 below.

[122] With biological developments in medicine, perhaps, like S Firestone, 1971, the emphasis could be on genetic engineering to change these biologically "determined" natures?

[123] Further, it has been argued that the numbers studied by C Gilligan are small and there was no indication of how representative the examples are when two responses are compared; some of her chapters are based on findings of women's thinking on abortion – not a good subject to choose to compare men's and women's reasoning; Gilligan interprets talk of rights as negative rights and conflates that with individualism and selfishness – see SM Okin "Gilligan's Work: Thinking Like a Woman" in D Rhode (ed), 1990, p 156–7.

[124] C Card " Review Essay: Women's Voices and Ethical Ideals: Must We Mean What We Say?" (1988) *Ethics* 125.

[125] See MC Nussbaum 1999, who warns against simply accepting given norms and preferences which have been formed under oppression – expressing a very sympathetic reading of the work of MacKinnon and A Dworkin in her chapter 2.

women disadvantaged in, for example, workplace structures and domestic arrangements, in international development and international justice.

But surely it is right to highlight the often massive contrast between male and female subjectivity in respect of the empirical conditions under which each is constructed?[126] It has been asked whether values emanating from ethic of care work and a focus on relationships should be used as a way of reconstructing social, political and legal institutions, even if they have developed out of the necessity for survival in a world where women have been powerless, because the values are intrinsically important in themselves and say something about the way in which individuals look at themselves. This process can itself be one of reconstruction.[127]

The perception that standard models of moral subjectivity do not apply to women (or only in problematic ways) has brought a dawning recognition that what is distinctive in women's social experience is worthy of exploration in its own right. An acknowledgement needs to be made, without self-contempt, of the social reality of femininity yet, at the same time, any naïve celebration of feminine characteristics which would be more accurately regarded as effects of oppression needs to be avoided. A detailed moral reflection is needed to work out what to accept and what to reject.

The recognition of traits, characteristics and a way of thinking which arguably more women than men are seen to demonstrate is important for taking seriously the realities of those women's lives and experiences. Listening to someone and taking into account their views is an important part of recognising them as human beings worthy of respect. If they think, feel and speak in a way not recognised as of value by the norms dominating society, they will feel shut out, excluded, not respected as persons. It is important that all feel they are included in the category of human by being so respected.

If women have emphasised relationships because historically the only way a woman has "amounted to anything" has been through her relationship to "some man", this does not preclude valuing relationships but it does mean that existing relationships should be subject to critical examination.[128]

Although care and emotional, interconnected and relational ways of being are not inherently part of some sort of female "nature" or "essence", those characteristics are important elements of what it means to be human in *all* human beings, increasing potentiality to lead a fuller life. These things are not intrinsically part of "women's wisdom" but they are important in contributing to a fuller, more adequate conception of what it means to be human. Although often voiced by women, this feminist care ethic promises a social order which could help provide an alternative model of human relationships generally and a new societal blueprint.[129]

---

[126] E Frazer et al, 1992.

[127] See C Menkel-Meadow in E du Bois et al, 1985, and C Menkel-Meadow "Portia in a Different Voice" (1985) *Berkeley Women's Law Journal* 1.

[128] As expressed by CA MacKinnon, 1989.

[129] This has been described as producing a standpoint for social critique and a site of resistance to a male-orientated, patriarchal vision of society, but one which carries a promise

Thus abstract universal qualities of all can be reconciled with the social relatedness aspects of humanity highlighted by ethic of care theorists and the social constitutiveness of individuals. The ethic of care is best understood as providing caring insights into universal abstract reasoning and as a relational interconnected way of viewing humanity. The two need not be incompatible.

Many liberals have sought to deal with factors which structure individuals', including women's, choices and do say that capacities are dependent on social circumstances.[130] This has been expressed as liberal thinkers seeing more deeply and consistently: rejecting purely formal equality.[131] What liberals fundamentally advocate is that people be able to choose a life in accordance with their own thinking. It is for that very reason that liberals seek to justify a social order which will permit the capacities of individuals to be increased to exercise those choices. The distribution of resources and opportunities needs to be investigated to see how well each person is doing, seeing each person as an end in themselves, worthy of concern.[132] It has also been noted that when liberals have ignored background factors they are not being true to liberal principles and are simplifying the choices people make in this way. Explaining away substantive sex inequality on the basis of choices women make in a sexually unequal society is not being true to liberal principles.[133]

Any version of human existence in which individuals are always and inevitably opposed, egotistic, competitive, solipsistic and selfish, afraid of others (who are just as selfish as themselves) is inadequate. While this is, to some extent, based on liberal theorists, it largely derives from Hobbes, and while accurate for many presentations of the liberal tradition, it over-emphasises the isolation and "atomistic" nature of the individual.[134] It also fails to take account of the emphasis on the human capacity for pity and sympathy and on the social constitutiveness of individuals at a psychological level stressed by liberals like Adam Smith, David Hume, L T Hobhouse, T H Green, Rawls, Ronald Dworkin and Joseph Raz. The modern liberal theory of the person has been described as inclining heavily in the

---

for the future realisable only if this different voice is heard. See M Drakopoulou, 2000, at p 205.

[130] M Nussbaum says that some liberal thinkers have an evidently social and other-inclusive psychology, building the needs for others into the foundation of their accounts of human nature. She cites JS Mill and D Hume, A Smith and J Rawls – See M Nussbaum 1999, at p 50. See also the work of S Benn *A Theory of Freedom* (Cambridge: Cambridge University Press 1988); W Kymlicka, 1990, and W Kymlicka "Rethinking the Family" (1991) *Philosophy and Public Affairs* 20; (ed) *Justice in Political Philosophy* (Oxford: Oxford University Press 1990); *Liberalism, Community and Culture* (Oxford: Clarendon Press 1989); *Multicultural Citizenship* (Oxford: Clarendon Press 1995); R Dworkin, 1997, 1985, 1994, 2000.

[131] M Nussbaum 1999, p 68. Her favoured way of doing this is through equality of capabilities.

[132] As expressed by M Nussbaum, 1999, p 62.

[133] E Frazer and N Lacey say that liberalism itself explains away substantive sex inequality on this basis (1993). A Jaggar would argue similarly (1983).

[134] A Jaggar, 1983; N Lacey, 1998.

direction of emphasising the potential harmony and mutual dependence of individual development with equal liberty embedded in a democratic polity and co-operative economic order.[135]


## Creative Ways of Thinking

Much work emanating from the ethic of care debate and an attempt to construct a woman-centred subject, presents radical departures from simply accepting the given norms in society and the norms of how things are usually viewed. To be able to do this, the capacity for self-reflection is needed. It is not enough to care for everyone and everything. Individuals need to be able to decide for themselves what is worthy of their care. If a practice therefore condones or tolerates traditional communal norms of gender subordination or oppression, it is unacceptable.[136] This encouragement of a creative and paradigmatically different way of thinking is a very positive aspect of the work of ethic of care theorists which is a capacity to be encouraged in all and will only happen in societies where conditions are available to enable humans to realise this potential.

For example, the paradigm of mothering as the foundation of society and the social contract has been used instead of independent, self-interested or mutually disinterested and self-sufficient individuals.[137] While it is explicitly doubted that morality should be based on any one type of human relation, the possibility is raised that this may be *an important stage to go through* in reconstructing a view of human relationships that will be adequate from a feminist point of view. Thus theories of rational choice (supposedly applicable to all human activity and experience) makes these same basic assumptions about individuals.[138] Feminists

---

[135] GF Gaus *The Modern Liberal Theory of Man* (London: Croom Helm 1983) at p 274.

[136] An excellent analysis of this point is given by M Friedman "Feminism and Modern Friendship, Dislocating the Community" in S Avineri and A de-Shalit (ed), 1992. See also SM Okin "Is Multiculturalism Bad for Women?" in J Cohen, M Howard and MC Nussbaum (eds) *Is Multicuturalism Bad for Women? Susan Moller Okin with respondents* (Princeton New Jersey: Princeton University Press 1999) and M C Nussbaum 1999.

[137] V Held, 1993, p 111. For Held, the whole tradition that sees respecting others as constituted by non-interference with them is most effectively shown as inadequate when looked at in terms of mothering. It assumes people can fend for themselves. This Robinson Crusoe image of "economic man" is, she says, false for almost everyone and is totally false in the case of infants and children: at p 129.

[138] To begin to think about things in a radically different way, Held suggests replacing economic men with mothers. Try to imagine, she says, what society would look like if the paradigm of economic man was replaced, and substituted by, the paradigm of mother and child. Before there were any self-sufficient, independent men in a hypothetical state of nature, mothers had to exist. However, it has been supposed that while contracting is a specifically human activity, women are engaged in an activity which is not specifically human (mothering) and have therefore been thought to be closer to nature than men, to be enmeshed in a biological function involving processes more like those in which other

focusing on a different caring moral voice highlight that such assumptions are highly questionable, and indeed may be presenting what some might call impoverished views of human aspirations.

Thinking creatively creates new types of persons. So using the example of mothering as the foundation leads to the conclusion that for even adequate levels of social cohesion, persons are tied together by relations of concern, caring, empathy and trust rather than merely by contracts. The emotional satisfaction of a mothering person is a satisfaction in the well-being and happiness of another human being and a satisfaction in the health of the relation between the two persons, not the gain that results from an egoistic bargain.[139]

A new concept of the human could be envisaged who will have a significant impact on conceptualisations of the supposedly "impersonal" and "public" domain. But accepting the importance of the moral norm of caring does not mean automatic acceptance of a division along gender lines which assigns particularised personalised commitments to women and universalised rule-based commitments to men.[140]

Different perspectives, focusing on moral and legal concepts from a different and often highly imaginative point of view ought to be acknowledged and taken into account in formulations of what it is to be a human to then be used for the purposes of law.

Concepts of autonomy, rationality, choice, self-determination and freedom are retained but are recognised as best developing in societies where care, love and empathy and the connectedness of humanity are emphasised. This will lead to new, more meaningful, interpretations and applications. This retention of human subjectivity and self-respect demands that all be treated as persons who are responsible and deserve respect.[141] Yet this is not fully possible unless it is

---

animals are involved than like the rational contracting of distinctively human "economic man" – Held, 1993, page 118.

[139] V Held, 1993, p 125, 127–128. The rights and interests of individuals seen as separate entities and equality between them all should not exhaust our moral concerns: at p 128. The flourishing of shared joy, of mutual affection, of bonds of trust and hope between mothering persons and children can illustrate this as clearly as anything can. Harmony, love and co-operation cannot be broken down into individual benefits and burdens. They are goals we ought to share and relations between persons.

[140] M Friedman, 1992, p 109.

[141] See D Cornell, *At the Heart of Freedom: Feminism, Sex and Equality* (Princeton: Princeton University Press 1998); R Dworkin, 1997, 1985, 1994, 2000; MC Nussbaum, 1999; S Sevenhuijsen, 1998, and J Tronto *Caring for Democracy: A Feminist Vision* (Utrecht 1995). Sevenhuijsen advocates radical pluralism, the aim being to achieve judgements in a situated way, interpretative dialogic and communicative moral epistemology. To do so requires a minimal degree of normative reasoning and well-considered political choice – a political recognition of basic humanistic values and human rights and a legal order guaranteeing these. Liberal values like equality and freedom are crucial. For Tronto, care is the mean between excessive reliance upon others for our maintenance and excessive self-reliance – between excessive dependency and autonomy, cited by Sevenhuijsen at p 67.

appreciated that everyone is equally entitled to this demand given the importance of relationships and others in determining their own self-worth and given their interconnection with each other. This involves appreciating the particular other but in a universalised form. In this regard, some work by contemporary feminists focuses on reconceiving notions of the autonomous subject: explaining the importance of relationships in developing the capacity of autonomy which I explore in Part II.[142]

In contrast to an atomistic view of human nature, ethic of care work has highlighted the relational self, a moral agent who exists in concrete relationships with other people and who acquires an individual moral identity through interactive patterns of behaviour, perceptions and interpretations. Individuals are no longer seen as atomistic units with a pre-determined identity: identity and selfhood are formed in specific environments, thus the self is not a "finished" or "unified" self from birth. So instead, for example, Sevenhuijsen has called the human subject a *"protagonist in a biography which can contain all kinds of ambiguities and unexpected turns"*. This type of work takes a narrative approach to moral subjectivity.[143] A narrative approach refuses to separate needs from the people who are their subjects and takes as its starting point the idea that people themselves can have knowledge about their own subjectivity. It takes seriously people's stories about what they need to live well. The central values of the ethic of care, responsibility and communication, lead to a commitment to deal with differences, not only between individuals and social groups, but within the self. This makes it possible, and even normal, not to assume that one's own values and world view are self-evident and to continually question the ability of one's moral framework to enhance the quality of life. This has been described as implying a radical break with the idea of the pre-social self in liberal ethics.[144] However, I do not see this as contradictory or in opposition to the pre-social ideal: the two are dealing with different ideas. The pre-social is a universal ideal norm of equality and freedom, the continually developing self is that which is allowed to form because of a belief in the freedom and equality of all individuals to live in a society which allows a fully human person to exist and develop.

However, certain feminist ethic of care theorists have rightly pointed out that such a relational image of human nature rejects a radical separation between self and other or subject and object, and replaces this with an interactive image of moral subjectivity, care and responsibility.

Some try to use a feminist ethic of care as a complement to postmodernism to provide for the capacity to deal with diversity and alterity, with the fact that

---

[142] See, in particular, J Nedelsky's work including J Nedelsky, 1989, and C MacKenzie and N Stoljar (eds), 2000.

[143] M Griffiths *Feminisms and the Self: the web of identity* (New York and London: Routledge 1995); H Reece *Divorcing Responsibly* (Oxford and Portland: Hart 2003); L McNay *Gender and Agency: Reconfiguring the subject in feminist and social theory* (Cambridge: Polity Press 2000), see also Part II below.

[144] S Sevenhuijsen, 1998.

subjects are different and in this sense both strange and knowable to each other.[145] Any alliance between postmodernism and feminism is explored in the next chapter where I deal with the question of whether it is possible to retain a feminist politics if the postmodern death of the subject is accepted.

## Conclusion

While the social, interconnected, relational aspects of the human need to be emphasised to prevent a deficient account of human identity from being presented, this is different from, and does not preclude, abstract, universal reasoning, showing the shared common aspect of humanity. Further, such interconnection is not inherently female, it is human and such abstract reasoning is not male, it is human. Both capacities need to be developed and fostered in a caring, loving, empathetic environment as will be shown in Part II.

Before that is examined however, the impact of postmodern views of the human will be explored in the next chapter. Whether the legal subject is an autonomous individual endowed with equal rights or a caring one embedded in a web of relationships and responsibilities, it may still be insufficient.[146] If women are not all the same, but are different, in situation and experience with social class, race, religion, ethnicity, sexual orientation, how does this impact on the so-called unity of the woman-centred subject? It is to such alternative views that I now turn.

---

[145] See S Sevenhuijsen, 1998.
[146] M Drakopoulou, 2000, p 213–4.

Chapter 3

# The Postmodern Subject and Feminism

*"Feminist Politics is at a fundamental level posited on the modernist metanarrative of personal emancipation."* L McNay[1]

## Feminism, Normativity and the Postmodern Subject

In the previous two chapters, analysis was provided of feminists' critiques of the traditional Western philosophical conception of the human to include women or to create a separate "woman-centred" subject. However, many feminists are unhappy with both these moves. The very possibility of both a human subject or a "woman-centred" subject able to articulate "true" and objective knowledge claims about the category human or woman is questioned. It is claimed that these presentations of such a woman-centred subject can be as authoritarian and norm creating – in an exclusionary form – as the male norm of the human which feminists had originally critiqued. What is described as the essentalism of much feminism, and then the very existence of such an essentialist category of "woman", is therefore disputed and often denied. Instead, subjectivity is seen as the outcome of numerous discourses and discursive practices and the human subject is seen as neither male nor female, generalised or concrete. In fact, there is no certainty whether it exists at all.[2]

In this chapter, analysis of the human subject continues by moving away from ideas of any unity of the subject either as a universal or as a woman-centred subject – through deconstruction, postmodernism and poststructuralism.

I start with a short definition of postmodernism (in the context of my emphasis on the human subject), followed by an analysis of some specific postmodern views on gender and sexuality.[3] The analysis shows that deconstructing the subject is not in itself a problem, and in fact is a useful tool.

---

[1] L McNay *Foucault on Feminism: power, gender and the self* (Cambridge: Polity Press 1992) at p 123.
[2] M Drakopoulou, 2000, p 214–5.
[3] D Cornell, 1998; D Cornell *The Imaginary Domain: Abortion, Pornography and Sexual Harassment* (New York and London: Routledge 1995); D Cornell *Beyond Accommodation: ethical feminism, deconstruction and the law* (New York and London: Routledge 1991); D Cornell *The Philosophy of the Limit* (New York and London: Routledge 1992. L Irigaray *This Sex that is Not One* (Ithaca: Cornell University Press 1985); E Marks and de Courtivron (eds) *New French Feminisms* (Brighton, Harvester 1981); J Butler, 1990; C Smart *Feminism and the Power of the Law* (NY and London: Routledge 1989).

However, for feminist politics to remain, that subject needs to be capable of agency with a normative purpose behind the deconstruction to give it any meaning.

Recent feminist work has re-opened debates that question the usefulness, or otherwise, of postmodernism to feminist jurisprudence, echoing doubts intermittently raised in the last decade or so on this topic.[4] In my analysis here, particular focus rests on the contribution of feminist postmodern techniques to analysis of the human. The position is taken that feminist jurisprudence, like other political and potentially radical critical theories in law, cannot evade normative foundations for human subjectivity. The reason for this position is that feminist jurisprudence, at its broadest and most general level, is necessarily concerned with creating or finding better ways of being and living for women and men. Whilst it is acknowledged that feminist jurisprudence has other, perhaps more easily obtainable goals, such as highlighting and critiquing law's gender bias through analysis of existing laws, its ultimate goal surely is for women to be allowed to live, and to have, better lives?[5] Feminist jurisprudence therefore needs to contribute to providing idea(l)s and conceptions of human subjectivity which assist that aim. This necessarily entails looking at the lives women lead, seeing that women not only suffer disadvantage as women, but also suffer this to differing degrees depending on how their sex and gender intersects with other sources of disadvantage.[6]

This chapter sets out some postmodern analysis to highlight that feminists need to retain normative foundations of human subjectivity if they are to coherently produce better ways of being for humans. The analysis therefore queries certain postmodern theories of the subject or self which have anti-normative views of the subject with regard to analysis of the human on which to build feminist freedom.

## A Return to Normativity?

Recent feminist jurisprudence work has advocated a return to normativity. For example, it has been argued that feminist scholarship is instilled with normative ideas and acknowledges that feminism springs from normative preoccupations:

---

[4] CA MacKinnon "Points Against Postmodernism" (2000) 75 *Chicago-Kent Law Review* 687; MC Nussbaum "The Professor of Parody" (1999) *New Republic* 22 Feb 1999 at 37; R West *Caring for Justice* (New York: New York University Press 1997); R West *Re-Imagining Justice* (2003); A Barron "Feminism, Aestheticism and the Limits of Law" (2000) 8 *Feminist Legal Studies* 275; J Conaghan, 2000; B Marshall 1994; S Benhabib, 1992; L McNay, 1992; L Nicholson (ed), 1990.

[5] For general information on what feminist jurisprudence is trying to do, see F Olsen (ed) *Feminist Legal Theory* Vol 1 and 2 (London: Dartmouth 1995); N Lacey "Feminist Legal Theory" (1989) 9 *Oxford Journal of Legal Studies* 383; H *Barnett Sourcebook on Feminist Jurisprudence* (London: Cavendish Publishing Ltd 1997).

[6] See a recent summary of this intersectionality in E Jackson and N Lacey, 2002; A Harris "Race and Essentialism in Feminist Legal Theory" (1990) 42 *Stan L Rev* 581.

its history, focus, concepts, methodologies, political and intellectual objectives, are all imbibed with an overriding sense of wrongness, of violation, exploitation and repression, of silenced and excluded Others.[7]

This recent work calls for a recognition of these normative and transformative aspirations, challenging the emergence of an "anti-essentialist" norm in feminist discourse and reaffirming the value of "women-centred" feminist approaches.[8] This call is made against the background of a reticence amongst feminist scholars towards such normative aspirations which has been attributed to various sources.[9]

Many feminists are either returning to, or newly emphasising the value of feminist projects of reconstruction.[10] Some argue such projects are problematicised, but not prevented, by the postmodern deconstruction of the subject.[11] For example, although queries are raised as to how people can be free to pursue their normative aspirations if they are not unified, rational, self-present subjects (which has been described as the liberal subject) but products of discourse (described as the postmodern subject), it has been argued that there is still room for the postmodern subject and normativity.[12] However, it has not been clearly and convincingly argued how.

These calls for a return to normativity within feminist jurisprudence are welcome but, to substantiate a normative agenda, although it is not necessary to believe in an "essential woman", or "unified" subject concerned with satisfying their own preferences, a retention of a concept of strong subjectivity is needed. If postmodernism means the death of man, the death of any self-reflective subject, it is incompatible with feminist politics.

## The Postmodern Subject?

Postmodernism, its connection with, and the possibility of alliances with, feminism, is a vast subject and I do not purport to argue that postmodernists

---

[7] J Conaghan, 2000, p 375. However, Conaghan does not develop the point as to how to include others or whether the issue is with the idea that there are "others" per se.

[8] J Conagahan, 2000, p 384–385.

[9] See Conaghan's summaries of these: (i) an epistemological concern with how knowledge or norms are legitimated given their social construction and absence of foundational justifications; (ii) questions of agency, in that, how can individuals be said to be free to pursue their normative aspirations if they are not unified, rational, self-present subjects but products of discourse; (iii) concern as to the regulatory and ideological effects of normativity if they are assumed to be "pre-given": J Conaghan, 2000, p 387–391.

[10] K Knop (ed) *Gender and Human Rights* Oxford: OUP 2004); E Jackson and N Lacey, 2002; E Jackson "Abortion, Autonomy and Prenatal Diagnosis" (2000) 9 *Social and Legal Studies* 467–494; S James and S Palmer (eds), 2002; D Cornell, 1998.

[11] S Sevenhuijsen, 1998; J Conaghan, 2000.

[12] J Conaghan, 2000.

present some sort of identifiable coherent stance.[13] The purpose here is simply to set out a few basic postmodern positions regarding human subjectivity which I will then analyse in the context of their interrelationship with ways of being for humans.

Postmodern relations of power render claims of truth or falsehood illegitimate and aim to displace the unified category of "woman" as a subject. Focusing on the formation of subjectivity through linguistic usage, postmodernism has, as one of its primary goals, the aim of freeing itself from overarching philosophical givens, to ground social criticism within specific contexts and locales. However, if one of the significant aspects of the postmodern condition is the dissolution of what postmodernists call the "myth" of autonomous subjectivity, this will have a bearing on feminist articulations of subjectivity which often depend on notions of liberation.

Postmodernists reject the commonly held concept of the idea that humans contain some sort of "essence" a concept already mentioned in Chapters 1 and 2. Certain radical theories, including Marxism and various "brands" of feminism present the view that this "essence" has been repressed by society. As such, a pre-existing supposed "true" self can be found through "consciousness raising", a method which will reveal and liberate the true self through the removal of "false consciousness".[14]

Essentialism has been a particular bane for feminist jurisprudence. Is it necessary to "essentialise" women, thus emphasising the similarities amongst women in a way that some argue box women into a corner, preventing changes that could makes their lives better? Various characterisations of essentialism abound. Main examples of essentialism are *biological* and *philosophical* essentialism. The first argues that women's biology purportedly gives them their essence. This often translates into embracing women's biological specificity as providing a woman-centred valorisation of femaleness.[15] The second explores how culture cuts off the feminine body from the possibility of transcendence and highlights women's enslavement.[16]

Postmodernists view such essentialist claims as false. They take the position that there is no "self-contained" subject separable from social reality, and

---

[13] For some of the debates on the interrelationship between postmodernism and feminism, see L Nicholson (ed) 1990; S Benhabib and D Cornell, 1987; C Smart, 1989; J Butler and J Scott (eds*) Feminists Theorise the Political* (New York and London: Routledge: 1992); S Benhabib, J Butler, D Cornell and N Fraser *Feminist Contentions* (New York and London: Routledge 1995); G Lloyd (ed), 1984.

[14] See J Schroeder's analysis of CA MacKinnon in J Schroeder "Taming the Shrew: the Liberal attempt to mainstream radical feminist theory" (1992) 5 *Journal of Law and Feminism* 123 and "Catharine's Wheel: MacKinnon's Pornography Analysis" (1993) 38 *New York Law School Law Review* 225. This type of thinking is also evident in much of the burgeoning personal development industry.

[15] S Firestone, 1971; A Rich, 1976; R West 1987; R West 1988. However, West's more recent work suggests this interpretation of her work is restrictive and now out of date, see West, 1997, 2001, 2002.

[16] S de Beauvoir, 1997; M O'Brien, 1981.

no conception of the subject as a unitary agent which has been described as *"the capacity to get behind one's discursively constituted contexts of interaction to a privileged vantage point from which those contexts could be understood and controlled."*[17] Instead, for postmodernism, the "subject" is never unitary, never complete; it is a social construct, the product of multiple structures and discourses.[18] This view therefore rejects not only the liberal conception of the "nature" of the human subject, it rejects *any* philosophical ideas of a true inner nature or "natural" or "true authentic" self for society to liberate or oppress. Society constructs, rather than represses, the "true" "inner" self and then represents it as somehow natural and as having been always already there.[19] As many have highlighted, although seemingly rejecting universalism, this postmodernist claim seems to be universalist in itself.[20] Such positions on the death of the subject are extremely problematic for feminist views of the human and when feminists try to use these ideas in conjunction with feminist jurisprudence, the incoherence of the postmodern "subject" becomes clear. Before showing how this manifests itself, I want to analyse the use that can be made of deconstructive method for feminist legal theorists.

## Method

Many feminist theorists have sought to use postmodernism, perceiving its methods to be useful in being wary of generalisations that transcend the boundaries of culture and region.[21] Although I am critical of the death of the subject in postmodernism, its deconstructive method can, and has been, usefully employed by some feminists as an instrument or tool to better ways of being through deconstruction, but this must be followed by reconstructions of subjectivity. For deconstruction to be of such use, it should not involve throwing away or destroying, instead it is a way of undermining authoritarianism within the idea of the *"determinateness of the meaning of concepts in general"* by delineating their histories, identifying their multiple meanings in the present, and attempting to foresee the possible political consequences of employing or elaborating any of these meanings in specific ways in the future.[22] Such deconstruction involves

---

[17] A Barron 1993, p 80.
[18] See M Foucault *The History of Sexuality: An Introduction* (Harmondsworth: Penguin 1978); see L McNay, 1992.
[19] J Butler, 1989.
[20] A point made by R West, see above at note 15; N Lacey, 1998, and S Benhabib, 1992. As Benhabib has expressed it, while dismissing the norms of autonomy and rationality, postmodernists rely on them, assuming hyper-universalist and superliberal values of diversity and otherness.
[21] L Nicholson, 1990, p 5–7.
[22] See L Nicholson *The Play of Reason: from the modern to the postmodern* (Buckingham: Open University Press 1999) at 3–4. Looking at the ethic of care Kohlberg/Gilligan debate (see C Gilligan, 1982), Nicholson is critical of both Kohlberg's and Gilligan's methods. Kohlberg selected a certain type of thinking: abstract formalism, from the historical context

analysing how power operates in diverse uses of such concepts and trying to understand how such uses make possible certain forms of human interaction and suppress or marginalise others, thus reifying and privileging some views and concepts, while others are devalued and suppressed. This therefore provides a valuable tool for oppressed peoples to argue forcefully against existing norms and privileged viewpoints.

Warning to guard against the tendency of claiming "feminist truth" as better than other truths, some feminists prefer instead to deconstruct the notion of truth.[23] The "truth" of feminist jurisprudence, as represented in works of feminists like Catharine MacKinnon and psychoanalytical feminists who point to a stage of child development at which the feminine has not been *"colonised by the structures of patriarchy"*, is questioned, asking whether such theories ever lead to "truth".[24] Instead, feminists are encouraged to deconstruct the naturalistic gender-blind discourse of law by constantly revealing the context in which it has been constituted: law being grounded in patriarchy, class and ethnic divisions.

It is important not to reproduce dogmatic authoritarian theories to replace the patriarchal "truth" that dictates what being a human means and can mean. However, it is possible to say that some positions are better than others, that some positions are right and others wrong, that there is a truth to certain situations and beliefs and not to others, that there are just and unjust positions. It is important for feminist politics that feminists are not reticent in taking such stands against injustice.

Deconstructive method can assist in learning which positions to accept and which to reject, what has been described as *"the pursuit of justice"*.[25] Accordingly, it can assist as part of a critical reasoning process for individuals to make informed choices. However, deconstructive analyses can be of no use *unless the deconstructive arguments assume the existence of an alternative: one that is more just than the one being deconstructed* (even if it, in turn, can be subjected to further deconstruction).[26] Deconstructive argument itself is a rhetorical practice that can be used for good or bad. All positive norms can be deconstructed, therefore the critical use of deconstruction must postulate a transcendental value, such as justice, for all. The fact that a conceptual scheme is deconstructible cannot by itself be a reason for rejecting it because all texts are deconstructible.[27] There

---

that fostered this way of thinking and construed it as desirable. Gilligan commits a similar mistake, says Nicholson, in that her theory was silent about which girls and women her claims addressed.

[23] See C Smart, 1989.

[24] C Smart, above note 3; see analysis by N Lacey, 1998. CA MacKinnon, 1989.

[25] See JM Balkin "Being Just with Deconstruction" (1994) 3 *Social and Legal Studies* 393–404; "Deconstructive Practice and Legal Theory" (1987) 96 *Yale Law Journal* 743; "Transcendental Deconstruction, Transcendent Justice" (1994) 92 *Michigan Law Review* 1131.

[26] For this view, see JM Balkin, 1994a.

[27] JM Balkin, 1994a, at 395. This can be seen clearly in Balkin's examination of Jacques Derrida's deconstructive method. In Derrida's example of attacking apartheid, Balkin explains there is nothing in the nature of deconstructive techniques that prevents Derrida

are particular reasons for deconstructing some texts and positions while leaving others alone. The reason has to do with the deconstructor's *pre-existing moral and political commitments*. Deconstructive arguments must come to an end at some point, although they are potentially endless.

Deconstruction for its own sake is ultimately nihilistic but the method is useful and has potential to create better ways of being through subsequent reconstruction of a more inclusive human subjectivity. However, such reconstruction depends on normative moral and political commitments as the motivation and driving force behind the deconstruction to give it any meaning. Some of these moral and political commitments can be shown to be right and some wrong.

## How is it Possible to have the Death of the Subject and Feminist Politics?

Certain prominent feminists use postmodern or poststructural method in their theories.[28] In this section, their work is drawn upon to illustrate that normative ideas of subjectivity need to be retained if feminist politics is to succeed in making women's lives better. Their work is driven by strong critical normative commitments to justice and freedom for women. While some use postmodern methodology, emphasising the importance of language and deconstruction, what results is often concrete proposals for law reform in the form of rights. Other theories fail because they use postmodernism and end up with the death of a self-reflective subject.

Deconstructive method has been used to produce a *"utopian moment"* – the potential for future imaginings in the yet impossible in the work of Drucilla Cornell, a theorist whose work usefully deconstructs the subject but provides alternatives to reconstruct it.[29]

Cornell builds on Lacan's psychoanalytical theory, arguing that individuals see themselves as intrinsically sexed, not easily re-envisioning their "sexuate" being.[30] The term "sexuate being" is defined as the sexed body of the

---

from doing the opposite (that is, supporting apartheid). It is simply because of Derrida's commitment to anti-apartheid.

[28] D Cornell "Institutionalization of meaning: Recollective Imagination and the potential for transformative legal interpretation." (1988) 136 *University of Pennsylvania Law Review* 1135; D Cornell, M Rosenfeld and D Carlson (eds) *Hegel and Legal Theory* (New York and London: Routledge 1991). In Cornell's work, Hegelian ideas of freedom, self-recognition and awareness through other others is the starting point. See also the references above at note 3.

[29] D Cornell, above note 3.

[30] J Lacan "The Mirror Stage as Formative of the Function of the I" in *Ecrits: A Selection* (Trans. A Sheridan. London: Routledge 1977); E Wright, 2000. In Lacanian theory, the subject is split on the imposition of language, between its symbolic identity and the body that sustains it. The splitting of subjectivity produces a sexual division. It has been claimed that Lacan has provided a powerful critique of stable identity without getting rid of it

human being when engaged with a framework with which persons orient themselves.[31] This analysis is supplemented with Kantian practical reason, as interpreted by John Rawls's Veil of Ignorance and his principles of justice, and Ronald Dworkin's equality theory.[32] The idea is that no-one starts from scratch, all are socially constructed and born into ideas of the good life culturally available to them. Individuals cannot therefore be the fully original source of their own values. However, the argument is made for a normative recognition of women and men as agents of choice, accepting Kant's ethical supposition that all persons have the capacity for reason. Persons should be politically recognised as if they are *"fully authenticating sources of [their] own values"*, normatively being recognised as abstract ideal persons who are agents of choice and sources of value.[33] This is the "imaginary domain", the ethical defence of which is made by an appeal to Ronald Dworkin's grounds of liberalism: that all are of equal worth as persons and that all are uniquely responsible for their own lives. This political and legal recognition comes in the form of "the right to equivalent evaluation". This right amounts to women being evaluated as free and equal persons.

Following Kant, the freedom of every member of society as a human being should be privileged. For women, it is this freedom that has historically been denied. Further, the equivalent evaluation of sexual difference should be demanded so that women are included in the moral community of persons, providing for fair and equitable treatment wherever and whenever sexual difference needs to be taken into account.[34] Law and other basic institutions need to recognise that each person is unique, has one life to live with integrity and freedom, including the freedom "to be".[35] This theory thus intertwines postmodern deconstruction of the subject with liberal rights theory, to enable a reconstruction of subjectivity in a way aiming to strengthen women's rights. Its value as a feminist theory with a political purpose is therefore retained because it keeps a conception of subjectivity which is coherent.

Similarly, French feminist Luce Irigaray deconstructs but then reconstructs.[36] In her theory, language is described as phallogocentric: women constitute the unrepresentable, the sex that cannot be thought, a linguistic absence and opacity with both the subject *and the other* being masculine, eluding the feminine altogether.[37] However, like Cornell, she concludes a rights programme is

---

altogether – see, for example, E Wright *Lacan and Postfeminism* (Cambridge: Icon Books Ltd 2000).

[31] D Cornell 1995.

[32] D Cornell 1998, p 64; J Rawls, 1971; R Dworkin, see Chapter 2 above for general analysis of Kant and Rawls in terms of universalism.

[33] D Cornell 1998, p 38.

[34] Cornell 1998, p 11.

[35] By way of example, she is critical of "difference" analysis of pregnancy laws, which views women's reproductive capacity as a real difference from men.

[36] L Irigaray, 1985.

[37] See E Marks and I de Courtivron (eds), 1981; M Whitford (ed) *The Irigaray Reader* (Oxford: Basil Blackwell 1991); N Lacey, 1998; see also J Butler's analysis in J Butler, 1990, p 9–10.

the way forward: rights are needed for women, the right to human dignity and human identity. The idea behind deconstruction is again to reconstruct with the goal of improving women's ways of being.

The having of rights is normally based on having capacities and geared to entitlements on a contractual model: rights to have things in the masculine language of performance, measurement and control.[38] By contrast, Irigaray focuses on the need for rights to reflect *being* rather than *having*, and on the relational aspects of rights.

The work of these feminists can be criticised for resulting in rights programmes which inevitably lead to the fixing of identities, sometimes invoking arguably conventional stereotypes of femininity, for example, the right to virginity.[39] The answer is to balance the danger of essentialising and stereotyping women with the aim of making concrete proposals which will improve women's lives in the existing system.

Some have also criticised attempts to juxtapose rationality with the seemingly contradictory theory of Lacanian psychoanalysis.[40] Indeed, it has been stated that when Cornell does normative jurisprudence, she is not doing postmodernism.[41] Such a statement seems accurate to the extent that it is difficult to reconcile a subjectivity which presents persons as normatively recognised abstract ideal persons capable of choice, of equal worth and responsible for their own lives, if they are postmodern discourse-produced "subjects". However, this theory can be interpreted as discussing two different conceptions of human subjectivity. One is the psychologically developed experiencing human subject and the other is the transcendent, somehow all encompassing ideal conception of the human subject, the ideal for the purposes of political rights. The two are concepts or representations, they are not real particular people. The basic idea of reasonableness in political liberalism is that each person accords the other the recognition that each is to be treated as a free and equal person before both the law and other basic institutions of society.[42] It is not that all are, in actual political, social and legal practice, free and equal: the point is that persons *should* be treated *as if* they are.

As can be seen in this type of work, feminist jurisprudence needs norms and freedom and rights discourse to make concrete changes possible in the present, while balancing with future possibilities. There is an awareness that recognising such ideas through "rights" has the potential to close future possibilities for liberation and potentially reinforce existing power structures.[43] However, utopian

---

[38] L Irigaray, 1985.

[39] N Lacey, 1998, p 213–5. Nicola Lacey describes Irigaray as moving between two voices or styles: imaginary and the language of an institutional programme for legal and political reform.

[40] See R Sandland, 1998; R Sandland "Between Truth and Difference: Poststructuralism, Law and the power of feminism" (1995) 3 *Feminist Legal Studies* 3.

[41] See A Barron, 2000.

[42] D Cornell 1998, p 175. See also J Rawls (1971) and R Dworkin, 2000.

[43] A criticism lucidly made of D Cornell's work by N Lacey, 1998, at her Chapter 8.

reconstructions assert the right to future possibilities and remain driven by normatively charged ideals. Although it will always be difficult to balance the possibility of a rights programme fixing identities and making meaningful change, it is nevertheless necessary to speak the language of the world's discourse if that is to happen. Rights discourse is a dominant discourse which provides a chance to make a possible difference to women's lives. Ultimately, feminist work which reconstructs rights in this way illustrates that deconstructive method can be used while retaining a normative theory, based on a strong conception of human subjectivity, with the importance of freedom and the need for human beings to be treated as agents of choice being stressed.[44]

Some feminist work has sought to use postmodern method and while dismissing normativity, seems to be driven by normative beliefs.[45] The main target of their criticism is essentialism and its potential to fix identities. In such arguments it is claimed that what is assumed to be natural about gender identity is almost non-existent. What is therefore needed is to undermine conventional gender expectations, opening up the possibility of new forms of gender relations that are not structured by biological imperatives or a hierarchical dichotomy between male and female.

This feminist work draws on theorists Friedrich Nietzsche and Michel Foucault, and argues that, instead of searching for the origins of gender or the inner truth of female desire, the political stakes in designating as *an origin and cause* those identity categories that are in fact *the effects* of institutions, practices and discourses, ought to be investigated.[46] The law produces and then conceals the notion of a subject before the law in order to invoke that discursive formation as a naturalised foundational premise that subsequently legitimises that law's own dominant regulation. On this view, there may not be any subject who stands "before" the law waiting to be represented in or by it.[47] Instead the law and the "regulatory hegemony" creates this subject.[48] The presumed universality of a "unitary" view of the subject is criticised for leading to exclusions.[49] While doing this, such work explicitly rejects normative ideals: "identity" is a normative ideal rather than a descriptive feature of experience.[50] The subject is decentred, dispersed and constituted in a multiplicity of power relations that produce meanings. This is

---

[44] See K Knop, 2004; R West 2003.

[45] See J Butler, 1990; W Brown, 1995. See analysis in K Weeks *Constituting Feminist Subjects* (Ithaca and London: Cornell University Press 1998) at p 125 ff.

[46] J Butler, 1990, p ix.

[47] J Butler, 1990, p 2.

[48] Butler is therefore critical of state of nature theories as they claim an ontological integrity of the subject before the law which, in her view, does not exist; for example, as can be seen in the diverse works of T Hobbes, 1960; Locke, 1988; and Rousseau, 1974.

[49] J Butler, 1990, p 4–5.

[50] J Butler, 1990, p 16.

contrasted with the humanist conception of the subject who assumes a substantive person: a bearer of essential and non essential attributes.[51]

Following Nietzsche's idea that there is no being behind the doing, and instead the deed is everything, it is argued that there is no gender identity behind the expressions of gender, identity is performatively constituted by the very expressions that are said to be its results.[52] Following Foucault, it is argued that a literature of femininity would not involve the problem of truth (uncovering "true" identity) but it would be a practical ethical issue of exploring the potential of new identities.

Thus the subject is dissolved. With the dissolution of the subject, agency is in danger of disappearing, leaving no room for the transformation of relations of domination to take place. This awareness appears to be evident and agency is stressed as important for that very reason. Therefore what is advocated as the way forward is to make "gender trouble", not through strategies presenting utopian visions, but through the mobilisation of those constitutive categories that seek to keep gender in its place by posturing as the foundational illusions of identity.[53]

Although criticisms of any notion of feminine identity as the foundation for feminist politics can be well-founded because it can, as Butler expresses it, obscure the field of power through which the feminine subject is formed,[54] such a view does not mean that the subject needs to be dissolved. The concept of the human subject as it has been conceptualised to date can be deconstructed in ways ably done by many feminists but it then needs to be reconstructed to ensure a strong sense of identity, self and subjectivity for all human beings, a notion which is of particular relevance to those historically denied such a sense of subjectivity or self, including women. A sense of dissolution of the subject without foundation leads to a sense of chaos and meaninglessness: something which those groups historically oppressed are all too familiar with and which is exactly the opposite of what they really need if their lives are to be better and they are to have improved ways of being.

Anti-essentialist critiques have been described as causing "*palpable feminist panic*".[55] Why does putting the subject in question – decentring its constitution, deconstructing its unity, denaturing its origins and components – cause much feminist hostility? Some think that hostility is caused by feminist attachment to the idea of a subject that is more critically bound to retaining women's experiences, feelings and voices as sources of political truth. Those feminists who want to dispense with or reject the unified subject argue that such rejection does not mean that women cease to be able to speak about their experiences as women, only that their words cannot be legitimately deployed or

---

[51] Butler critiques feminist essentialism by particular reference to the work of Simone de Beauvoir and Monique Wittig. See S de Beauvoir, 1997; and M Wittig *The Straight Mind and Other Essays* (New York: Harvester Wheatsheaf 1992).

[52] J Butler, 1990, p 25.

[53] J Butler, 1990, p 34.

[54] J Butler, 1990, p 109.

[55] W Brown, 1995, p 39.

construed as larger or longer than *the moments of the lives they speak from* – they cannot be authentic or true.[56]

Feminists who believe in the social construction of gender but preserve some variant of consciousness-raising as a mode of discerning and delivering the "truth" about women are particularly criticised by those who want to dispense with the subject. It has been asked why the standpoint of women should be used as a foundation if women are socially constructed? On this view, consciousness-raising, as or like confession, does not deliver the hidden truth of women and women's experience. Postmodernity has been described as unsettling feminism because it erodes the moral ground that the subject, truth and normativity co-produce in modernity.[57] However, such postmodernists claim that politics can thrive without a strong theory of the subject, without truth and without scientifically derived norms: postmodern feminist politics requires cultivated political spaces for posing and questioning feminist political norms rather than false essentialism.[58] This is unconvincing.

Given feminism's political underpinning, it is not surprising that questions have been raised as to whether a radically critical project such as postmodernism can sustain feminist, or any similar kind of, politics, including the ideal of reconstruction which has so long been accepted as part of feminism.[59] Thus there is a wariness of an alliance between postmodernism and feminism. It has been suggested that postmodernism is a theory whose time may have come for men but not for women in that postmodernism expresses the claims and needs of a constituency (white, male, middle-class) that has already had an enlightenment for itself and is now ready and willing to place that legacy under critical scrutiny.[60] Since men have had their enlightenment, they can afford a sense of a decentred self but for women doing such decentring would mean weakening what is not yet strong and feminist politics would suffer. It has been asked whether the adoption of postmodernism really entails the destruction of feminism since surely feminism depends on a relatively unified notion of the social subject "woman", a notion postmodernism would attack.[61] Although feminists have used postmodernism, there remains a strong driving sense of moral and political commitment behind their theories of the subject inconsistent ultimately with the postmodern death of the subject.

The point has also been made that objects of postmodernism's critical and deconstructive efforts have been the creations of a similarly specific and partial constituency in that mainstream postmodern theory has been remarkably blind to the questions of gender. Concerns have been voiced that the postmodern project, if seriously adopted by feminists, would make any semblance of a feminist politics

---

[56] W Brown, 1995.

[57] W Brown, 1995.

[58] W Brown, 1995, p 50–1.

[59] N Lacey, 1998, p 181; S Benhabib, 1992.

[60] See C Di Stefano "Dilemmas of Difference: Feminism, Modernity, and Postmodernism" in L Nicholson (ed), 1990.

[61] C Di Stefano, 1990.

impossible and, to the extent feminist politics is bound up with a specific constituency or subject, namely women, the postmodernist prohibition against subject-centred inquiry and theory undermines the legitimacy of a broad-based organised movement dedicated to articulating and implementing the goals of such a constituency.[62] Particular concerns are validly raised that just as previously silenced populations have begun to speak for themselves and on behalf of their subjectivities, it is worrying that the concept of the subject and the possibility of discovering or creating a liberating "truth" become suspect.[63]

The realities of women's lives seen at global, national and local level include sexual and physical violation and such violation can be analysed as being gendered, systematic and organised.[64] It is of particular concern that the foundation for feminist responses to that do not dissolve into different and multiple subject positions providing excuses for perpetrators of such wrongs and violations and crimes against women. This issue will be explored further in the global context in Part III.

The postmodernist contention that the subject is dead prevents holding perpetrators of crimes against women accountable for what they do.[65] This is of particular relevance in the context of international humanitarian, criminal and human rights law.[66] The postmodern alliance with feminism has starkly been described in the following terms:

> We cannot have this postmodernism and still have a meaningful practice of women's human rights, far less a women's movement…Ironically…just as women have begun to become human, even as we have begun to transform the human so it is something more worth having and might apply to us, we are told by high theory that the human is inherently authoritarian, not worth having, untransformable, and may not even exist – and how hopelessly nineteenth-century of us to want it.[67]

As identified in Chapters 1 and 2, feminist work has been invaluable at showing how the human subject of modernity has been insufficient in including women within its definition. It needs to continue to transform and reconstruct that concept to include women, to ensure that subjectivity is retained and used in a way that is

---

[62] C Di Stefano, 1990, p 76.

[63] N Hartsock "Rethinking Modernism: Minority vs majority theories." (1987) 7 *Cultural Critique* 187–206.

[64] See, for example, KD Askin and DM Koenig (eds), 1999–2004; CA MacKinnon "Crimes of War, Crimes of Peace" in S Shute and S Hurley (eds) *On Human Rights: The Oxford Amnesty Lectures* (New York: Basic Books 1993); J Gardam "A Feminist Analysis of Certain Aspects of International Humanitarian Law" (1992) 12 *Australian Yearbook of International Law* 265; "Women and the Law of Armed Conflict: Why the silence? (1997) 46 *ICLQ* 55; J Gardam and M Jarvis, 2001.

[65] See CA MacKinnon, 2000. For other examples of feminist theories which focus on basing feminist theory on the realities of women's situations see b hooks "Theory as Liberatory Practice" (1991) 4 *Yale Journal Of Law and Feminism* 1; R West, 1988.

[66] See KD Askin and DM Koenig, 1999–2004; and J Gardam, 1992 and 1997.

[67] CA MacKinnon, 2000, p 710–711.

to women's advantage. However, postmodernist work that hails the subject as dead, at the very least, regresses this project.

Additionally, some feminists have astutely argued that many women's experiences reverse the postmodern description of individual awareness of the social construction of selfhood. What many women experience is not socially constructed subjectivity or *selfhood*, instead they experience socially constructed *lack of self*.[68] The social existence for many women world-wide is not one of subjecthood or selfhood, but the opposite: one of objecthood or otherhood, a sense of selflessness, experienced as incapacity. Those who experience such an existence are *falsely* and *wrongly* in this position. Whilst many, including many feminists, may find this view sweeping, evidence of the devastating effects of oppression on women's lives can be demonstrated from almost every country in the world, obviously with geographical, class, race and ethnic variations in, to name but a few examples, unequal education; unequal pay; discrimination at work; sexual and physical violation; domestic violence; political under-representation; lack of power in all avenues of public life and disproportionate poverty.[69] What women therefore need is to become aware of this oppression, leading in turn to the construction of a strong sense of self within each one of them. As such, women's experience and a feminist understanding of subjectivity has been described as utterly incompatible with the postmodernist's understanding of the self.[70]

Becoming more aware of structural inequality, of the reality of hierarchical gender alignments and the presence of power skewed against women is important for individual women as a part of women's conceptions of themselves. The aim is for feminist jurisprudence to retain ideas of subjectivity not dissolve them out of existence. This does not need to constrain the formation of new identities as will now be shown.

## No Agency Without the Subject

Ideas of "essentialism" amongst women can result in imposing restrictions and constraints on women's ways of being. At the same time as addressing this, feminism needs more than a view that women's experiences – of, for example, rape and sexualised torture anywhere in the world –relate only to the *"moments of the lives they speak from"*.[71]

If the subject is evaporated out of existence, why should anyone bother to mobilise anything – what is the point in resistive strategies? Why make "gender trouble" at all? Whilst some valid critical points have been made by feminists using postmodern methods concerning the imposition of fixed subject identities, making socially constructed features appear "natural", this can be avoided if the common quality of each human being is seen as their *potentiality* and not some

---

[68] R West 1997, p 285.
[69] See all references at Introduction, note 5.
[70] R West, 1997, Chapter 5.
[71] W Brown, 1995, see analysis above.

fixed core essential unified self. This potentiality and freedom can include the potential for free identity formation, the freedom to be one's own person. Normative subjectivity, individual power and a coherent sense of identity is kept. This acknowledges the effect that social conditions have on preferences and wants and people's sense of who they are and what choices they therefore make. Yet it retains a common potential shared by all which normatively ought to guide political and legal imaginings: that individuals ought to be encouraged to develop their potential to exist meaningfully. If this idea of existence rather than essence is used seeking an expansion of human potentiality, the problem of fixed constraints on identity are removed. The concepts of individual freedom and autonomy need not be based on assumptions of unitary unchanging essences. Such concepts need not require agents to be completely self-transparent and psychically unified; nor assume that only a pure will, free from all empirical determination, can be self-determining, or enforce a "hegemonic" identity.[72]

Individuals can form their new self-understanding imaginatively out of the materials available to them by taking advantage of the spaces within what is there. In this process, new meanings will emerge as their imaginative dimensions are expanded. Freedom and consciousness exist with the power to consider things as they are, as they are not, to imagine situations which are different from the actual situations in the world and form plans to change what is there: ideas more fully developed in Part II.[73]

The continuing challenge for feminists, where much valuable work is being done in this area, is to reconstruct the notion of freedom or autonomy so as to uncover its emancipatory liberating potential, breaking down the distinction between transcendence and immanence or between the desire for autonomy and the recognition of one's dependence on others. However, in the final analysis, the idea of a postmodern feminism is unviable, because, at some basic level, feminist critique rests on normative judgements about what forms legitimate and non-legitimate forms of action, resting on the political goal of overcoming the subordination of women.[74]

As has already been shown, much of the criticism of the "unified" subject can be seen as a mischaracterisation and inaccurate representation of a great deal of liberal thought on the individual, perhaps more accurately being accredited to Thomas Hobbes and certain neo-classical or utilitarian liberals.[75] However, such criticisms are valid to the extent that theorists portray individuals as separate from each other, interested in their self-preservation, self-interested and motivated to maximise their own welfare, always inevitably in conflict. Such a presentation of

---

[72] As expressed by C MacKenzie and N Stoljar, 2000, p 10–11.

[73] See S de Beauvoir, 1997; M Warnock *Existential Ethics* (London: Macmillan 1967). See also Dilman "Sartre and Our Identity As Individuals" in D Cockburn (ed) *Human Beings* (The Royal Institute of Philosophy Supplement 29) (Cambridge: Cambridge University Press 1991); S Motha and T Zartaloudis "Review Article: Law, Ethics and the Utopian End of Human Rights" (2003) 12 *Social & Legal Studies* 243.

[74] L McNay, 1992, p 117.

[75] See analysis by MC Nussbaum 1999, chapter 2.

human nature is inaccurate as a psychological portrayal of humanity.[76] However, a conception of the human subject can be retained without accepting that that subject has to be always "unified, rational and self-present", isolated and atomised, wholly apart from (and even opposed to) society and exclude relationships with others, without deconstructing the subject out of existence as many postmodernists will have us do.

Retaining the subject who is capable of autonomous reflection does not inevitably lead to a belief in the Cartesian idea that consciousness can be transparently self-aware or to the Kantian view of persons as rational self-legislators. The persistence of such views can assist in upholding structures of domination and subordination, in particular aiding suppression of others, for example, women, "colonial subjects", ethnic minorities and other minority groups, who are somehow deemed excluded and thus incapable of achieving rational self-mastery.

The type of critical questioning that allows for deconstruction can only exist when individuals have been encouraged to develop such capacities and are therefore free within the society in which they live to develop these capacities and then to express such views. Selecting and affirming aspects of existing conditions and present practices to serve as the ground or foundation of a theory involves an active intervention, a conscious and concerted effort to reinterpret and restructure people's lives.[77]

Those postmodernists who seek to deconstruct and claim to have an aversion to normative agenda fail to explain why such agency and critical reflection is important. They also fail to show how it will be encouraged and allowed to flourish without normative goals and aspirations: to live in societies where the freedom to express these views is allowed and, additionally, actively encouraged. Postmodernists have given no reason why a discourse-produced, socially constructed subject should or ought to have any critical self-reflexivity. For example, they are keen to illustrate the injustice in laws, the power of the oppressor against the oppressed, while at the same time removing the tools for explaining why some positions (including their own) are better than others. They seem to be in favour of such capacity yet fail to show why it is important that such a capacity should exist and be allowed to develop. If resistance is so important (as it seems to be to them), surely this capacity is paramount to enable such resistance? Why is struggle preferable to submission according to postmodernists? They have not explained where the standards come from to provide this critical self-reflexive knowledge and why these *should* exist. If individuals lived in a society where they were not allowed to develop this capacity, postmodernists do not have the tools to explain why this would be "wrong" if their view is that the "subject" is only a product of discourse. Only with the introduction of some normative notions can postmodernism begin to explain what is wrong with modern power and why it should be opposed.[78]

---

[76] The feminist critiques of such a concept of humanity are numerous and from many perspectives. See Chapters 1 and 2 above.
[77] See K Weeks, 1998.
[78] B Marshall, 1994, p 111.

It is possible to deconstruct ideas which present human subjectivity as always the same and unified and reconstruct a new subjectivity out of existing formulations of the human subject. But is this "doing postmodernism"? Projects aiming to hold onto some of the insights of postmodernism, yet retaining a human subject and norms, produce reconceptualisations of the human subject, not the dissolution of the subject through postmodernism.[79] A postmodernism which does not allow for normative agenda can only lead to deconstructing the subject out of existence as many have already argued: resistance politics are meaningless without a normative aim.

This negative approach against universality and the human subject causes problems for feminist lawyers who need claims to be capable of enforcement and observation, making some sort of appeal to universality and concepts of justice and rights necessary.[80] Feminists purporting to be postmodern often continue to use liberal concepts to describe normative ideals (for example sexual equality, social justice and individual self-development) while dismissing them. The reason for this is that such language is inevitable – the language of freedom has to be used because freedom is what feminism is all about – the freedom to be treated as full moral persons, to allow women to be and to live, to become their own persons, in the community, which is evident in returns to normativity within feminist writing and in returns to liberalism as evidenced recently in the work of many prominent feminists.[81] In calling for norms and a return to normativity in feminist legal theory, the norm of freedom and the concept of the human subject with agency cannot be avoided.

As will be more fully explained in Part II, it is this freedom and potentiality for meaningful subjecthood which all humans share in common that has been suppressed in women. Feminism needs to hold onto that hope or potential and reclaim it for women. This does not need to entail a belief in an inner *essence* in the sense of an unchanging foundational core that is prohibitive, in that it can be used to justify placing constraints on new ways of being. Instead, it can be expressed as the *potential* to form projects and exist in the world in a meaningful way with the recognition by others of each human subject's full humanity.

Given the fragmented and unstable nature of identity as it is constituted in modern society, the "postmodern subject" is unable to produce a strategy, or utopian alternative, to transcend the chaos of everyday life.[82] Of course, the postmodern death

---

[79] See, for example, Peter Goodrich's response to A Barron: P Goodrich "Barron's Complaint: A Response to 'Feminism, Aestheticism and the Limits of Law'" (2001) 9 *Feminist Legal Studies* 149–170. In his view, Barron's criticism of postmodernism has resulted in her rejection of it (at 151).

[80] This claim is Anne Barron's: A Barron, 2000, p 276. Barron uses and reconstructs Kantian ideas on aesthetics concluding that a normative jurisprudence fully responsive to preoccupations of postmodern legal feminism might be developed through the elaboration of a model where *feeling* is the very condition of claims of legal right though only to the extent that it is amenable to possible universalisation. This is a thought-provoking and interesting idea which cannot be fully explored here.

[81] See also analysis in E Jackson and N Lacey, 2002.

[82] See A Giddens *Modernity and Self-identity: Self and Society in the Late Modern Age* (Cambridge: Polity Press 1991); S Benhabib "Sexual Difference and Collective Identities: the New Global Constellation" in S James and S Palmer (eds), 2002.

of the subject is a metaphor not the extinction of a living sentient human being. However, living in an age of instability and potential crises of individual identity, arguably the last thing people need is a decentring and dissolving of subjectivity without reconstruction as it inevitably leads to questioning and analysis of their self-identity and existence with a lack of better alternatives. Criticisms of the present should always be juxtaposed with a notion of *what ought to be* and no matter how non-prescriptive this "ought" is, it rests on some kind of normative assumptions, for example, what constitutes the legitimate and illegitimate use of power. In order to respect difference and to incorporate this respect into a systematic programme of social transformation such as is demanded by feminism, it is necessary to work within some kind of normative framework. Postmodern theories of the subject lack such positive normative guidelines. For many feminists, it appears too easy to slide from a crisis of subjectivity into a void or irretrievable fragmentation of subject positions.[83]


**Conclusion**

Feminist jurisprudence must remain a normative project: creating alternative interpretations, envisioning different futures and possibilities and being concerned with women transforming their own identity and becoming empowered.[84] To produce societies which are more just than those that already exist involves the presence of *active* and *intentional* subjects. Feminists cannot embrace the postmodern "subject" (that is, a rejection of the subject) because, as Barbara Marshall has stated, women as subjects have not been accorded the coherence, autonomy, rationality or agency of the subject which forms the basis of modernism and which postmodernism has deconstructed out of existence.[85] So, not only do normative foundations need to be sustained in feminist jurisprudence, the idea of an active and intentional, critically self-reflexive subjecthood needs to be retained, and indeed strengthened, particularly for individual women.

The postmodern death of the subject is ultimately unconvincing, hindering feminist ideals of liberation for women. Some deconstructive method with a normative aim is useful. Some postmodern ideas against essentialism are well-founded in avoiding "naturalising" tendencies to fix identities and restrict the freedom of human subjects. However, deconstructing the subject out of existence can be damaging when what is needed is a strengthening of the conception of human subjectivity which will be more inclusive and lead to better more flourishing lives for all.

In Part II, I explain more fully my arguments of a conception of the human being which will be more inclusive and lead to better more flourishing lives.

---

[83] L McNay, 1992, p 192–194.
[84] See A Phillips, 1993.
[85] B Marshall, 1994, p 148.

# PART II
# FREE EXISTENCE

# Introduction to Part II

*"The least extreme expression of gender inequality, and prerequisite for all of it, is dehumanization and objectification."* CA MacKinnon[1]

Given the cul de sac of the ultimate conclusions of theories of both essentialism and the death of the subject, a re-examination is suggested. This will involve examining the inseparable and intertwining relationship between the norms of society and structures, including law, which help create, develop, sustain and enforce the rights of the inclusive human subject and that human subject's empowerment through agency which in turn gives those norms flexibility to be changed, with the paramount concern resting on the human subject's capacity to be a free person in the community.[2]

This Part of the book provides a theory to increase individual freedom through the removal of internal and external obstacles with women being treated as free human beings or persons: a norm to guide feminist imaginings, discourse amongst persons, the structuring of institutions, and provide a political and legal framework for societies. This is a feminist project because women more than men have not been allowed to be, and have not been treated as, free persons historically and currently in social reality.

The importance of seeing women as subjects in the sense of being moral persons in their own right to be accorded equal dignity, respect and concern is emphasised: the language of egalitarian liberalism and the enlightenment project. Presenting a strong view of subjectivity ensures that there are no problems in coherently proposing normative theories for feminist legal theory and correspondingly agenda for feminist politics. However, it is important to develop these ideas in a way which is not normalising and privileging any particular groups' experience of the world and is therefore exclusionary.

The aim is to show how individual freedom can be radically increased to allow for more authentic choices to be made. Human beings will be more fulfilled if they experience a fuller human realisation and freedom which comes about from a recognition of interconnection one with each other, and with their environment, including the social, political and legal structures. A concept of positive freedom, emphasising the external structures that create, develop, sustain and then enforce the rights of all individual human subjects, will lead to a fairer, more just, ethically improved world. A human subject whose freedom is increased in this way, showing them how to make free informed real choices, will improve the lives of individual women and men.

---

[1] CA MacKinnon, 1989, p 243.

[2] Because identity and subjectivity are formed through interaction and relations with others, institutions are needed which allow this freedom to be realised.

This combination – the interdependence of the human subject's agency and the norms they imagine – will assist individuals to control their lives to make their own authentic choices and decisions, to be taken seriously, valued and treated with equal concern and respect within the society in which they live: surely all shared feminist aims? Following on from the previous chapter, it is therefore argued that any normative feminist jurisprudence needs to retain the sense of the subject, who has a capacity for agency, and an inviolability as a person, if feminism's transformative power is to have any real meaning. However, a subject whose common feature is potentiality is not essentialist and fixed with the attendant postmodern and feminist criticisms of such a subject.

## Retaining and Strengthening the Agency of the Subject through Freedom

To make any claims for normativity, a better way, an ideal to reach, it is necessary to retain a concept of the human subject who is capable of agency: leading to a belief in the importance and inherent dignity of all human subjects as persons.

It has been shown how the "liberal individual" – to the extent it is presented as being atomistic and separate from other individuals – is a deficient representation of human psychology. Such a presentation gives an inadequate view of the human condition. However, this is not the same as the idea of abstraction which is a device that can be used to show the critical evaluative capacity all humans can potentially have if developed clearly in a social environment. Removing internal obstacles to freedom in a social context will increase the freedom of individual human subjects.

As consciousness is created, in large part, by the social conditions individuals find themselves in – and when born and growing up most have little or no choice as to these social conditions, they need to be taken into account to ensure that they are structured in such a way as to allow for the development of a consciousness that will increase the freedom of every human being – freedom in the sense of the potentiality to be the author of one's life. Existing consciousness, and in turn choices made, and the social conditions which form that consciousness, are thus fundamentally connected and interdependent. What is often described as human "nature" is not a natural pre-social condition all are somehow born with but it depends largely on the way in which social structures shape individuals and regulate human relationships.

Who individuals are now, with inequalities and lack of freedom, is not a result of human "nature" or some "essential" male or female "nature" within, but depends on the way social structures shape individuals into who they are, who they are allowed to be and become. But often social constructionist arguments end up with such a socially determined entity that it seems extremely difficult to explain how individuals can extract themselves from their current condition, why they might want to, and what, if anything, they have in common with other people. For feminism to re-engage with normative ethics of human flourishing, to assist in creating a better place for women (and men) to live freely, human identity should be such that it allows individual freedom to determine the path of one's own life, plans and projects. If individuals are to be what they are capable of being, to realise their potentiality, they must not accept the given social situation as the only or inevitable way without question, especially as the existing social situation is structured and formed within a hierarchical gender system. Instead, the capacity to see that there are new ways of regarding themselves and others should be encouraged to develop.

This Part of the book expands on points highlighted by some feminists and examined in Chapters 1 and 2 that feminists are concerned with freeing women to shape their own lives, to define themselves, rather than accepting the definition given to them by others.[3] The social conditions in which individuals live and are formed are fundamental to this process of re-definition. It is therefore necessary to ensure that social conditions are adequate to enable each human being to find a *"self which is acceptable to itself"*.[4]

The idea of the human subject, meaning the agent who has responsibility over his or her own life needs to be retained. Structures and an environment that allow human beings the chance to think about what is possible for their lives are therefore required. Forming part of this process is taking women seriously by listening to, and believing them, according them respect and doing something about their concerns and problems. Feminism needs to retain conceptual resources adequate for criticising all forms of male dominance, thus a conception of political and moral agency within each person has to be retained, enabling a space for the self who subverts and conforms to and revolutionises social practices.[5]

Whether or not free will actually exists, most act as if it does and evaluate each other and live their lives on the basis of their ability to make what they believe to be genuine choices (they just disagree over to what degree). As persons, they seek not only material comfort but also respect and recognition from others: they believe that they are worthy of respect because they possess a certain value or dignity. They ought therefore to be treated as morally free persons. In this regard, Hegel's *Phenomenology of Spirit* is analysed in more detail in Chapter 4.[6] In the Hegelian master and slave dialectic, the slave only conceives of the idea of freedom: there is a discrepancy between his *actual* condition and his *idea* of freedom.[7] He must consider freedom in the abstract before he can enjoy it in reality and must invent for himself the principles of a free society before living in one.

---

[3] J Nedelsky, 1989, p 2–3; CA MacKinnon, 1989.

[4] M Griffiths, 1995.

[5] See S James and S Palmer (eds), 2002, p 7. In this volume of essays, Seyla Benhabib proposes a narrative view of the self while Moira Gatens suggests the limitations of liberal approaches and politics of differences where identities may be fixed may be overcome by drawing on Spinoza's philosophy and a feminist understanding of the self as embodied.

[6] GFW Hegel, 1977; D Cornell, 1988; K Hutchings, 2003; M Davies "Feminist Appropriations: Law, Property and Personality" (1994) 3 *Social and Legal Studies* 365–391.

[7] I use the male pronoun throughout when describing Hegel's master/slave dialectic as used by him.

The slave therefore has self-consciousness – being reflective of himself and his own condition.

These ideas can be considered and developed using a conception of freedom closely linked to positive freedom. People do not become free by being left alone, and the positive aspect of the choices people are able to make rather than the negative idea of non-interference will be emphasised.[8] In liberalism, two traditions of freedom have been identified. Often described as negative and positive freedom or liberty, most famously expounded by Isaiah Berlin in the late 1950s.[9] However, the distinction between the two types is often over-emphasised and after the downfall of the Soviet communist bloc and the thawing of the Cold War, such a distinction is, perhaps, of less relevance today than when Berlin was writing.

In Chapter 4, the idea of positive liberty of the liberal tradition is examined, as contrasted with negative, and Berlin's ultimate dismissal of it is then critiqued. Positive liberty provides for a fuller more flourishing liberal framework within which the human is formed and encouraged to be free in connection with other people thus removing the arguments that critiques of the liberal subject have of atomism, opposition to others, selfishness. It can also form the basis of a more inclusive human to which international humanitarian law can apply.

In Chapter 5, these views are applied in the context of the way women's preferences or wants are shaped by environment. The use of imagination and the development of a critical consciousness for human beings to change preferences and the importance of others in the formation of individual conscious desires, wants or preferences is then analysed. It is shown that even when oppressed by a hierarchical gender structure, and faced with seemingly intractable, no hope situations, individual women are undoubtedly capable of agency. Individual humans are capable of imagining the abstract possibility of being recognised as a

---

[8] A good example of a theorist who develops such a theory (without any consideration of gender) is R Norman "Does Equality Destroy Liberty" in K Graham (ed) *Contemporary Political Philosophy* (Cambridge: Cambridge University Press 1982). Norman argues that liberty and equality are interdependent. People do not become free by being left alone, liberty requires positive prerequisites – material, social and intellectual. What is essential is the exercise of choice. Meaningful and relevant choices are thus needed. For Norman *"freedom [is] the availability of, and capacity to exercise, meaningful and effective choice."* Power, wealth and education enable us to make choices ourselves and therefore enjoy greater freedom. In virtue of wealth, individuals have many more possibilities for choice open to them and can direct their lives in accordance with their own desires and intentions. Norman points out that political power, economic wealth, education and experience are all positive sources of freedom. The absence of these is a major impediment to freedom and the distribution of all of these can be changed by human action.

[9] I Berlin "Two Concepts of Liberty" in *Four Essays on Liberty* (Oxford: Oxford University Press 1969); L Seidentop "Two Traditions" in A Ryan (ed) *The Idea of Freedom: essays in honour of Isaiah Berlin* (Oxford: Oxford University Press 1979), most notably highlighting the contrast between the continental and Anglo-American traditions; M Ramsay, 1997; J Gray "On Negative and Positive Liberty" in *Liberalisms: Essays in Political Philosophy*; C Taylor "What's Wrong with Negative Liberty" in A Ryan, 1979.

free person with worth and dignity. This is empowering and is assisted by the use of imagination, autobiography and narrative but that capacity needs to be developed. This is where a Hegelian account of the formation of identity is used, through the development of self-consciousness and the importance of recognition by others, to suggest that individual consciousness is intimately connected with society and how individuals are perceived by others, thus stressing the importance of developing fair structures, systems and institutions to enable all to be free within them. Hegel's "man's" sense of self-worth and identity is intimately connected with the value that other people place on him. So individuals not only want to be *recognised* by others but additionally want to be *recognised as persons of worth* by others.

# Chapter 4

# Positive Freedom

*"We need to explicitly articulate and recognise that individuation is a project and one that needs legal, political, ethical and moral recognition if it is to be effectively maintained."* Drucilla Cornell[1]

## Negative and Positive Liberty

There are differences amongst liberal thinkers as to which conception of freedom or liberty they favour but a common presupposition of liberalism is that a coherent conception of liberty is available to all human beings.[2] A conception of positive liberty has been important throughout the liberal tradition but arguably it has not been the most dominant one which has been negative liberty or the freedom not to be interfered with and to be left alone.[3] Positive liberty is concerned instead with the wish to be autonomous, to be in control of one's own life, to be author of one's own fate.

Berlin's description encapsulates the positive conception as a...

> wish above all to be conscious of myself as a thinking, willing, active being, bearing responsibility for my choices and able to explain them by references to my own ideas and purposes. I feel free to the degree that I believe this to be true and enslaved to the degree that I am made to realise that it is not.[4]

I interpret such positive liberty as grounding a strong subjectivity, enabling human beings to be and to become what they want as an ongoing process of self-development. Such a free subject will be capable of making authentic choices on an informed, non-constrained and non-fearful basis.

---

[1] D Cornell, 1998, p 64.
[2] See J Gray's analysis in J Gray *Liberalisms: Essays in Political Philosophy* (Milton Keynes: Open University Press 1986).
[3] Although the modern liberal theory of "man" has been described as emphasising the potential harmony and mutual dependence of individual developments, focusing on equal liberty embedded in a democratic polity and co-operative economic order. See GA Gaus, 1983, p 274. This is, however, not typical. See also analysis of theories of freedom in A Lyon (ed) *The Idea of Freedom: Essays in Honour of Isaiah Berlin*, (Oxford: OUP 1979).
[4] I Berlin, 1969, p 131.

Negative and positive liberty have been described as historically developing in ways as to come into direct conflict with each other,[5] the idea being that positive freedom is derived from discovering one's "true" or "dominant" or "higher" self. As is evident from Chapter 1, this "self" has most notably been identified with reason and as an entity therefore possessed by all human beings. Some argue that certain people have a more developed "higher" self than others, so that entity, in the form of the collective or "organic single will", could logically impose upon or coerce the other, less enlightened, members of society in the name of some goal, most notably seen in Rousseau's famous diktat that individuals could, and should be, *"forced to be free"*.[6]

Such a positive conception of freedom with its suggestion of a person divided against themselves has historically allowed for a splitting of individual personality into two – the *"transcendent dominant controller"* and the empirical bundle of desires and passions:

> This demonstrates (if demonstration of so obvious a truth is needed) that conceptions of freedom directly derive from views of what constitutes a self, a person, a man.[7]

On this analysis of positive liberty, consideration of a human being's relations with others will be necessary because if individuals wish to be free to live as their rational wills or their real self commands, so must others be. How are collisions with their wills to be avoided? If a person is rational, it is said that they must acknowledge that what is right for them must for the same reasons be right for others who are rational like them.[8] As this freedom is not freedom to do what is irrational or stupid or wrong, to force empirical selves into the right pattern is not tyranny but liberation.[9] All human beings will thus have *one true purpose* – that of rational self-direction – and the ends of all rational beings must, of necessity, fit into a single universal, harmonious pattern because any conflict is due to the clash of reason with the irrational. Such clashes are avoidable in that when all have been made rational, they will obey the rational laws of their own natures which are one and the same in them all. They will be wholly law abiding and wholly free. As will be explained shortly, such a conclusion towards one harmonious pattern is ill-founded and unconvincing.

It is correct to say however that positive liberty is concerned with the fact that insofar as individuals live in society, everything they do inevitably affects, and is affected by, what others do. Individuals' material life depends upon interaction with others and their identity is largely created by social forces. In addition, some,

---

[5] I Berlin, 1969. LQ Skinner 'The Idea of Negative Liberty: Philosophical and Historical Perspectives' in R Rorty et al (eds) *Philosophy in History* (Cambridge: Cambridge University Press 1984); M Kramer *The Quality of Freedom* (Oxford: OUP 2003). Kramer's analysis is beyond the subject matter of this chapter and will not be directly dealt with here.
[6] JJ Rousseau, 1974.
[7] I Berlin, 1969, p 134.
[8] I Berlin, 1969.
[9] I Berlin, 1969, p 145–154.

perhaps all, of an individual's ideas about themselves, in particular a sense of their own moral and social identity, are intelligible only in terms of the social network in which they are an element. So, human beings wish to avoid being ignored, patronised, despised, taken too much for granted or not being treated as an individual, having their uniqueness insufficiently recognised, being classed as a member of some featureless amalgam, statistical unit without identifiable specifically human features and purposes of their own.[10] The status accorded to individuals as human beings and the recognition they receive from others is paramount. This recognition is given by members of society to which historically, morally, economically and perhaps ethnically, those individuals feel they belong.

The idea is that human beings do not wish to be ruled as being not quite fully human and therefore not quite fully free. Despotism is an insult to an individual's conception of him or herself as a human being determined to make their own life in accordance with their own purposes and to be entitled to be recognised as such by others. If individuals are not so recognised then they may fail to recognise, and doubt, their own claim to be a fully independent human being. For what individuals are is, in large part, determined by what they feel and think and what they feel and think is determined by the feeling and thought prevailing in the society to which they belong. An individual may feel unfree in the sense of not being recognised as a self-governing individual human being but they may feel it also as a member of an unrecognised or insufficiently respected group and therefore wish for the emancipation of that class or group.[11] The idea of a dominant self and of all wills coming together to the same conclusion is not the necessary consequence of positive liberty.

Ultimately dismissal of positive liberty often occurs because it is viewed as liable to lead to oppression. Such reasoning progresses from positive liberty as self-mastery and self-direction, to one rationality for all which inevitably leads to a totalitarian regime.[12]

This is an unnecessary accompaniment to positive liberty as "self-mastery". It is not necessary for an advocate of positive liberty to assert or assume a single universal harmonious pattern into which the ends of all rational beings must fit.[13] It is not logically necessary that just because one individual thinking rationally wants certain things, in certain ways, that everyone ought to think and want exactly the same things if they too were as rational and "enlightened". It is not necessary for a proponent of positive liberty as self-direction – enabling individuals to be purposive beings – to say there must be a *"true plan – the one unique pattern*

---

[10] The language is Berlin's, 1969, p 155.

[11] For Berlin, this is similar to but not quite freedom and is sometimes called social freedom. Berlin is in favour of pluralism as he sees human goals as many, not always commensurable and sometimes in perpetual rivalry. In the end, he argues that people choose between ultimate values. Berlin, 1969, p 171.

[12] I Berlin, 1969, p 171. Berlin favours instead a pluralist political system, recognising that human goals are many and not all of them are commensurable.

[13] CB Macpherson *Democratic Theory: Essays in Retrieval* (Oxford: Clarendon Press 1973).

*which alone fulfils the claims of reason*".[14] It is only a requirement for the particular individual to think that way – and then they should be able to change their views if they have reasons for doing so.

In any event, totalitarian regimes would be excluded from the terms of positive liberty because the prerequisites of positive liberty fundamentally include the exercise of *free* choice. Coercion is thus automatically excluded. Forcing anyone to think or behave in a certain way because others think it is enlightened and true would not be permitted. It is a requirement of positive liberty that individuals exercise their own choice to discover for themselves what they want to be, do and become.

The totalitarian conclusion to positive liberty emerges from a failure to see positive liberty as an absence of impediments or restrictions to human beings' developmental powers. Positive liberty has been described as virtually the same as an individual's power in the developmental sense.[15]

Freedom seen as the absence of humanly imposed impediments including the coercion of one individual by another, direct interference with individual activities by state, and also lack of equal access to the means of life and means of labour is a more accurate description.[16] Thus the distinction between negative and positive liberty becomes blurred.

In contrast to traditional negative freedom, the extent of social or political freedom consists in the absence of obstacles not only to individuals' actual but also to their *potential* choices. That is, being able to act in a particular way if they choose to do so.[17] Liberty, identified as a field of free choice allowing for self-realisation is closer to positive liberty.

JS Mill's less negative liberty, that is, freedom from social pressures to allow individuals to develop their human potential and capacities to the full, was taken up by TH Green, B Bosanquet and LT Hobhouse who saw that freedom as *self-direction* and *self-development* clearly meant government *had to intervene* in the lives of its citizens to increase their freedom. A more meaningful version of liberalism rests in a sense of oneness, providing the foundation of social solidarity and the bond which, if genuinely experienced, would resist conflict.[18] Such a version of liberalism sees growth as the foundation of liberty, life is learning.

What is absorbed by individuals depends on the energy they expound in response to their environmental surroundings; educating individuals to develop their own selves in a harmonising way with others and their surroundings, enabling individuals to be capable of directing their own lives.[19] This would provide an *organic* conception of the relation between the individual and society – the

---

[14] Berlin, 1969, p 147.
[15] CB Macpherson, 1973, p 96.
[16] CB Macpherson, 1973, p 96.
[17] I Berlin, 1969, p xl.
[18] LT Hobhouse, 1964, p 65. See also TH Green *Lectures on the Principles of Political Obligation* (London: Longmans 1941) and B Bosenquet *The Philosophical Theory of the State* (London: Macmillan 1965).
[19] Hobhouse, 1964, p 66.

individual's life would be utterly different if he or she were separated from society: indeed, a great deal of that individual would not exist at all. Such liberal ideas are clearly very different from positivist views that any law is an impediment or restriction on individual freedom.[20] As CB Macpherson says, if the starting point is having no laws, each law that prevents some type of invasion increases the aggregate liberty.[21] Further, laws like this are needed to protect those who are less powerful – whether historically, physically, psychologically, socially or economically. This includes women because of their social categorisation as women in a hierarchical gender system. "Non-interference" in systems already hierarchically arranged simply strengthens existing power structures. Thus' a recognition is needed that inequalities in wealth, social power and education, including those arising from the hierarchical gender structure, affect human beings' ability to take advantage of political and legal rights and their opportunities for self-development.

As described in Chapter 1, an additional problem in the gender context is that the concept of the "universal citizen" or neutral rational agent has traditionally and historically not been universal or neutral but masculine. The debate concerning the rational self and the actual self, with desires and passions, has recurred throughout political philosophy and has often been gendered with men or masculinity correlating with rationality, and women or femininity correlating with desires and passions. This division is removed if the common potentiality of humans is the focus rather than an emphasis on "rationality" in opposition to "desires and passions".

Put simply, positive liberty is the freedom to act as a fully human being. It is this conception of freedom I am concerned to develop here as an inclusive human subject who is free will be active, self-aware and will allow for self-development in connection with others. The *social conditions* which exist are fundamentally important to fully maximise the developmental powers of human beings, the potential which all share. Access to the means to be free or social conditions of freedom is essential including access to claims as a rights holder to enforce human rights and international laws to increase individual subjectivity and freedom from violation. Emphasis is therefore placed on the capacities and conditions that make human beings free to do what they choose. Positive liberty requires that the development of any one individual not be at the expense of any other.[22]

## Hegel, Self-Consciousness and Recognition By Others

As shown earlier, according to many, the standard liberal conception of freedom involves providing individuals with the freedom to be left alone, not interfered

---

[20] See Chapters 1 and 2 above.
[21] CB Macpherson, 1973, p 117.
[22] CB Macpherson, 1973. See also analysis in the context of feminism and individualism by V Held, 1993, p 182.

with, able to choose as they please. In this section, Hegel's theory of the formation of self-consciousness is examined as it presents a much deeper understanding of the nature of individual freedom. He thought the standard negative conception was inadequate as it fails to ask the more complex question: why do individuals make the choices they do? Hegel saw these choices as often determined by external forces controlling individuals. To be left alone to make their own choices without 'interference' by others is not to be free, it is merely to be subjected to outside control. Real freedom begins with the realisation that instead of allowing these forces to control them, individuals can, at least try to, take control of the forces for themselves.

Hegelian ideas of identity formation highlight the importance of the structural institutions and social framework and relations with other people within which human freedom thrives.[23] In using Hegel's ideas, I am certainly not agreeing with everything he said, in particular, his relegation of women to the private sphere. Therefore, although Hegel refers to "man", and sees "woman" as closer to nature, confined to the private sphere, it is possible to use his theory to include both men and women.[24] Further, the Hegelian end goal of the true realisation of freedom and the "end of history" in actual human society is unrealistic, but has value as a utopian goal. A utopian goal is, by its very definition, unattainable.[25]

In a Hegelian conception of freedom, the opposition between social necessity and individual freedom disappears. Hegel's ideal is not a condition in which individuals are means to an end but rather a community in which, like a living organism, the distinction between means and ends is overcome, everything is both means and ends. The Hegelian fully developed state has been described as incorporating the principle of the individual rational will judging by universal criterion, uniting the radical moral autonomy of Kant and the expressive unity of the Greek polis.[26] Humans are not determined by their "nature" in exercising freedom, their very humanity consists in their ability to overcome or negate that "nature" so the particular characteristic common to humans is their capacity for

---

[23] The theories of recognition, central to identity politics and communitarian political philosophy and misrecognition in Lacanian psychoanalysis, are described by Douzinas as direct descendants of Hegel's understanding of identity formation. See C Douzinas "Hegel and Human Rights" (2002) 29 *Journal of Law and Society* at p 380.

[24] For reasons as to why the traditional division into public and private is detrimental to human flourishing, see Chapter 1 above. On Hegel, see also K Hutchings, 2003.

[25] In this context, Cornell's interpretation of his theory into her "recollective imagination" is useful. See D Cornell, 1988. While using his theory, Cornell is critical of Hegel for tying humanity to "*the rock of the past*" as she sees no final culmination of the interpretative process. However, Hegel's account of the development of self-consciousness through mutual recognition and intersubjectivity is used and seen as importantly recognising that the individual entitlement to be a person is embodied in the law, and the rule of law, itself. See further analysis of Cornell's work in Chapter 3.

[26] See C Taylor *Hegel* (Cambridge: Cambridge University Press 1975) p 384–388. For Hegel, history reaches its culmination in a community which is in conformity with reason or one which embodies freedom.

free moral choice.[27] *What makes persons distinctively human is this freedom.* Freedom emerges only when humans are able to transcend their natural existence and create a new self for themselves.

The aim is to reconcile individual freedom and its institutional framework, seeking a synthesis between individuals' concrete ethical nature formed in a specific community and the rational aspect of their being.[28] This leads to a community in which each would find their own fulfilment while contributing to the well-being of the whole.[29] Not only do individuals experience sharp conflicts between reason and passions within themselves, they also experience themselves opposed to other individuals and to the larger political order.

Overcoming the divisions amongst individuals, and between them and the larger political order, will achieve genuine freedom: thus understood, freedom is the defining goal of human life. Such harmonious freedom is a humanly created achievement. The right institutions are needed to make this harmony possible. Hegel's individuals do not see themselves as isolated from, or imprisoned by, his ideal social institutions but see themselves as expressed and realised by them.[30]

Reciprocal recognition is the way Hegelian freedom is realised in interpersonal life. It involves reciprocal acknowledgement that the others one encounters are fully self-conscious like oneself. The process of achieving this enriches self-consciousness. Hegel identifies three stages of development. The first reaction of the desiring self when faced with the other is immediate satisfaction. This is the "master-slave" stage of encounter in which individuals violently struggle with each other to prove their superiority. The outcomes of these battles leave at least one party unrecognised and dominated by the other. Though such domination initially seems to achieve the aspirations of self-consciousness, it does not do so.[31] The second is to accept dependence on the other, but to keep one's

---

[27] F Fukuyama *The End of History and the Last Man* (London: Penguin 1992) at p 150.

[28] This is interpreted as Hegel accepting Kant's claim that action is not truly one's own if one follows the commands of others or if one unthinkingly conforms to tradition. Kant gave philosophical expression to the modern obsession with the separation between subject and object and between self and the world. Hegel's main task was to heal this rift and to reclaim the unity of existence. Douzinas, 2002, p 380.

[29] So being and nothing as opposites require to be brought together under the synthesis, *becoming*. See T Honderich (ed) *The Oxford Companion to Philosophy* (Oxford: Oxford University Press 1995).

[30] GW Hegel *The Philosophy of Right* 1821 105–10: see analysis by WR Schroeder "Continental Ethics" in H La Follette (ed) *The Blackwell Guide to Ethical Theory* (Oxford: Blackwell 2000).

[31] In the Hegelian master and slave dialectic, Hegel's explanation for this stage in the development of self-conscious subjectivity, the slave only conceives of the idea of freedom – there is a discrepancy between his actual condition and his idea of freedom. He must consider freedom in the abstract before he can enjoy it in reality and must invent for himself the principles of a free society before living in one. The slave has self-consciousness – being reflective of himself and his own condition. Recognition of the master's identity by the slave is corrupted by the fact they are unequal and the slave's labour leaves the master's talents

relations with the other external. The third is mutual recognition, accepting the other in his or her own identity and difference from self, with the recognition that self is integrally related to the other.[32] Prior to social acknowledgement, self-consciousness is still forming, after the process of acknowledgement, the identity of each participant as both living and self-conscious is ratified. In becoming socially recognised, one becomes more actual for oneself – more fully self-conscious.[33] Achieving reciprocal recognition means that people experience a deeper harmony and no longer see each other as alien but establish a genuine community.[34] The state and other social institutions therefore play a central role in Hegel's theory because they make individual freedom possible.

## The Reconciliation of Self and Others

Institutions that are irrational or inconsistent will undermine the achievement of this freedom.[35] Institutions and political organisation are essential to ethical life because they provide the proper environment for achieving expressive, integrated lives.[36] It has been argued that asserting rights as a human has an essential conceptual background in some notion of the moral worth of certain properties or capacities, without which it would not make sense.[37] Rights are ascribed to people because they are the beings who exhibit certain capacities that are worthy of respect. The primary capacity is one of choice where individuals rise to the level of self-consciousness and autonomy and can exercise choice, not simply live under some code prescribed by others. It has been argued that if there is any proof that these capacities can only develop in society or in a society of a certain kind, then that society or kind of society ought to be sustained. The question of the proper conditions for the development of these capacities arises.

What is important is that one is able to exercise autonomy in the basic issues of life and this develops within an entire civilisation. This has been described as an identity, a way of understanding themselves, which individuals are not born with, but have to acquire.[38] Thus the *social conditions of freedom* are extremely important. This developed freedom requires a certain understanding of the human subject or self: one in which the aspirations of autonomy and self-direction become conceivable but this understanding of the human subject is not something individuals can sustain on their own. Identity is partly defined in

---

underdeveloped. Only with the modern overcoming of the master/slave relationship can the complete human person come to life. Hegel, 1977.

[32] C Douzinas, 2002, p 384.

[33] GW Hegel, 1977, p 111–13.

[34] C Douzinas, 2002, p 378–9.

[35] GW Hegel, 1977, p 266–78.

[36] C Douzinas, 2002, p 380.

[37] See C Taylor, 1992,. See also Taylor's analysis of Hegel in C Taylor, 1975, and his expansion of these ideas in C Taylor, 1989.

[38] C Taylor, 1992.

conversation with others and through common understandings which underlie the practices of society. The identity of the autonomous, self-determining individual requires such a social matrix, as the free individual or autonomous moral agent can only achieve and maintain his or her identity in a certain type of culture.

Hegelian identity formation, showing that the self is constituted reflexively and is radically dependent on the actions of others, has a direct relevance to international humanitarian and to human rights law.[39] Lack of recognition or *misrecognition* undermines human beings' sense of identity, by projecting a false, inferior or defective image of the self. The typical harm of defective recognition is a split between someone's self-image and the image that social institutions or others project upon that person.

Harms which law commits and tries "to heal through human rights"[40] are the harms imposed by patriarchal society upon a large amount of women. Acknowledgement of the vital contribution others make to the constitution of self reconciles individuals (or alienates them in case of non-recognition) with the world. But the other's recognition of an individual's being or identity makes the individual aware of their specificity and difference from all others on an ongoing dynamic basis and helps their individuation. Part of the self is always outside itself (embodied human life depends for survival on the external world), with the human subject being an amalgam of self and otherness, of sameness and difference. A recent analysis in this area concluded that the word "human" cannot be fully and finally pinned down to any particular conception because it transcends and overdetermines them all, carrying enormous symbolic capital.[41] As related to human rights, such definitions of the human are vital. Having human rights has been described in modernity as synonymous to being a human, but such rights must be claimed. If new rights claims are to succeed, claimants must assert their similarity and difference with groups already admitted to the dignity of humanity, thus appealing to the universal and the particular, the dilemma between the two having been discussed in Chapter 2. An important point raised is that a claim to difference without similarity can establish the uniqueness of a particular group and justify its demands for special treatment but it can also rationalise its social or economic inferiority.[42]

It is necessary to make appeals to universality and similarity to others (in some respect) who are already admitted to the category of human to which human rights apply. In Part III this point is developed through the need to recognise the individual subjectivity of women by recognising their rights as humans within

---

[39] See recent analysis of Hegel and human rights in C Douzinas, 2002. Douzinas's analysis is helpful, revealing many interesting insights, but the conclusion, applying Hegel to postmodern jurisprudence is less than convincing: Hegel's philosophy is far from postmodern. Links are made to International Humanitarian law in Part III below.

[40] C Douzinas, 2002, p 396.

[41] C Douzinas, 2002, p 399–403.

[42] C Douzinas, 2002.

international human rights and particularly, humanitarian law. Before doing so, I want to explain more fully how human freedom and potentiality can be achieved for women.

# Chapter 5

# Human Potentiality

*"Imagining a society without gender oppression involves imagining persons in inherently social relationships acting together to foster human development."* Virginia Held[1]

## Shaping Wants and Preferences

If the emphasis is on human beings' capacities developing through social conditions which will increase their freedom, the internal consciousness of human beings is of the utmost importance. Will they be free if they simply satisfy their desires? If so, could eliminating such desires simply lead to just as much satisfaction?[2] It is evident that obstacles or impediments to freedom can be "internal" as well as external. This means that individuals could easily be doing what they want in the sense of what they can identify as their (socially formed) desires (or things they think they desire) but by doing so actually *entrench* their freedom. For women, this can include accepting the wants and preferences that have developed through living in hierarchical gender structures in patriarchal societies.

But how can individuals identify which wants or preferences are to their own good or advantage, and which are not, without reintroducing opposition between their rational (so-called male) "nature" and their desiring (so-called female) "nature"? Freedom has been identified as involving and making qualitative distinctions between which desires and motivations are important.[3] *Motivational conditions* have been highlighted as necessary for freedom in that individuals must be able to discriminate between desires and *exercise a capacity to evaluate* wants, not just to satisfy them.[4] Existing desires shaped by social forces can often operate as *internal constraints* of which individuals are unaware through ignorance or simple acceptance without questioning of social conditioning and lack of knowledge of any available alternatives. In such circumstances, individuals cannot be said to be exercising free choice.[5] Some self-awareness, self-understanding, moral discrimination and some ability to discriminate, evaluate and identify their own purposes is thus needed in this conception of freedom. There is a commitment

---

[1] V Held, 1993, p 187.
[2] See I Berlin, 1969, p xxxviii.
[3] C Taylor, 1989.
[4] C Taylor, 1989.
[5] See M Ramsay, 1987, p 55.

to allowing "*a critical creative conscious search for coherence*" to develop and the resources to allow this to develop in individuals lies in the cultures or societies in which they live. Free action requires that an individual knows what he or she is about and understands his or her action in some coherent sense.[6]

Freedom is important because human beings are *purposive* beings. Individuals doing what they want in the sense of following their strongest desires is not sufficient to establish that they are free. Human beings have to see their lives as sometimes made up of mistaken or ill-judged desires and feelings. Such desires may frustrate their deeper purposes, plans and projects. Freedom therefore involves an element of being able to overcome or at least neutralise motivational fetters as well as being free of external obstacles.

Sometimes human beings have become so embedded in the social practices of the community in which they live that it is virtually impossible for them to question the fairness of their situations. This may be because of the social construction and power dynamics involved. Because of the gender structure, this can be especially so for women. This is why it is important to ensure that conditions appropriate to re-examining ways of life and life plans and projects are readily available.

As analysed in Chapter 2, communitarians question the aim of liberal society striving for a place where human beings would decide for themselves who or what they want to be or do. Instead, they favour discovery within an existing social matrix. Although, as examined in Chapter 2, some of the insights of communitarian thinkers (developing at the same time as many feminist critiques of the liberal self) have some degree of similarity with certain feminist analysis of the social formation of identity, the social self of the communitarians is not the same as the relational self of feminist theory.[7] Discovery of one's place within an existing social matrix will more often than not be detrimental to women because of the patriarchal system. The communitarian view provides a weak basis for oppressed members of actual communities to break away from, and out of, the traditions that contribute so much to their oppression and "*a primary aim of feminism is to end the oppression of women*".[8]

Seeing individuals as first and foremost members of families, religious traditions or ethnic groups rather than as human beings capable of choice and freedom may hinder the achievement of a flourishing life for those individuals. It has recently been re-argued that feminism needs to operate with a general notion of the "human core" without forgetting that this core has been differently situated and also shaped in different times and places, for if feminism denies the value of the whole idea of a human core, it gives up something vital to the most powerful feminist arguments.[9]

---

[6] See S I Benn, *A Theory of Freedom* (Cambridge: Cambridge University Press 1988) at chapter 9 "Autonomy and Positive Freedom".
[7] V Held, 1993.
[8] V Held, 1993, p 90.
[9] MC Nussbaum 1999, p 71.

Feminism definitely needs to retain a normative progressive political programme based on women as human beings retaining an idea of a common shared humanity. However, often an unnecessary division arises in feminist legal theory because of ideas of the "human core" which has been hotly debated in feminist legal theory in recent times in terms of essentialism and fixed identities as outlined in Chapter 3.

This "essentialism" or the essence of men and women can be seen in radical feminists' "essential woman" or socialist and liberal feminists' "essential human nature" all of which are in need of liberation and reclamation. However, this division is unnecessary. If the human "core" is seen not as a *core or essence* which needs to be reclaimed but instead is seen as *human potentiality* through existence, the division evaporates. This, I argue, is both consistent with Butler's theory (but not her conclusion that there is then no human subject which in turn leaves no foundation for feminist agenda for change) and explicitly liberal feminist theories, like Okin's and Nussbaum's. These arguments are set out more fully below.

In terms of the preferences people have, it needs to be acknowledged that all humans are social beings. However, desires that are subjectively valuable, and those that are objectively important, need to be distinguished: that is, what is desired and what is worth desiring and worthy of satisfaction. This requires the ability to achieve a critical distance from individuals' existing social situations.

It has been argued that liberals and corresponding rights' discourse tend to overlook the social significance of relations of power in certain spheres: liberal theory begins with the conviction that all persons are equal in essential respects and ends with the normative conviction that they should be treated equally.[10] This normative gender neutrality means that liberals do not see and take account of the realities of power exercised along these dimensions and the resulting disadvantage to individuals. To analyse how social order is possible requires an interpretation of the relations of dominance, submission and aggression in society.

Liberal theorists have often failed to consider the significance of domestic, cultural and sexual power. Arguments about the pervasiveness of power and the questions of legitimacy need to be acknowledged; including how the private sphere is political and how power inheres in structures and practices rather than merely in individual persons or person-like institutions. Therefore power structures that already exist need to be examined to see if they inhibit and restrict some human agents' liberty while increasing that of others.[11] Equalising power equalises freedom and *"freedom is always relative to power"*.[12] Free and informed consent will only occur in a context of much greater equality than already exists because equalising power allows for reciprocal recognition of each person as inherently worth recognising as a "subject" or "end" in themselves. It follows that a redistribution of power will radically increase the freedom of many individuals who had previously been powerless or certainly less than powerful, for a fair

---

[10] E Frazer and N Lacey, 1993, p 76–77.
[11] See R Tawney *Equality* (London: Unwin Books 1964) chapter 5.
[12] R Tawney, 1964.

redistribution will improve the chances of an atmosphere of free informed choice occurring.

Once the social conditioning of wants and the limits of individual knowledge and rationality are acknowledged, some have argued that it is difficult to maintain the sovereignty of individual desires and the nature of freedom as want satisfaction.[13] For, if wants and preferences are socially conditioned by power relationships, then acting on those wants shows a lack of freedom and lack of self-determination rather than the freedom and autonomous choice that is usually portrayed. A theory such as that of neo-classical economists, which treats people's subjective preferences and desires as simply given, is therefore inadequate.[14] However, it is possible to critically examine one's wants and preferences, re-evaluate and change them if necessary and to be more in control of one's life. Theory must be modified by empirical evidence subjected to critical evaluation. Empirically, it has been demonstrated that people's desires and preferences respond to their beliefs about social norms and about their own opportunities.[15] Emotions, desires and preferences are not given or "natural" but are often shaped instead by social norms many of which subordinate women to men. So the idea of freedom as making choices must take into account the social formation and *deformation* of preference, emotion and desires.

The clearest example of a feminist who focuses on this aspect of women's social formation is Catharine MacKinnon.[16] Although MacKinnon expresses her disdain for what she interprets as liberal equality, her theories can be interpreted as providing an internal critique of formal equality and an extension of liberalism that can usefully show how women's preferences have often been formed against their better interests. The social context of such formation is due to the failure of liberal states to live up to their promise of allowing all to become full human beings or persons.[17]

---

[13] M Ramsay, 1987, p 233–5.

[14] In this sense, I agree with MC Nussbaum's analysis (1999).

[15] MC Nussbaum argues that the recognition of a social dimension in desire/preference formation is not alien to the liberal tradition: MC Nussbaum, 1999, p 11–12.

[16] CA MacKinnon, 1987; 1989; 2000; and CA MacKinnon "Feminism, Marxism, Method and the State: Toward Feminist Jurisprudence" (1983) 8 *Signs: Journal of Women in Culture and Society* 635; CA MacKinnon *Only Words* (Cambridge Mass: Harvard University Press 1993); "Reflections on Sex Equality Under the Law" (1991) 100 *Yale Law Journal* 1281 (1991a); "From Practice to Theory, or What is a White Woman Anyway?" (1991) 13 *Yale Journal of Law and Feminism* 13 (1991b); "Crimes of War, Crimes of Peace" in S Shute and S Hurley (eds) *On Human Rights: The Oxford Amnesty Lectures 1993* (New York: Basic Books 1993); "Legal Perspectives on Sexual Difference" in D Rhode (ed), 1990; "Rape, Genocide and Women's Human Rights" (1994) 17 *Harvard Women's Law Journal* 5.

[17] That is also one of the main reasons in my opinion why MacKinnon has had such an influence on mainstream jurisprudence See also A Loux "Idols and Icons: Catharine MacKinnon and Freedom of Expression in North America" (1998) 6 *Feminist Legal Studies* 85 and J Schroeder "The Taming of the Shrew: the Liberal Attempt to mainstream Radical Feminist Theory" (1992) 5 *Journal of Law and Feminism* 123.

My reading of MacKinnon's theory contrasts with the interpretation of those theorists who view her as a radical social constructionist, presenting women as victims who are effectively man-made, and as some sort of essentialist who homogenises women, ignoring their differences. Such criticisms show her as *hostile* to female responsibility and agency, reluctant to confront the consequences of her depictions of women. It has led some to believe that she views women's agency under oppression as insufficiently important to defend, in addition to presenting all women in the image of white middle-class women.[18]

Although most do not see MacKinnon's work as internally critiquing liberalism, or of being capable of accommodation within a liberal framework, some have, at least to a certain extent. For example, her work has been described as part of a larger feminist enterprise of reconstructing concepts, like autonomy, allowing political debate to go forward and her law reform projects have been compared to JS Mill's concept of harm.[19] In a similar vein, her view of subjectivity (together with that of collaborator Andrea Dworkin) as related to pornography and sexuality has been compared to a Kantian conception of the person.[20] In defending liberalism from certain feminist critiques, it has been argued that, in a similar way to MacKinnon, Kantian liberalism insists that individuals' desires are frequently distorted by self interest and JS Mill recognised that gender hierarchy deformed the desires of men and women.[21] MacKinnon has been credited with adding to Kant's and Mill's insights the new insight that sexual desire is socially shaped, in that, men eroticise domination and learn to achieve sexual satisfaction in connection with its assertion while women come to eroticise submission and learn to find satisfaction by giving themselves away. MacKinnon is described as having developed Mill's central idea which challenges liberalism to conduct a rigorous examination of the social formation of desire.[22]

Such a project can therefore be read as a deeply normative one: what ought to be, but what is not, that is, the truth of women's real selfhood that has been suppressed by society's construction of women, preventing them from freely exercising this sense of self or autonomy by being unable to freely shape their own wants and preferences:

---

[18] See K Abrams "Sex Wars Redux: Agency and Coercion in Feminist Legal Theory" (1995) 95 *Columbia Law Review* 304 p 326–329. However, Abrams' conclusions seem to arrive at a similar position to where I see MacKinnon by a combination of dominance theory supplemented by an agency critique. See also S Gibson "The Discourse of Sex/War: Thoughts on Catharine MacKinnon's 1993 Oxford Amnesty Lecture" (1993) 1 *Feminist Legal Studies* 179–188 and E Jackson "Catharine MacKinnon and Feminist Jurisprudence: A Critical Appraisal" (1992) 19 *Journal of Law and Society* 195 and C Smart, 1989 (in particular p 76–89); M Mahoney "Women and Whiteness in Practice" (1993) 5 *Yale Journal of Law and Feminism* 217.
[19] N Lacey, 1998, p 170.
[20] MC Nussbaum, 1999.
[21] MC Nussbaum, 1999.
[22] See MC Nussbaum, see 1996 and 1999.

I have learned that feminism – in the form of a tacit belief that women are human beings in truth but not in social reality – has gone deep into women and some younger men.[23]

Women are in fact not full people in the sense men are allowed to *become*.[24]

If a woman feels anger at not being treated as a full person, this surely refers to social definitions of personhood, possibly even liberal ones to which men routinely experience entitlement without being subjected to class-based critique.[25]

The concern expressed is that women be allowed to live within the existing structure without fear of violation etc, including by using existing laws. At the same time, women should aim to be freely determined: free to live the lives they want to live without their wants and preferences being socially determined by patriarchy. So, a group's characteristics, including empirical attributes, should be included in the definition of the fully human, not be defined as exceptions to, or as distinct from, the fully human.

The institutionalisation of inequality through the hierarchy of the gender system has limited and continues to limit, the chances of women conceiving goals of their own and realising them. MacKinnon's work makes explicit to women what many liberals have advocated for all humans but have often then restricted to men, mainly for reasons to do with the family and what is seen as women's "nature". That is, it makes clear that women have too rarely been treated as ends in themselves and are too frequently treated as means to the ends of others.[26] Men's sexual *objectification* of women creates a central problem in women's lives in that women "*can grasp self only as a thing*".[27] This objectification is bad because it cuts women off from full self-expression and self-determination – from in effect, their humanity.[28]

Focusing on women as persons, and retaining an idea of human potential which individual women possess, ensures that feminist normative agenda are not lost. The need to hold onto a strong sense of women as individual subjects, something which cannot be violated and ought to be built up, is emphasised as strengthening such feminist agenda and enabling a vision of feminism's normative and transformative power to have any real meaning.

While such feminist views do not express an essentialist concept of the feminine, they could easily be interpreted as having an essentialist concept of the human. For MacKinnon, speaking of social treatment "*as a woman*" is not to invoke any universal essence or homogeneous generic or ideal type, but to refer to the diverse material reality of social meanings and practices such that to be a

---

[23] CA MacKinnon 1989, p 216.
[24] CA MacKinnon, 1989, p 103, my emphasis.
[25] CA MacKinnon 1989, p 52.
[26] MC Nussbaum 1999, p 63.
[27] CA MacKinnon 1989, p 124.
[28] MC Nussbaum 1999, p 214. See also MC Nussbaum "Objectification" (1995) 24 *Philosophy and Public Affairs* 249; R Langton, 1990.

woman "*is not yet the name of a way of being human*".[29] On this interpretation, the subordination of women to men is socially institutionalised, shaping access to human dignity, respect, resources, physical security, credibility, membership in community, speech and power.[30] With all its variations, the group women can be seen to have a collective social history of disempowerment, exploitation and subordination, extending to the present.[31] To use MacKinnon's language, what women need (and what they are socially prevented from having on the basis of a condition of birth) is a chance at productive lives of reasonable physical security, individuation, self-expression and minimal respect and dignity.

Whilst deeply socially constructionist, in that gender is socially constructed and enforced to the detriment of women, a view of the "human core" is presented that can best be described as Kantian autonomy and a right to self-determination. The Kantian demand has been interpreted as seeking that women be treated as ends in themselves, centres of agency and freedom, rather than merely adjuncts to the plans of men.[32] On this view, woman is excluded from the concept of the true free universal subject but should be included. This has led some to question where this leaves women. But does this "authenticity" forming the basis of all human existence need to rely on a *pre-social* self or inner core in need of liberation? Can it not be described in terms of a *potential*?

The danger with presenting a view of the "human core" which is always there and can somehow be reclaimed or discovered (through, for example, consciousness raising) consists in fixing and constraining identity, taking us back to ideas of human nature or function. It allows the more powerful to tell people what a true essence is and so try to persuade others to think in certain ways about their identity that will purport to enable this "true inner essence" to be fulfilled (in a similar way to Berlin's analysis of the one harmonious whole of rationality). If, instead of a human essential nature, an idea of a "female nature" is presented, this is arguably more damaging in that it can be used as the basis for imposing oppressive (stereotypical) social conditions on women. However, if the idea of *existence* is used rather than *essence*, seeking an expansion of human potentiality, this removes those dangers. Social patterning of difference including group characteristics can then be examined to ensure that all human beings are given the potential to be who they want to be, to be fully free. This point is developed further in the analysis of existential freedom below.

---

[29] MacKinnon 1991, p 1299. R Rorty: "Human Rights, Rationality, and Sentimentality" in S Shute and S Hurley (eds), 1993.

[30] Her project reverberates with echoes of Isaiah Berlin's positive liberty:
"*I wish to be somebody, not nobody; a doer – deciding, not being decided for, self-directed and not acted upon by external nature or by other men [sic] as if I were a thing, or an animal, or a slave incapable of playing a human role, that is, of conceiving goals and policies of my own and realising them…*" (I Berlin, 1969).
Because of the socially constructed unequal division of society into male and female genders, women are very often "objects", "nobody", "decided for", "acted upon by external nature or by other men [sic]".

[31] CA MacKinnon 1991, p 15.

[32] MC Nussbaum 1999, p 20.

In the gender system, femininity is subordination. Men are dominant not in the sense that biologically they are destined to dominate in a hierarchical political and social structure but in the sense that the gendered identities made available within the present social order are identities that situate persons in a certain hierarchy of power. This restricts the freedom of women and makes it harder to attain a right to be treated as free persons with their own subjectivity.

As has been explored in Chapter 2, some argue that women's "different or caring voice" has been constructed to suit men's interests: women care for men and others due to the social construction of women as caring for men in patriarchy, constructing women's subordination.[33] But as mentioned in that chapter, even if this is true, work on the ethic of care, trust, love and empathy is important because a society where these virtues are sustained and nurtured amongst its citizens is one which will assist in the formation of potentially a strong sense of morality and respect for others within those citizens, making it difficult for persons to treat each other in an objectified and disrespectful way.

The idea of choice or preference as a human capacity carries with it the idea that individuals rise to the level of self-consciousness and autonomy where they can exercise choice and not be determined by traditional forces around them. A society which nurtures a caring and interconnected, interdependent environment will be one which assists in the development of such self-consciousness and autonomy, these are not mutually exclusive concepts.

The experience of care and caring is important in social relationships. As shown in Chapter 2, ethic of care theorists have convincingly argued that individuals' inherent interconnection with each other needs to be acknowledged: although I reiterate my views that such interconnection is not inherently within women or some sort of female nature. A moral sense cannot be developed in individuals who are isolated from each other. An ethic of care with its emphasis on moral capacities and dispositions provides an account of the origins of moral motivation and an insight into the social conditions necessary to develop these motivational forces. Empathy, love and care and a sense of responsibility are necessary for moral motivation – to want to act morally. Individuals are motivated to act with care and concern because of their social experiences of relationships and ties to other people.

What might be a natural tendency of human beings to share the feelings of others as a natural fact of human psychology, is also part of individuals' social nature which depends on people's relationships to facilitate sympathetic identification.[34] But for such reciprocal care to flourish, a co-operative community is required which correlates with the Hegelian formation of self-consciousness and human freedom examined in Chapter 4.

One of the roots of the problem as regards gender relations is the disparity of power in society's existing structures, as embodied by law and social institutions. As already discussed in Chapter 2, one of the most interesting and provoking aspects of ethic of care work is that it encourages thinking in

---

[33] CA MacKinnon, 1991; E du Bois et al, 1985.
[34] See also JJ Rousseau, 1974.

paradigmatically different, more creative and imaginative ways, presenting radical departures from simply accepting the given norms in society and the norms of how things are usually viewed. To be able to present such views, the capacity for self-reflection is needed to discern who and what to care for.

Using insights about the contribution of community and social relationship to self-identity, yet opening up for critical reflection the moral norms of those communities and identifying the sorts of communities which will provide non-oppressive and enriched lives for women to decide more freely the lives they wish to live is key. The important element in this analysis is the ability to *choose* which morals and norms to *accept or reject*. It is necessary to have the type of political and legal structure that will enable such a human subject to flourish to enable such choice to occur.

Allowing the path for personal redefinition necessitates the encouragement within society of a critically reflective stance and the freedom to be, to be active and to form projects and plans that will then be encouraged and put into action. It is not enough to recognise "different" voices within the existing structure as some difference feminism wants to celebrate. Structures need to change and be reconstructed based on revised ideals. Changes cannot simply be made to accommodate women's existing experiences and leave things there. Doing so is simply making laws fit reality without questioning why reality is as it is, and in a hierarchical, power-based structure, it reinforces the status quo.

Affirming certain human capacities like choice has normative consequences. That is, the belief exists that such capacities *ought to be* fostered and nurtured. As Charles Taylor has highlighted, if there is proof that these capacities can only develop in a society of a certain kind, then that kind of society ought to be sustained. Most people who want to affirm the primacy of individual rights are interested in asserting the right to freedom and the freedom to choose life plans, to dispose of possessions, to form one's own convictions and, within reason, to act on them. These capacities do not simply belong to individuals just by being alive but require proper conditions for their development.[35]

Individuals' ability to exercise choice in the basic issues of life, regarding identity and a way of understanding themselves is an ability that is acquired. The free human being can only achieve and maintain this type of identity in a certain type of society. This developed sense of freedom requires a certain understanding of self: one in which the *aspirations* to autonomy and self-direction become conceivable and this self-understanding is not something sustainable in isolation.

The reality is that individuals do not live in a society structured to allow this identity to flourish for all human beings and certainly not when there is a hierarchical gender system. Human beings, and women in particular, are often not free to determine for themselves the shape their individual lives will take. The institution of inequality through the gender system has limited and continues to limit women's real choices.

---

[35] See C Taylor, 1992. See also Chapter 4 above.

Although the aim is individual freedom, it will never be possible to reach completely. The ideal is not what is usually represented as the classical liberal "rational maximiser" – the autonomous man aiming for abstract individualism and economic preference or want satisfaction. I am talking about the ability to think for oneself, not to be bound by social fetters and restrictions, to be able to resolve issues and make plans as a purposive agent. Such a creation is not possible without the necessary social conditions: *"my individual self is not something which I can detach from my relationship with others."*[36]

If individual wants, desires and preferences have been shaped by sexist and hierarchically gendered social norms, women, and men, need to question the beliefs and norms they see around them. To do that involves a critical capacity, critical scrutiny, self-conscious questioning. In a recent analysis, the liberal tradition has been presented as profoundly opposed to the "accepting" view of women being emotional and caring, giving to others and men being governed by cool rationality:

> the mother had better think, and teach her child to think. She had better think critically, asking whether the norms and traditions embodied in the emotions are reasonable norms.[37]

The importance of persons critically reflecting on the traditions and community in which they find themselves is clear. Such capacity for critical reflection needs to be developed in a particular type of society where want and preference formation are freely allowed for both men and women.

Autonomy means that individuals have control over their own lives to make their own choices and decisions: to be taken seriously, valued and treated with equal concern and respect within the society in which they live. Social conditions are necessary for this – social and institutional powers, material and economic requirements and proper education, the ability to acquire knowledge and expand it – so increasing the sources of their capacity to exercise choices for themselves. These are prerequisites to freedom because access to them greatly increases the chances of making choices for themselves. Autonomy can also be gendered and situationally related: for example, bodily decisions will take different paths for men and women in many cases but bodily autonomy will be important for all human beings.[38]

But autonomy is nonetheless needed. Women have suffered from a lack of a sense of self and have too rarely been treated as ends in themselves and too frequently treated as means to the ends of others.[39] As mentioned in Chapter 1,

---

[36] I Berlin, 1969, p 156.

[37] MC Nussbaum 1999, p 75–6.

[38] See J Nedelsky, 1989: what enables people to be autonomous is not isolation but relationships that provide support and guidance. Relatedness is not the antithesis of autonomy but a precondition of autonomy and interdependence is a constant component of autonomy: at p 120.

[39] Obviously a Kantian notion. See MC Nussbaum 1999, p 63.

certain feminists rightly highlight that where women and the family are concerned, liberal political thought has not been nearly individualistic enough – through a lack of interference with the family; and a failure to see that it is not always an organic activity involving a harmony of interests amongst family members.[40]

Recent explicit engagements with liberalism by some feminists have presented views that liberal selves do not only consent to maximise their own welfare and when they do they usually take others into account when working out what is best for their own welfare.[41] Yet the importance of the idea of self-sufficiency, depending on oneself, encouraging women to care for themselves and be economically situated to survive on their own, thus being able to care for others best is appreciated too.[42] This is unlikely to be fostered by any idolisation of self-sufficiency and isolation. Specific forms of dependence and interdependence may be morally valuable, even a source or precondition of developing strong abilities to act and to act autonomously.[43]

Subjectivity and personal autonomy can be retained while allowing for interconnectedness, stressing the way that people develop their identity in large part out of social relations. Autonomy can be seen as formed by human interactions which allow it to develop and flourish.[44] The starting point is the individuality of human beings and their social nature, with a need to find the optimal relation between the individual and the collective to understand the core of human autonomy and the forms and scope of collective activity that will foster it. So feminists need to reconstitute autonomy, not abandon it. To be autonomous, a person must feel a sense of their own power. Societal structures need to attend to what gives persons a sense of autonomy; what makes them feel competent, effective, able to exercise some control over their lives, as opposed to feeling passive, helpless and always dependent.[45] Specific forms of dependence can be morally valuable, as sources or preconditions of developing strong abilities to act and to act autonomously.

Such capacity for critical reflection is linked to imagination which has a place in expanding future possibilities. In the context of developing ideas of a global future, the global and international aspects of the view of subjectivity presented here are developed in Part III. However, I would like to analyse the positive role imagination has to play in developing an interconnected world at a

---

[40] MC Nussbaum 1999, p 64–5; SM Okin 1979 and 1989.

[41] MC Nussbaum 1999.

[42] MC Nussbaum 1999, above note 8 at p 61–2. She argues also that even if liberals did hold that individuals' most basic desires can be satisfied independently of relationships to others, the normative conclusions about self-sufficiency would not follow. Moral theories frequently demand that people do things against the grain – she cites Bentham as an example of a theorist with an extremely self-centred psychology but with a normative altruism. Liberals can and do highly value benevolence, family concern, social and political involvement, even if they hold that individuals must control strong selfish inclinations.

[43] See O O'Neill *Bounds of Justice* (Cambridge: Cambridge University Press 2000) at p 49.

[44] J Nedelsky, above note 37.

[45] J Nedelsky above note 37; see in particular p 21–25.

local and global level here, focusing on individuals' common humanity. J B White describes the situation eloquently:

> There is no easy way to imagine ourselves out of the world of deep and violent injustice we have created, and that we recreate every day. But that is our task, and we shall have a much better chance of doing something right and valuable if we can find ways of talking and thinking, ways of telling our national story, that will do justice to its meaning.[46]

Inquiries stimulated by imagination and then social interaction based on the ideas created are what shape moral questions and their answers.

Consciousness is created by putting the world at a distance from oneself, leading to the possibility of thinking or acting as one chooses. The emptiness has to be filled by whatever the individual plans to do, thinks or wants to be.[47] Freedom and consciousness are therefore both identified with the power to consider things as they are, as they are not, imagine situations which are different from the actual situations in the world and therefore form plans to change what there is.[48] This consciousness needs potential agency from individuals. Such freedom correlates with the ability to see things as possibly other than they are or with human imagination. One of the powers conscious beings have is emotion. Consciousness will be explicable only if it is viewed as a project for an individual, the plan or purpose of a particular human being. The difference between knowing, doing and feeling becomes indistinct.[49]

As already explained, human beings are socially constructed and born into ideas of the good life culturally available to them, they cannot be the fully original source of their own values. However, they are capable of self-reflection and able to critically examine the roles they find themselves in and the norms governing their societies. To enable and allow this capacity to develop, it is necessary to live within a certain kind of society.

There are two strands to the role of imagination. The first is the possibility of making a claim to have a capacity for imaginative reflection to develop within each individual into some type of legal right. The second is developing imaginative capacities regardless of having such a legal right.

### A Legal Right to have an Imaginative Capacity

In combination with feminist work that shows how women's wants and preferences are often shaped to their detriment and in men's interests, Drucilla Cornell's idea of the *"utopian moment within deconstruction"*, (which contends that words and ideas in some sense exist in the very moment in which they are

---

[46] JB White "What's Wrong with Talking About Race?" (2002) 100 *Michigan Law Review* 1927 at p 1953.
[47] M Warnock, 1967, p 21.
[48] M Warnock, 1967, p 21.
[49] M Warnock, 1967, p 26.

repressed) can be advanced to change the landscape of ideas.[50] Changing people's ideas of the possible is a crucial element in reformism and part of rhetorical strategies' capacity to dislodge dominant conceptions of various discourses on, for example, autonomy, freedom and equality.[51]

It has been argued that each person's psychic and moral space in which each individual is allowed to evaluate and represent who they are ought to be a legally protected right.[52] In Cornell's *"imaginary domain"*, that is, the space in which individuals imagine who they might be if they made themselves their own end and claimed themselves as their own person, and her theory of recollective imagination projects forward, as an ideal, the principles it reads into the past, suggesting a creativity that seems beyond discourse, with reason enhancing innovative capability to provide the ability to re-imagine the world and each individual's place in it.

As explored in Chapter 3, such work is premised on a poststructuralist view of the openness of language. Worlds can exist in the very moment in which they are repressed.[53] Thus the world can be imagined differently. Normative concepts which allow individuals to shape their world – like rights, justice, equality – can be re-imagined and reconstructed in radically different ways. Such reconstruction rests on the use of liberal principles and ultimately has a normative purpose which requires that a strong sense of self be encouraged within individuals to believe they have this right to an imaginative capacity and to exercise it.

*The Possibility of Developing Individual Imagination without a Legal Right*

Imagination can be developed and used by individuals to make the best of themselves, their community and their world, enabling them to think themselves better to a certain extent. The danger some may see with this is that individuals will simply accept their lot in life and therefore no structural changes need take place. Although a danger, as long as the awareness of not doing this is kept in mind, the actual imagining, and then sharing thoughts with others, can lead to structural changes. This happens through changing the discourse of ideas that are so powerful in affecting how individuals think and feel about things. It is these ideas that lead to structural institutional changes at a concrete level in parliament, laws and a global future. What people have thought in their imagination leads to a change in discourse which leads to change in and of itself of how individuals live and think alone and converse and live together. In turn, this leads to structural changes which are needed to sustain that developed thought. It is always conceivable for the individual or group awareness to stretch beyond its horizons into future possibilities.

---

[50] D Cornell 1995.
[51] See N Lacey, 1998, p 246–247.
[52] D Cornell 1995.
[53] N Lacey, 1998, p 233ff. Lacey makes the comparison between Cornell's work and Derridean deconstruction.

Moral consciousness reveals the active attempt of individuals to grasp or make sense of their situations in ways that are novel and indeed it may be this very activity upon which future hopes inevitably must be founded. It is the human activity of making sense of life in a social environment that leads to moral concepts and language. Morality is a matter of personal development requiring sensitivity in dealing with oneself and the others with whom life is shared.

Reality and imagination are bound up together, new self-understandings can be formed imaginatively out of the materials provided by taking advantage of the spaces within what is there. New meanings will thus emerge as the dimensions of insight are opened out and discovery will be made of the sources of moral inspiration for use in the future. Individuals' capacity to imagine themselves otherwise, to abstract and extract themselves from their present situations, imagining what it might be like to be somewhere else, doing something else, and at the same time, imagining what it is like for others, is a central part of that. Indeed imagining themselves otherwise is seeing themselves as "others". The "othering" involved here does not have to be negative – it simply acknowledges the fact that any individual, as a self or subject, has boundaries which necessarily entails there are others: individuals have an internal consciousness, a part of them that is private and inaccessible to others (although largely formed, developed and sustained through their relationships with others). Because this is so, there is a need to formulate norms to ensure that that capacity is allowed to flourish in society's structures.

One way of achieving a more fully realised view of freedom and the subject to encompass all of human beings' lives is through the interpretative process, individuals aiming to make themselves the best they can, focusing on a striving for an ethical unity of the subject and community or the other.

The norms are freedom and equality of persons. All ought to show an awareness that others are entitled to basic respect as subjects and equal persons (for they in turn are subjects in their own right).[54] These norms will be more fully realised through a transformation of the concept of the subject, and human beings, by seeing the world as made up of people talking to each other, as a language, a community. Through conversations, individuals constitute and transform their cultures, characters and communities.

Also important is the power of narrative: a power by which the self maintains its integrity in the face of threats of total destruction.[55] The work of black feminist theorists focusing on the use of the narrative method as a recognition of who individuals are and how this leads to empowerment is insightful here.[56]

---

[54] JB White *Heracles' Bow: essays on the rhetoric and poetics of law* (Madison Wis: University of Wisconsin Press 1985) at p xi and xii.

[55] JB White, 1985, p 172. See also R West 1993; I Ward *Law and Literature: Possibilities and Perspectives* (Cambridge: Cambridge University Press 1995). M Griffiths, 1995.

[56] P Williams *The Alchemy of Race and Rights* (Cambridge: Cambridge University Press 1991); *Seeing a Color Blind Future: the paradox of race: the 1997 Reith Lectures* (London: Virago 1997); see also PH Collins *Black Feminist Thought: Knowledge, Consciousness and the Politics of Empowerment* (2nd Edn New York and London: Routledge 1991); K

Retaining the idea of the subject, not only allows individuals to be "*agents of choice and sources of value*",[57] but it also carries responsibilities. As individual women are encouraged to express their views and are listened to, knowing that when they do so someone might listen and believe them, they will become more empowered, with the hope that this will lead to positive change. The discourse of human rights, and including those women in the human of such human rights assists in the search for freedom through the establishment of their individual identity. As Patricia Williams says:

> For the historically disempowered, the conferring of rights is symbolic of all the denied aspects of their humanity: rights imply a respect that places one in the referential range of self and others, that elevates one's status from human being to social being.[58]

## Increasing Women's Real Choices

These theories of freedom, critical reflection and imagination can be used in analysing and trying to change the gender system and identity formed under conditions of oppression by the use of existentialist thought where the distinct individuality or identity of a human being is self-actualised.

Structural institutions and societies ought to allow for self-conscious mutual recognition and aim for a harmony between the individual and the community to which they belong, thus creating harmonious freedom – a humanly created achievement. The creation of this consciousness and identity is an ongoing process of creation and is constitutive of an individual's being. So a human being is who he or she is in the sense they make of things and their relations with others. The very possibility of self-criticism presupposes the reality of a self founded in certain beliefs and relationships.[59] This is an important insight in the lives of women, for, as has been shown, often their identity is formed under conditions of oppression and against their interests.

Women's sense of self needs to be built up and reconstructed rather than deconstructed. The "authentic" self which emerges will grow in the person's life as he or she makes it something better, through their commitments and projects.[60] By gaining a sense of one's own identity, individuals become *existing* human beings with the role of choice being fundamental. This sense of authenticity can only be

---

Crenshaw "Race, Reform and Retrenchment: Transformation and Legitimation in Anti-Discrimination Law (1988) 101 *Harvard Law Review* 1331.

[57] D Cornell 1998, p 38.

[58] P Williams 1991, above note 55 at p 153. Williams makes the important point that, to the privileged, rights talk may seem decadent and unnecessary, something to be critiqued and deconstructed, while to the oppressed it is a forceful tool: at a symbolic level and in terms of enforcing actual legal rights.

[59] Dilman, see Chapter 3, note 74 at p 262.

[60] Dilman, 1991, p 264.

attained within a community practising mutual respect valuing the aspiration for each person to become an individual.

If "woman" is the object and "man" the subject as created by social reality containing two genders in a hierarchical power-based system, to free "woman" means women have to be seen as independent human beings, as human subjects in their own right, not as defined in their relation to men. This can lead to mutual recognition of each other as subjects. In order to explain limitations in the lives of women, women's situation as a matter of history must be invoked, not a "mysterious essence", thus the future remains largely open to change and is therefore more hopeful.[61] It is possible to rise above the "other and self" dichotomy if each individual freely recognises the other, each regarding him or herself and the other simultaneously as object and subject in a reciprocal manner.[62]

As other people bring individuals into their real existence in that they contribute to the existence they have, individuals are conscious of how they are perceived by other people, this knowledge of being an object to them is a fundamental part of their awareness of the world and of themselves. The wider the gulf is between their view of themselves and other people's view of them, the more they are in danger of losing their identity.[63]

This type of freedom can increase the probability that choices are seen as an individual's own, and that individuals can make them knowing they are free and not suffering under some kind of controlling forces. When women are struggling to reconstitute their community into one that includes themselves as equal members, such a strong sense of self, consciousness and freedom will be of great assistance. If particular focus rests on the lives of women, it is *wrong* that life chances are often determined by being a member of a "second-class sex" rather than being determined as persons. Women's life chances are often determined by their status as a member of this group attributed to them in a social, political and legal sense rather than as full human beings in the community. This is particularly so on a global scale where women often do not even have formal rights under their national laws. It is important that women (as well as men) – as human subjects – be treated as persons or selves or individuals with agency and responsibility, and as persons in the community, treated with respect and as free moral persons. Hegel says *"what it [the person] is potentially it may not be actually"*.[64] It is this potential or capacity to be fulfilled which is the "authentic" self – the true self in being, not some inner "essence" or core that is there to be uncovered.

The self is understandable as constituted intersubjectively, in interaction with others, in a process of becoming. *"How does this finite embodied creature constitute into a coherent narrative those episodes of choices and limitation, agency and suffering, initiative and dependence?"*[65] An account of the construction

---

[61] See S de Beauvoir, 1997, p 723.
[62] S de Beauvoir, 1997, p 172.
[63] M Warnock, 1967, p 36 on Sartre. See also analysis by C Douzinas, 2002, and as discussed in Chapter 4 above.
[64] See M Davies, 1994, p 381.
[65] S Benhabib, 1992, p 162.

of the self needs to show how social circumstances, material circumstances (including embodiment) change and growth all come together to make a self.

## Conclusion

In the ongoing development of human beings' freedom, I have argued that imagination needs to be expanded, while the interconnection between the self and others into mutual recognition needs to occur, particularly in the context of the hierarchical gender structure where women are seen as the other. The importance of the freedom and common potentiality of all humans developed internally needs to be encouraged to exist and then thrive by external structures. One way of doing this is globally, through international law, and ideas of globalism to which I now turn.

# PART III
# GLOBAL APPLICATIONS

# Introduction to Part III

Because of the intimate interconnection between internal and external obstacles to the realisation of freedom, it is necessary for structural changes to occur to actualise the increase in each person's inner freedom.

In Chapter 6, this external structural framework is laid down in the form of global ethics, international human rights, humanitarian and international criminal law: one of the ways to assist a new global order to come into existence is through the development of global institutions.[1] In Chapter 7 this is analysed in the context of the enforcement of international humanitarian law through the jurisprudence of the ICTY as it relates to rape and sexual violence.

External structures are all interconnected with internal ones because of their importance in consciousness forming. External structures like these areas of law need to ensure that each person is treated as of equal worth, so increasing the sources of their capacity to exercise choices for themselves, to live freely, to be, to be themselves and to grow. How these are structured will thus increase individuals' internal sense of power and agency over their own lives and make them feel competent and effective as opposed to feeling hopeless, helpless, passive victims. This is a feminist agenda because of the empirical historical oppression of women as a gender. In particular, I look at the way these laws treat and view women who have been raped and sexually violated, particularly in times of armed conflict. This focus on some of the most ultimate violations of personal integrity and freedom shows the need to retain a universal subject as rights holder to enforce claims against violators and also, the subject as wrong doer with responsibility for his deeds. Such an international humanitarian discourse also provides a means for upholding a common shared humanity but there must remain an awareness of fixing and privileging certain types of identities.

---

[1] See T Franck, 1995. The ICTY and the International Criminal Tribunal for the atrocities in Rwanda (the ICTR) and the International Criminal Court (ICC) are part of this process.

# Chapter 6

# Globalism and Potentiality

*"Women want...the possibility of living lives of dignity, free from domination and violence. In this struggle, the recognition of women's rights as human rights can play an important role."* Charlotte Bunch[1]

## Introduction

Legal globalism finds its philosophical basis in the idea of law which is applicable globally and to everyone. It implies an idea of international law that bases the international legal community on two beliefs: the moral quality of human beings and the moral unity of humankind.[2] As well as internal obstacles to freedom, external obstacles in politics and law impede the moral growth and fulfilment of humans. Accordingly, political and legal conditions are important to allow this moral quality and moral unity to thrive and come to its full potential. Claims for social recognition and equality have been largely played out in terms of claims for legal rights. The importance of such claims in an international context is emphasised particularly where national law insufficiently protects the individual human rights of women or where that national law or the state system is the problem in the first place.

This chapter shows the link between the failure of the concept of the human being in Western philosophical thought to encompass women and the male-based features of the human on which international human rights and humanitarian law (the law of armed conflict or *jus bello*) is based.[3] It seeks to show how women need to be fully included not only in the concept of the human but also in the human of international human rights and international humanitarian law. However, it is argued that, just as ideas of human subjectivity should not be discarded, so these areas of international law should not be discarded. Indeed, they can, and should be, used and expanded to provide a fuller realisation of human potentiality globally.

Recognition is needed that inequalities are not the result of human nature but depend on the way social structures shape human "nature", including, as has

---

[1] C Bunch "Women's Rights As Human Rights: Toward a Re-Vision of Human Rights" (1990) 12 *Human Rights Quarterly* 486 at p 498.
[2] See M Saward "A Critique of Held" in B Holden (ed), 2000, p 32ff.
[3] International humanitarian law has been described as the part of human rights law that is applicable to armed conflict and there is an overlap in the underlying theory behind the systems of law. KD Askin, 1997.

been shown in the previous chapter, individual wants and preferences, and regulate human relationships. These structures include national laws, the structure of international law, international human rights and humanitarian law. These external structures, amongst others, set out what rights and claims individuals have, regulate human relationships, set out who individuals are allowed to be, what standards will apply, who will be protected and how, who will be accorded dignity and claims as a person rather than as a seemingly deficient or deviant human. In particular, I concentrate on the treatment of rape and sexual violence during times of conflict, showing how rape is one of the ultimate violations of personal integrity and freedom as a world-wide issue.

Progress will be made towards a more inclusive conception of the human by ensuring that women are included in the definition of human and seeing rape and sexual violence as violations of the human rights and of the humanity of women as humans, of their subjectivity and sense of self.

The ideal is an interconnected, interdependent world, involving world governance, in a caring, loving, empathetic environment along the lines developed in Part II, largely based on Hegelian freedom and care ethics, allowing free human potentiality to grow and lead to free existent individuals, creating a global world order constructed in a way that will enable all individuals to be free to create what has been called *"a moral consciousness of humanity"*.[4] Once rooted, this constitutes the best barrier against the enemies of human dignity. However, in the meantime, and to help get there, there needs to be an engagement with existing discourses and political structures. One of the most useful tools to the empowerment of individual subjectivity is international human rights and, at times of conflict, international humanitarian law, aiming to attain at least a certain level of global social justice and safeguards from the human rights abuses of women. In this context, after looking at ideas of global ethical governance, I briefly examine the theory behind the external structures of international human rights and humanitarian law; feminist critiques of these, and then how these frameworks can be used to lead to global improvements. Developments in the field of women's rights as human rights are analysed only briefly in the context of my argument that this area of law illustrates the necessity of feminists retaining normative ethics, normative feminist agenda, and a concept of strong human subjectivity. This context shows that retention of a universal subject as rights holder is needed to enforce claims against violators and also to hold responsible the human subject as wrongdoer with responsibility for his deeds. Additionally, the retention of these concepts upholds ideas of common shared humanity.

Although the limitations of human rights and humanitarian law are recognised, they can function in an instrumental way in assisting to attain that (necessarily unattainable) goal of a caring global order while also regulating existing conditions.[5] It is argued that women, as much as men, are entitled to full

---

[4] The expression is in CS Nino *The Ethics of Human Rights* (Clarendon Press Oxford 1991).
[5] See Part II as to why this is necessarily unattainable.

protection of their rights and freedoms because they are human beings and that the human rights of women have yet to be fully attained.[6]

## Ethical Global Subjectivity and Citizenship

With a developing global order, the idea of the consciousness of a global citizen, together with a global ethics, is increasingly emerging. All human beings are, it is said, global citizens by virtue of the rights and duties all have as humans. This idea involves belonging to, and participating in, a wider community than an individual's immediate geographical environment.[7]

With increasing communication, technology, financial and/or multi-state organisations, space exploration, environmental resources, inter-state co-operation and more regional governance, arguably there is a reduction in the role of the nation state relative to that of various other units and actors on the global stage.[8] So the sovereign state in which people happen to find themselves born and/or living is not the only arena in which citizens' values are cultivated. Citizens' values and judgements are now formed in a complex web of national, international and global cultural exchange.[9] Within the human rights and humanitarian law framework, it is clear that governments and states are no longer free to treat their citizens as they think fit and, correspondingly, some of the most fundamental forces and processes which determine the nature of life chances within and across political communities are now beyond the reach of nation states.[10] It has been argued that if the idea of cosmopolitan democracy is to be realised, each citizen must learn to become a cosmopolitan citizen – what has been described as a person capable of mediating between national traditions, communities, and alternative forms of life through dialogue.[11] Discourse with others will aim to expand the horizons of one's own framework of meanings and prejudices and increase the scope of mutual understanding.

Have the events of September 11th 2001 rendered ideals of citizenship irrelevant as countries and regions retreat into preoccupations with security, reducing their commitment to tackling global problems, posturing over and entering into war and global conflict?[12] Or have the ideals become even more important, as global solutions are sought to the world-wide threat of terrorism,

---

[6] See K Tomasevski *Women and Human Rights* (London: Zed Books UN Non-Governmental Liaison Service 1993) page ix–x.
[7] See N Dower "Global Citizenship: Yes or No?" in N Dower and J Williams (eds), 2002, p 40.
[8] M Midgley "Towards an ethic of Global Responsibility" in T Dunne and NJ Wheeler (eds), 1999, ch 5 at p 172; F Robinson, 1999.
[9] D Held "The Changing Contours of Political Community: Rethinking Democracy in the Context of Globalization" in B Holden (ed), 2000, p 18ff at p 23.
[10] D Held, 2000, p 25–6.
[11] D Held, 2000, p 29.
[12] As described by N Dower and J Williams, 2002, Introduction.

leading to a collective global tackling of the root causes of terrorism through co-operation and the promotion and strengthening of peace between people of goodwill from all faiths and nations?[13]

Whether people like it or not, these are undoubtedly times when it is virtually impossible not to think in a global context. If there are threats to individual security from global terrorism and increasing resort to arguments of regime change intervention on other states, it seems unarguable that this is a global age when increasingly all need to think globally, trying to relate, understand, and/or empathise with others who may have views very different from one's own, whether they live in the same city or on the other side of the world. It seems that in these times reference needs to be increasingly made to international humanitarian law.

As individuals seek to live globally, all should be empowered to realise their full potential. This has been described as the pursuit of self-definition.[14] However, this ought not to mean atomistic individualism with no concern for others. Instead, there is a link between individual responsibility and a just order in which everyone has an equal chance to reach their full potential as a human being.[15] This idea has been eloquently described as individuals increasingly thinking in terms of their common destiny: seeing humanity as a single species, sharing a common, finite and endangered speck of the universe.[16] International law makes and gives individuals an opportunity to play a creative role on a scale inconceivable a few decades ago: the arguments being that there is no longer any need to defend the *existence* of international law. Instead scholars can look to a *critical assessment* of its content and ask whether international law is *fair and just.*[17]

Opportunities have been described as available to shape a future where citizenship remains a meaningful idea linked to the protection of rights, a sense of community and duty and a respect for the value of human life and dignity everywhere, with a commitment to a transformation – both spiritual and material – premised on the wholeness and equality of humanity with humane governance being the aim. Human consciousness will be challenged and develop in this process.[18]

If a hierarchical gender system persists, with power differentials which devalue women and anything seen as feminine, seeing women as the other, such an order will never come close to being realised. The institutionalisation of inequality and injustice in this way needs to cease as its existence limits the chances of women conceiving goals of their own and realising them; of women being seen as persons in their own right. As a result of the unequal, dominant/superior (male) and

[13] N Dower and J Williams, 2002.
[14] See T Franck *The Empowered Self* (Oxford: Oxford University Press 1999) at p 255.
[15] See H Kung "A Global Ethic for a new Global Order" in N Dower and J Williams, 2002.
[16] See T Franck, 1995, p 6.
[17] T Franck, 1995, p 6.
[18] See R Falk "An Emergent Matrix of Citizenship: Complex, Uneven, and Fluid" in N Dower and J Williams (eds), 2002, p 15ff at p 27–28.

the subordinate/inferior (female) gender structure, the liberty of women is dramatically curtailed in societies throughout the world. Further, rape and sexual abuse are acts of violence and humiliation in which the victim experiences overwhelming fear for her, and sometimes his, very existence, as well as a profound sense of *powerlessness*. This disparity of power is embodied in laws and in social and political institutions. International law can assist in remedying this situation.[19]

Developments in international human rights, humanitarian and international criminal legal discourse are necessarily at odds with the commitment to respect the territorial supremacy of sovereign states, therefore these external structures can assist in creating a humanely governed world in which human consciousness can be changed, if these are used in the right way. It has been noted that many use their fellow human beings as just another resource to try to benefit themselves, using people as instruments. This is even more damaging if carried out by the powerful on the powerless but the recognition of rights of humans in these three areas of law can be described as the antidote to this.[20] The mere fact of being human proves in itself an entitlement to claim goods which are necessary for an autonomous and dignified life and this is a fact regardless of where one happens to be born or live. While the ultimate aim is the creation of a moral consciousness of humanity in a global context as the best barrier against the enemies of human dignity and against using persons as means rather than ends in themselves, given the moral consciousness created using positive freedom and care ethics, these areas of law provide stepping stones to striving for that (never ending) goal.

It has been shown how social conditions lead to individual consciousness and that how they are arranged can decrease or increase options for becoming a full person. If the concept of the human subject is changed, created in a caring, empathetic environment, with the potential to be free and make "authentic" free choices, then in the sphere of international human rights, international humanitarian and international criminal law concepts of the human on which these laws are based need to be conceptualised in a way to fully encompass this potentiality rather than exclude certain categories of persons who it is thought somehow do not fit within a fixed concept based on a certain type of male experience. It will of course be more difficult to apply the laws to such persons and thus the laws are discriminatory and sustain inequalities.

As was shown in Part II, individuals can increase their internal freedom because of their ability to transform themselves and their society through the power of the imagination, with ideas of empowerment being important as well as self-determination and positive self-definition. This is in the context of acknowledging intersubjectivity and the impact of external structures on freedom too. Persons cannot realise their potentiality if legal structures prevent them from fulfilling their potential and make it more difficult to claim their right to be treated as a person as opposed to another person who, for example, may happen to be of a different sex.

---

[19] For arguments that international law is gendered in and of itself, see H Charlesworth and C Chinkin, 2000.

[20] See CS Nino, 1991, p 1.

In international human rights, humanitarian and international criminal law, existing conceptions of the "human" have historically restricted women's ability to enforce rights they ought to have as full members of the human community. However, as will be developed later in this chapter, this is changing. Before looking at this, the identity of the subject of international law needs to be addressed.

## The Subject of International Law

Traditionally, the subject at international law has been the nation state, leaving individuals with no direct status under international law, instead having to depend on the support of national governments to bring cases on their behalf. [21] Thus individuals have been described as objects of international law and states as its subjects. [22] However, it has long been recognised that international law is the creation of human beings and its ultimate impact is on individual behaviour. [23] Special tribunals set up after World War II at Nuremberg and Tokyo did try individuals accused of war crimes, crimes of aggression and crimes against humanity. Such crimes were said to be crimes under international law for which an international tribunal could properly exercise jurisdiction. Further, increasingly, with globalisation, the expansion of international human rights discourse and legislation, international humanitarian law developments and ad hoc tribunals being set up in the 1990s, together with the development of international criminal law, the individual is now clearly a subject in international law in his or her own right. [24]

Within this framework, respect for the autonomy of the subject and for an extensive range of rights accorded to humans creates a new set of ordering principles in political affairs that delimit and curtail the principle of effective state power. [25] These three areas of law can have important functions internationally as statements of the elements of humanity.

International criminal law is an area of law where international human rights law intersects with international humanitarian law. The convergence of international human rights law, international humanitarian law and international

---

[21] In comparison to the cases before the Yugoslav Tribunal examined in Part 2 of this Chapter, the International Court of Justice (ICJ) heard the case of *Bosnia and Herzegovina v Yugoslavia (Serbia and Montenegro)* 1993 ICJ. Proceedings were therefore taken by one state against another under the Statute of the ICJ to which only States can be party. To prosecute individuals alleged to have committed crimes, the domestic courts of a State or an International War Crimes Tribunal are needed.

[22] R Falk, 2002.

[23] H Charlesworth and C Chinkin, 2002, p x.

[24] See T Franck, 1995, p 196 and Y Dinstein "International Criminal Law" (1975) 5 *Israel Y B Hum Rts* 55.

[25] See D Held, 2000, p 25.

criminal law has been described as progressing at an unparalleled pace.[26] Although these areas of law are different in theoretical and practical origins, they aim to protect the rights of the oppressed and can complement each other. The individual person who is normally hidden behind the "abstract entity"[27] of the legal personality of the state when using these areas of law clearly becomes the subject of international law. Many international crimes are now crimes under customary international law and therefore states and individuals are subject to it without having to be signatories to treaties. It can therefore no longer be said that international law is only concerned with the enforcement of the rights and duties of states.[28]

Despite these positive elements including the basic provision of universal and common humanity standards, such laws have been subject to feminist critiques which are now analysed.

## Feminist Critiques of the Subject of Human Rights and International Humanitarian Law

Although feminist critiques of rights have been described as remarkably rare in the literature on international women's rights, there has been much written critiquing the field of human rights law generally.[29]

Some feminist international law scholars have argued that a major reason why human rights and humanitarian law have insufficiently protected women in the past is because the laws drafted and interpreted are not truly universal, they are masculine.[30]

The main problem identified by rights critique which I want to highlight here is that following from the norms relating to the human subject of human rights and humanitarian law. As the norms of international human rights and humanitarian law are male-defined and cast in the male image, the human whose rights are protected is based on a gender specific (male) person. Therefore it is perhaps not surprising that the human whose rights are protected is based on a

---

[26] See D Koenig and KD Askin "International Criminal Law and the International Criminal Court Statute: Crimes Against Women" in K D Askin and D Koenig (eds), Vol 2, 2000, p 3ff at p 7. Although it is debatable whether or not there is a convergence.

[27] A phrase used at Nuremberg.

[28] See M Dixon and R McCorquodale *Case and Materials on International Law* (4th Edition, Oxford: Clarendon Press 2003) at p 299.

[29] The comment is made by H Charlesworth "What Are 'Women's International Human Rights?'" in R Cook (ed) *Human Rights of Women* (Philadelphia: University of Pennsylvania Press 1994) p 58ff at p 61, citing only K Engle, "International Human Rights and Feminism" (1997) 13 *Michigan Journal of International Law* 317 as such an example.

[30] CA MacKinnon 1994; H Charlesworth and C Chinkin, 2000, p 17 and 231ff; KD Askin, 1997, p 253; V Spike Peterson and L Parisi "Are Women human? It's not an academic question." in T Evans (ed) *Human Rights Fifty Years On: A Reappraisal* (Manchester: Manchester University Press 1998); C Bunch, 1990; K Engle, 1997.

gender specific (male) person. Inevitably, women, whose lives and experiences may not fit this model, will be failed.

In the same way as feminists highlighted the maleness of the human in Western philosophical thought, the human of human rights can be identified as male or masculine rather than universal. Reasons for this include the use of men's bodies, experiences and stereotypical attributes (reason, agency, independence), as the norm for the human in human rights. In contrast, women and women's bodies, experiences and stereotypical attributes (non-agency, dependence) are excluded from the "universal" and described instead as particular and partial.[31] Therefore men occupy the universal category of the human of human rights, and women the other. Human rights have often been men's rights and therefore exclusions, constraints and abuses more typical of women's lives are neither recognised nor protected by human rights instruments.

Criticisms have been made that because the gender division is largely socially constructed, but is presented as totally natural, discrimination that detrimentally affects women is not seen and analysed as violating their human rights.[32] Further, when men use their liberties socially to deprive women of theirs, it does not look like a human rights' violation but when men are deprived of theirs by governments, it does.[33] Rights have been described as being defined by the criterion of what men fear will happen to them.[34] This is because the violations of men's human rights better fit the paradigm of human rights violations because that paradigm has been based on men's experiences. The more feminised victims become, no matter what their gender, it has been commented that it is less likely that international human rights will be found to be violated no matter what was done.[35] Guarantees women specifically need due to sex inequality in society in order to live to a standard defined as human – like women having the freedom from being bought and sold as a sexual chattel, having autonomous economic means, reproductive control, personal security from intimate invasion, a credible voice in public life, a non-derivative place in the world – are not considered at all.[36] Women's refusal to settle for anything less than *a single standard of human dignity* as an entitlement has been described as having the potential to lead to positive equality which looks to social context and envisions an active role for equality law. This will promote a society of equal dignity and respect where a social, contextual, relational, anti-hierarchical equality jurisprudence operates.[37]

To ensure that women are not excluded from the definition of human rights, a definition is needed that is flexible enough to include women's lives and needs.

---

[31] See V Spike Peterson and L Parisi, 1998, p 132.

[32] See N Kim, "Toward A Feminist Theory of Human Rights: Straddling the Fence between Western Imperialism and Uncritical Absolutism." (1993) 25 *Columbia Human Rights Law Review* 49.

[33] See CA MacKinnon 1993.

[34] H Charlesworth, 1994, p 71.

[35] CA MacKinnon 1993, p 94.

[36] CA MacKinnon 1993, p 102–3.

[37] CA MacKinnon, 1993, p 102–3.

Following from my analysis in previous Chapters, the definition needs to be fully inclusive of all humanity, not simply built on existing stereotypes of what it means to be a man or a woman.

Existing provisions in human rights law, insofar as they provide specific protection for women, often do so in terms of their relationships with others. They have been criticised as outdated, instead of focusing on women as individuals in their own right.[38] Women are treated as the property of men: "their women". Indeed, such thinking could be seen as a contributing factor to rape and sexual violence occurring, with ideas of ownership, possession and power and some type of "revenge" on other men through the "use" of "their" women.

The individualism promoted by a traditional understanding of rights has been seen as limiting their possibilities by ignoring the relational nature of social life.[39] Further, rights have been described as undermining radical transformation by making contingent social structures seem permanent. Rights therefore could be seen as functioning to protect the most privileged groups in society. For example, rights such as freedom of religion or the protection of the family can justify the oppression of women.[40]

Further, feminist scholars have shown the operation of the public/private division in international law and demonstrate that the marginalisation of women by dominant legal systems is exacerbated by the structure of international law, with its emphasis on the abstract entity of the state and by the almost total exclusion of women from participation in its processes.[41]

The discourse of human rights has traditionally been advocated as assisting the oppressed, based on ideas of the freedom and equality of all human beings universally. Rights have been described as nothing more than the symbolic expression that one is equal in his or her freedom with everyone else or that one is a legal subject.[42] Rights consciousness requires experiences with the legal system that confirm the subjectivity of persons – that they are rights holders capable of enforcing their rights and are able to do so in the legal system. Rights have been described as bridging the moral and legal, with it being argued that the liberal rights tradition should be refashioned to provide defensible conceptions of the good society.[43]

---

[38] J Gardam, 1992; N Kim, 1993.
[39] See H Charlesworth, 1994.
[40] H Charlesworth, 1994.
[41] See H Charlesworth, C Chinkin and S Wright "Feminist Approaches to International Law" (1991) 85 *American Journal of International Law* 613 and C Romany "State Responsibility Goes Private: A Feminist Critique of the Public/Private Distinction in International Human Rights Law" in RJ Cook (ed), 1994.
[42] See C Douzinas, 2002, p 391.
[43] R West, 2001, p xii and xiv; see also analysis by N Lacey "Feminist Legal Theory and the Rights of Women in K Knop, 2004.

Feminist scholars have critiqued international human rights law to show how it excludes women from the human in human rights by reference to what is commonly known as the three generations of human rights law.[44]

The first generation of rights are civil and political, accorded in such documents as the 1948 Universal Declaration of Human Rights (UDHR) and the International Covenant on Civil and Political Rights 1966 (ICCPR).[45] The UDHR declares equality for men and women:

> Article 1: All human beings are born free and equal in dignity and rights. They are endowed with reason and conscience and should act towards one another in a spirit of brotherhood.
> Article 2: Everyone is entitled to all the rights and freedoms...without discrimination of any kind, such as...sex.[46]

The UN Charter has binding character on all signatories and possibly all of the provisions of the UN Universal Declaration rise to the level of customary international law.[47] Women have formal protection under these provisions. However, it has been argued that women are not included in the Civil and Political Rights codified in the UDHR and the ICCPR. The argument is similar to feminist critiques of the liberal individual and human in Western philosophical thought in that certain feminists see women as not being included in the Western, liberal, public sphere definitions of individuals that underpin this discourse of human rights. On this interpretation, citizens are implicitly male or masculine and enjoy civil and political rights while women can enjoy these only to the extent that they become like men.[48]

Linked to critiques of the public and private, it is shown that the focus in this generation of rights rests in the public sphere. As the abuse of women both physically and psychologically often takes place in the private sphere, it has been argued that women's human rights are therefore often not covered by provisions of these Charters. The UDHR does not affirm the right of women to freedom from masculine dominance and the structural violence it constitutes against women.[49]

The second generation of rights do not fare much better in feminist critiques. Such rights are contained in the International Covenant on Economic Social and Cultural Rights 1966 (ICESCR)[50] and emphasise socio-economic rights and, to a limited extent, cultural rights. They continue to focus on the public sphere

---

[44] See analysis in H Charlesworth and C Chinkin, 2000, and V Spike Peterson and Parisi, 1998.

[45] Charter of the United Nations 26 June 1945; International Covenant on Civil and Political Rights 16 Dec 1966 999 UNTS 171.

[46] Articles 2 and 3, relevant extracts.

[47] KD Askin, 1997.

[48] See V Spike Peterson and L Parisi, 1998, p 141. See Chapter 2 above.

[49] See V Spike Peterson and L Parisi, 1998, p 147.

[50] International Covenant on Economic, Social and Cultural Rights, 16 Dec 1966, 999 UNTS 3.

and have been criticised as failing to address economic, social and cultural issues of particular relevance to women's lives.

Insofar as women are secondary and not seen as fully adult members of society, it is argued that what they do is not taken as seriously as what men do.[51] Here the criticism again relates to the public-private division and women's seemingly "natural" role as reproducers and as family members. Women are not constructed as agents, subjects or persons in their own right or as full adults or decision makers in groups seeking inter-generational continuity. Women are relegated to the role of reproducers and there is a denigration of what is associated with the feminine. Women are marginalised instead of being treated as human agents in relation to economic, social and cultural practices. For example, rights to work presume a public sphere understanding of work.

Even the third Generation of Rights has been criticised as still failing to take seriously the human rights of women. These rights are collective or group rights which seek to preserve the integrity of a particular cultural, ethnic or indigenous group through the right of self-determination. Group rights are predicated on and legitimised by emphasising the cultural identity of the group rather than the rights and identities of individuals. The criticism is based on the fact that women do not enjoy the rights to self-determination that men in such groups may achieve through being accorded group rights.[52]

Some feminist analysis argues that emphasis on the collective is often detrimental to women as individuals and indeed there is much written on the potential conflict between multiculturalism and human rights as an important issue in these global times.[53] This has led to claims that no social group has suffered greater violation of its human rights in the name of culture than women.[54] Relevant questions need to be asked and answered, including how the group is to be defined and by whom; how membership is retained; what is the relationship between the rights of the group and rights of the individuals within the group and how conflict between them is to be resolved.[55] While cultural sensitivity is important, it needs to be remembered that culture is a series of social practices whose meanings are influenced by the power and status of their interpreters and participants.[56]

There are also international protections accorded to women in women-specific provisions most notably in the Convention on the Elimination of All

---

[51] V Spike Peterson and L Parisi, 1998, p 147. The authors of the article focus on the "heterosexism"of the existing gender system.

[52] V Spike Peterson and L Parisi, 1998, p 141–2.

[53] See SM Okin, 1999; A Phillips "Feminism and the Politics of Difference. Or, Where have all the Women Gone?" in S James and S Palmer (eds), 2002; B Barry *Culture and Equality* (Cambridge: Polity Press 2001).

[54] A Rao "The Politics of Gender and Culture in International Human Rights Discourse" in J Peters and A Wolper (eds) *Women's Rights Human Rights: International Perspectives* (New York and London: Routledge 1995) at p 167–175.

[55] See H Charlesworth and C Chinkin, 2000, p 241 and W Kymlicka *Multicultural Citizenship* (Oxford: Clarendon Press 1995) at Chapter 3. See B Barry, 2001, for a critical response to multicultural group rights from a liberal perspective.

[56] See A Rao, 1995.

Forms of Discrimination against Women.[57] Such protections do not entail the necessity of a separation of women's rights from human rights. However, some feminists have argued in the direction of separate women's rights (as opposed to the human rights of women).

While emphasising the importance of issues and problems specific to women's lives is essential, the difficulty in creating women's rights and setting them apart from human rights is that there is great potential for marginalisation. The under-resourcing and geographical division of women's rights from other mainstream human rights protections has been noted.[58] This problem can also be seen in the theoretical work of some feminists which could be seen to stereotype and fix women's identities, often making positive changes which would enrich the lives of women *harder* to achieve.[59] At the same time, mainstreaming can tend to ignore the fact that human rights norms are masculine and can often therefore have limited application to women in practical terms.[60] This is because human rights have not been interpreted in a way consistent to their founding principles of equality and freedom and to their ethical best. They will be so interpreted when they include the rights of all within their ambit. As I hope to show, the jurisprudence of the ICTY in its treatment of violence against women can be interpreted as showing positive movement in that direction. Further, it has been noted that since the early 1990s, there is an increasing trend toward treating gender discrimination as a violation of customary international law.[61]

The debate as to the extent of human rights being women's rights, by the system taking into account women's lives, has only recently been extended to the field of international humanitarian law.[62] This recent feminist critique focuses on the fact that, for reasons similar to failings in human rights law, international humanitarian law also privileges male norms. Indeed, it is likely to be worse given that its subject matter is armed conflict – an area predominantly focusing on combatants, mainly men – with civilians being given subordinate status.

The experience of women as civilians in times of war has not been the starting point, it has been man as a combatant that is the starting point and standard.

International humanitarian law itself is based on masculine chivalric notions.[63] This has been said to exacerbate the gender division hierarchy as in personnel terms combatants are largely male and most women are affected by war, and thus the provisions of international humanitarian law, as civilians. Limitations

---

[57] See also regional protection, most importantly perhaps in the Inter-American Convention on the Prevention, Punishment and Eradication of Violence against Women (Convention of Belem Do Para) 1994.

[58] See, for example, RK Smith *Textbook on International Human Rights* (2nd Edn, Oxford: Oxford University Press 2005).

[59] For example, see analysis of L Irigaray's work in Chapter 3.

[60] H Charlesworth and C Chinkin, 2000, p 218.

[61] KD Askin, 1997, p 230–1.

[62] See J Gardam, 1997.

[63] See J Gardam 1997, p 67–69.

on the existing body of international humanitarian law have been seen as even more deficient than human rights in taking into account the reality of women's experiences with the provisions of the former which seek to protect women being described as *"totally inadequate".*[64] Moreover, it is argued that international humanitarian law incorporates a gendered hierarchy in the sense that the rules dealing with women are regarded as less important than others and their infringement is not taken as seriously.[65]

In seeking to protect women, international humanitarian law focuses on their relationships with others, for example, seeking to protect women as mothers or in special need of protection of their honour. In reality, as has been stated, a woman's honour is a concept constructed by men for their own purposes: it has little to do with women's perception of sexual violence.[66] So, even within the rules protecting civilians, there is no equality in the treatment of men and women. The rules take the experience that men have of warfare as their starting point.

The fact that international law is a system of law largely developed by Western states has been the cause for criticism from some feminists, particularly in the developing world.[67] However, these feminists generally highlight the positive aspects of what a fuller realisation of international law standards can do for women world-wide, recommending *"the protection and realization of basic human rights in a holistic and democratic fashion".*[68] Although rape in warfare will impact differently on women depending on its cultural significance, it is surely right to say that it is experienced by all women as *"terrifying and painful".*[69] The view has been expressed that the task of finding a shared experience of women is easier in the area of armed conflict that in human rights and international law generally.[70] Sexual violence has been described as:

> ...encapsulat[ing] all the deficiencies of the law from the perspective of women. Sexual violence in warfare is the most obvious distinctive experience of women in armed conflict...and is almost universal in all types of warfare.[71]

Specifying rape as an attack on a woman's honour has a great deal to do with a male view of rape and very little to do with how women see it. Women experience rape as torture and it should be recognised as such by the legal regime: *"rules protecting women against sexual violence must mirror those that regulate the torture and mistreatment of men".*[72]

---

[64] J Gardam, 1997.

[65] J Gardam, 1997, p 56.

[66] J Gardam, 1997, p 58.

[67] J Oloka-Onyango and S Tamale "The Personal is Political" or Why Women's Rights Are Indeed Human Rights: An African Perspective in International Feminism" (1995) 17 *Human Rights Quarterly* 691–731.

[68] J Oloka-Onyango and S Tamale, 1995: a point I develop later.

[69] J Gardam, 1997 p 67.

[70] An assertion made by J Gardam, 1997, p 66–67.

[71] J Gardam, 1997, p 73.

[72] J Gardam, 1997, p 78.

For all the valid criticisms of rights and humanitarian law discourse from the point of view of taking account of women's needs and including them as humans, these discourses offer a recognised vocabulary to frame political and social wrongs. Rights talk has been accurately described as a constant source of hope: *"Rights is...still so deliciously empowering to say. It is a sign for a gift of selfhood".*[73] The empowering function of rights discourse provides a focus that translates into action and women should be encouraged to make "rights' talk" their own. Rights are defined by who talks about them and the language that is used.[74]

Linking together positive liberty, the social formation of the individual and the interconnection between the individual and the community, shows there is no need to have a negative conceptualisation of rights, constraining state action or preventing interference. Instead, rights can entitle an individual to some form of assistance or intervention. The right to be left alone and what has been described as the *"neurotic understanding"* of individuals on which this right rests has been called a late nineteenth and early twentieth century invention which is not required to be central to liberalism. Rights could as readily be grounded in a view of humanity that respects individuality while fully recognising the social nature of the human.[75]

Disowning rights has accurately been criticised as distancing the possibility of humanity being able to universally share and focus on universally held utopian aspirations.[76] Additionally, nihilistic critiques prevent exploration of positive rights talk. It is true that rights, whatever their content, are premised on the egalitarian assumption that all humans share something which universal norms follow.[77]

Feminists are right to continue to critique the failings in human rights and humanitarian law instruments but the overarching framework of a commitment to use these areas of law for women's benefit remains strong, even amongst their fiercest feminist opponents in the international field. What most of these critiques seem to be aiming for is a fuller realisation of the human for women. Retaining an isolated male-based individual as the standard, or using a subject based on women's existing experiences, or deconstructing the human subject out of existence, prevents any meaningful women's rights that can aid their human flourishing.

## On Rape and Sexual Violence

While many feminists have shown how human rights and international humanitarian law reinforce the second-class status of women as a special category of human since they, together with other "special" kinds of humans, are seen to be in need of special protection, in terms of provisions protecting against rape and

---

[73] P Williams 1991.
[74] See C Romany, 1994.
[75] R West, 2001, p xix–xxi.
[76] R West, 2001.
[77] R West, 2001, p xxix.

sexual violence, it has been noted that some movement has taken place away from male-based, chivalric-encoded and exclusive, gendered definitions of rape in recent UN Human Rights' instruments.[78] Instead, rape is seen as a crime of violence, defined in ungendered terms. This move is praised because it neither naturalises women as rape victims, nor depends on a cultural definition of women.[79] Importantly, it clarifies the dynamic of power and subjugation that rape involves, therefore making it difficult to think of rape as related to some sort of natural sexual desire. Thus a report into the atrocities in the former Yugoslavia describes rape as:

> ...an abuse of power and control in which the rapist seeks to humiliate, shame, embarrass, degrade and terrify the victim. The primary objective is to exercise power and control over another person.[80]

Rape and sexual violence is a world-wide phenomenon and affects women of all classes, ages, ethnic and racial groups. Fear of such a crime restricts women's activities, affecting the qualities of their lives, with rape, and fear of rape, being part of women's consciousness and operating as constraints on their freedom.[81] Gender-based violence – which is brutal, systemic and structural – must be seen as no less grave than other forms of inhumane and subordinating violence, the prohibition of which has been recognised as *jus cogens* (peremptory norms from which derivation by nation states is not permitted under international law).[82]

Further, the most pervasive violation of women's subjectivity is violence against women.[83] This violence is endemic and is an extension of the hierarchical relationships of power between men and women in society. Female subordination is viewed as inevitable or natural rather than as an effect of politically and socially constructed reality. Women, understood not as agents in their own right – full humans – but as reproductive members of the group or property, are subject to objectification and abuse. This abuse is both physical and psychological, with rape being one of the worst manifestations of this violence. In some countries, national laws (and, as shall be shown, certain international laws) mischaracterise rape as a crime against honour or custom and not as a crime against the physical integrity of the victim and thereby minimise its seriousness. It is often seen as what men do to women, an extension of their natural biological needs as men; often their marital right. It has been argued that the state is complicit in reproducing social relations

---

[78] See B Allen *Rape Warfare: The Hidden Genocide in Bosnia-Herzegovina and Croatia* (Minneapolis and London: University of Minnesota Press 1996) at p 115.
[79] B Allen, 1996, p 118.
[80] Mazowiecki's Report "The Situation of Human Rights in the Territory of the Former Yugoslavia" 1993 at p 73 quoted in B Allen, 1996.
[81] A Morris *Women, Crime and Criminal Justice* (Oxford: Basil Blackwell 1987) p 160 and 180.
[82] See R Copelan "Intimate Terror: Understanding Domestic Violence as Torture" in RJ Cook (ed) (1994) at p 116ff who questions why gender specific violations are absent from *jus cogens*.
[83] See C Bunch, 1990, p 489.

that promote the social control of women through the threat or actuality of sexual violence both by failing to intervene when such violence takes place in the private sphere and by defining rape from a male point of view in both spheres.[84]

## Women as Persons Globally

Instead of focusing on a shared "nature" leading to claims of essentialism, with its attendant problems of fixing identity, focus could rest on humans' shared sense of being and potentiality. The right of an individual to an independent and self-fulfilling life, and the commitment to the liberal conception of the independent and autonomous self has been explained as connecting political struggles for racial and sexual emancipation.[85] As discussed already, the best safeguard against human rights abuses is humane world governance. However, in the meantime, a democratic framework allowing all individuals to make free choices on an informed basis, in a caring environment is the next best thing.

The traditional definition of the liberal subject or human being has been inadequate and has sought to be neutral and representative of all humankind, while at the same time being largely defined in a masculine way, fitting with male experiences and thus sustaining patriarchy. However, its failure to encompass all identities does not mean that ideas of retaining the norms of equal respect and freedom ought to be relinquished. Instead, it needs to be stressed how there has been, and is, a failure to live up to them for various reasons, including the inadequacies of certain conceptions of the subject which have been, and do still, exist. So, arguing for a fuller definition of the subject does not mean that the concepts of the subject, rights and freedom are deconstructed out of existence. It means that a fuller realisation of the terms can occur so that they encompass every individual, not just certain sections of society or one particular gender.

Much valuable feminist work has contributed to a fuller, more encompassing formulation of the human subject than that traditionally associated with "liberal individualism" with its connotations of atomistic isolationism. At the same time, recent feminist work makes the important argument that women around the world (particularly in the developing world) are using the language of liberalism because their problems are often centred around a devaluation of women's personhood: three things being described as essential for personhood, namely, autonomy, self-respect and a sense of fulfilment and achievement – all terms of the liberal enlightenment.[86] At a strategic policy level, the important point has been made that, with the dramatic growth in the movement to recognise women's rights as human rights under international law, the radical feminist potential of liberal principles is just beginning to be realised.[87] In stressing the importance of seeing women as demanding to be treated as persons, women's

---

[84] MacKinnon, 1993, and V Spike Peterson and L Parisi, 1998, p 145–6.
[85] Z Eisenstein, 1981.
[86] See MC Nussbaum 1999, p 55–6.
[87] MC Nussbaum 1999, p 56.

agency, sense of self and tools for empowerment can be identified. To be effective in the world, as it currently exists, requires organisation and an ability to relate to it in a way recognised and understood by it. As Nussbaum says:

> [The liberal] reveres the capacity of persons to choose and fashion a life...Some liberal thinkers have in fact revered established distinctions of gender. But, insofar as they did, they did not follow the vision of liberalism far enough. It is the vision of a beautiful, rich and difficult world, in which a community of persons regard one another as free and equal but also as finite and needy – and therefore strive to arrange their relations on terms of justice and liberty. In a world governed by hierarchies of power...this is still...a radical vision, a vision that can and should lead to social revolution.[88]

The importance of retaining and strengthening ideas of the individual subjectivity of women need to be emphasised. If women around the world are being treated in ways which devalue their selfhood, what is needed is for it to be built up, not demolished. Thus human rights and humanitarian law can be used to women's advantage, showing how they fail to live up to their egalitarian principles. In the next chapter, I show how an international court is aiming to do that.

---

[88] MC Nussbaum 1999, p 79–80.

# Chapter 7

# International Humanitarian Law and the ICTY

*"A universal standard of human dignity is the only principle that completely repudiates sex-class exploitation and also propels us into a future where the fundamental political question is the quality of life for all human beings."*
Andrea Dworkin[1]

In this final substantive chapter, the jurisprudence of the ICTY is used as a case study. The aspects of international humanitarian law analysed here are those covered by Articles 2 to 5 of the statute which set up the ICTY.[2] Its jurisprudence is examined insofar as it deals with the subject of rapes and sexual violence in the former Yugoslavia to show how this particular area of law has progressed by beginning to recognise women as persons in their own right.

There could be a tendency to regard the sexual abuse in the former Yugoslavia as exceptional and not as a regularly occurring aspect of conflict. However, it is shown that this is not the case.[3] As such, it is not an exceptional case study with no broader relevance. Instead it can be used to show how women can be included in the concept of the human subject, and how such interpretations should continue in future court jurisprudence in ad hoc tribunals and in the International Criminal Court.[4]

It should become evident during the analysis of this case study that to retain a concept of the human subject who is a rights holder (for the victim) and one who retains a sense of rightness and wrongness, and a sense of individual responsibility for the choices made as human subjects (by the perpetrators) is vital.

This chapter builds on the ideas developed in Part II and Chapter 6, that feminist jurisprudence needs to retain normative ideals and a strong sense of the

---

[1] A Dworkin *Right Wing Women: The Politics of Domesticated Females* (London: The Women's Press 1983).
[2] Its full name is the International Tribunal for the Prosecution of Persons Responsible for Serious Violations of International Humanitarian Law committed in the Territory of the Former Yugoslavia after 1 January 1991: SC Res 827 (1993) reprinted in 31 International Legal Materials (1993) 1203. Relevant extracts from the Statute's provisions are set out at Appendix I.
[3] See PV Sellers "The Context of Sexual Violence: Sexual Violence as Violations of International Humanitarian Law" Chapter 7D in G McDonald and O Swak-Goldman (eds) *Substantive and Procedural Aspects of International Criminal Law* (2000).
[4] Rome Statute for an International Court 1998: see relevant extracts at Appendix II.

free subject to ensure that actual women's lives are not obscured and their voices and pains not silenced or ignored. The individual – man or woman – should be allowed to be free. Coercion and violation are the opposite of real choice. Treating individuals as objects is dehumanising, with rape being the ultimate example of a deprivation of selfhood or subjectivity and violation of personal integrity. An international commitment to a conception of individual subjectivity – both for perpetrators of crimes and for the victims of those crimes – shows a commitment to freedom which will assist in individual flourishing and, relatedly, global justice.

The development of International War Crimes Trials is a modern phenomenon with the Nuremberg and Tokyo War Crimes Trials, set up after the Second World War, representing the first major International War Crimes Tribunals. It was not until the 1990s that two further tribunals were set up to deal with atrocities committed in the former Yugoslavia and Rwanda.

## Background to the ICTY

The ICTY was established on 25 May 1993 by the United Nations Security Council to prosecute those responsible for violations of international humanitarian law in the territory of the former Yugoslavia committed after 1 January 1991.[5]

The Yugoslav conflict of the 1990s followed the breakdown of the former Socialist Federal Republic of Yugoslavia, declarations of independence by republics of that political state in mid-1991, followed by vicious ethnic conflict between the various ethnic racial groups within that former state.

Daily media and human rights organisations reports of atrocities, including the rape and other abuse of women, often on a systematic and planned basis involving the detention of women and girls for the specific purpose of forced impregnation to produce offspring of the perpetrators' ethnicity, led to a high level of public horror and momentum for the international community to alleviate such horrors.

At the same time as carrying out diplomatic negotiations, the Security Council of the United Nations took the following steps culminating in the establishment of the ICTY. At first the Security Council publicly condemned the atrocities as violations of international humanitarian law.[6] It then publicised the reported atrocities.[7] This led to the investigation of violations through a Commission of Experts in the hope that the first War Crimes Commission since World War II would deter abuses.[8] Its task was to prepare cases for possible prosecution in national or international courts. This culminated in the Security Council's determination that violations of international humanitarian law threatened international peace and security and therefore permitted them to issue a

---

[5] A similar tribunal was set up to deal with the atrocities in Rwanda (the ICTR): SC Res 955 (1994) Statute of the Rwandan Tribunal reprinted in 33 ILM (1995) 1598.
[6] SC Res 764 (13 July 1992) reprinted in 31 ILM at 1465.
[7] SC Res 771 (12 August 1992) reprinted in 31 ILM at 1470.
[8] SC Res 780 (6 Oct 1992).

mandate pursuant to Chapter VII of the UN Charter under which the Security Council has authority to take measures necessary to maintain international peace and security.[9] The Security Council announced the creation of an international tribunal to prosecute those responsible for violations of international humanitarian law in the former Yugoslavia. The resulting report of the Secretary-General was submitted including a draft statute for the tribunal on 6 May 1993 taking into account the views of thirty one states and several organisations.[10]

Pursuant to Articles 1 to 5 of the Statute, the ICTY has jurisdiction over grave breaches, other breaches of the laws or customs of war, genocide and crimes against humanity committed after 1 January 1991 in the former Yugoslavia. The law to be applied has to be relevant and well-established international law. The Statute requires that rules of procedure provide protection for victims and witnesses.[11]

Although the law stated by the Security Council and the ICTY is formally applicable only to the former Yugoslavia, its decisions are likely to become established fundamental normative norms of international humanitarian law. Accordingly, the positive jurisprudence arising from the ICTY's judgments on rape and sexual violence has the power to influence international norms, not only in international humanitarian law but also in international criminal and human rights law respectively.[12]

Sexual violence is only explicitly referred to in the Statute in Article 5 which refers to the crime of rape as a crime against humanity. When originally analysed by feminist legal scholars prior to the hearing of any ICTY cases, there were mixed reactions to the wording of the Statute.[13]

On the one hand, there was a positive reaction of optimism with the tribunal being described as holding promise and representing progress, its existence per se being of symbolic significance, sending out a powerful message. The explicit description of rape as a crime against humanity in Article 5 was applauded and it was noted that confirmation that rape can constitute a crime against humanity is both morally and legally of groundbreaking importance.[14]

On the other hand however, there was a certain amount of disquiet in the failure of the drafters of the Statute to include rape and/or sexual violence explicitly as grave breaches of the Geneva Convention, war crimes or genocide set out in Articles 2 to 4. Whilst the history of rape and the international crimes dealt

---

[9] SC Res 827 (25 May 1993) reprinted in 32 ILM (1993) at 1203.

[10] See further J O'Brien "The International Tribunal for Violations of International Humanitarian Law in the Former Yugoslavia" (1993) 87 *American Journal of International Law* 639 at 640–642.

[11] The procedures adopted have been favourably commented upon – see KD Askin, 1997.

[12] T Meron "Rape as a Crime under International Humanitarian Law" (1993) 87 *American Journal of International Law* 424 at p 428.

[13] T Meron "International Criminalization of Internal Atrocities" 89 *American Journal of International Law* (1995) 554 at 555. See also J O'Brien, 1993; CN Niarchos "Women, War and Rape: Challenges Facing the International Tribunal for the Former Yugoslavia" (1995) 17 *Human Rights Quarterly* 649 at p 680 and 689.

[14] T Meron, 1993, p 428.

with in those Articles was shown to allow for such an interpretation regardless of explicit reference, feminist scholars presented strong reasons why it would have clarified matters greatly to set this out explicitly.[15] Such scholars predicted that the ICTY's handling of such cases would test the commitment of the international system to women's human rights and determine whether women can participate as equals in an international legal system created by men.[16]

Now many years in operation, the court has resided over the interpretation of these Articles in leading international humanitarian law cases from which it is clear that all of these crimes can be committed through rape and other forms of sexual violence. The ICTY has developed the law in ways to seriously include women within the definition of the human to which International humanitarian law applies as will now be seen from the case law analysis.

**The Relevant Jurisprudence of the ICTY**

The relevant Articles of the Statute of the ICTY are set out in Appendix I. I deal with the jurisprudence by reference to Article 3, violations of the laws and customs of war, then Article 2, grave breaches. I move on to briefly examine Article 4, genocide, and then Article 5, crimes against humanity.

*Laws and Customs of War*

Although rape and sexual assault of women during armed conflict is not new, such rapes and sexual assaults have been marginalised and certainly not been centre stage in the legality of warfare or in the judgments of war crimes trials. However, rape by soldiers of civilian women has been illegal for centuries with rape being punishable under customary laws during periods of armed conflict since at least the fifteenth century. The earliest comprehensive code on the laws of war, the Lieber Code of 1863, considered rape by a belligerent to be a capital war crime.[17]

Rape was not mentioned in the Nuremberg Charter and not prosecuted in Nuremberg as a war crime but it was prosecuted in the Tokyo Trial as a war crime.[18] After the Second World War, four Geneva Conventions were drafted and adopted with the aim of controlling such war outrages as had been seen in that War.

The first Geneva Convention seeks to provide assistance to wounded and sick Armed Forces in the field; the second to the wounded and sick and shipwrecked at sea; the third provides for the treatment of Prisoners of War; and

---

[15] See generally C Chinkin "Rape and Sexual Abuse of Women in International Law" (1994) 5 EJIL 326; H Charlesworth and C Chinkin, 2000; CN Niarchos, 1995.
[16] CN Niarchos, 1995, p 690.
[17] T Meron, 1995, p 425.
[18] See T Meron, 1995, p 427.

the fourth relates to the protection of civilians.[19] The fourth Geneva Convention attempts to extend to civilians the rights and protections that have been afforded to prisoners of war and to sick and wounded belligerents but it has been noted that sometimes humanitarian law has made a distinction as to whom the crime is committed against, whether a friend or foe, in determining whether or not a war crime has been committed.[20]

Article 2 to all four Conventions ("Common Article 2") specifies when the four conventions are to apply. This includes all cases of declared war or other armed conflict arising between two or more of the High Contracting Parties.[21] This Article also specifies that the Conventions apply in addition to provisions which apply during times of peace. Most of the human rights treaties thus apply during times of war too.

The explicit reference in humanitarian law prohibiting violence against women in wartime is contained in Article 27 which reads as follows:

> Protected persons are entitled, in all circumstances, to respect for their persons, their honour, their family rights, their religious convictions and practices, and their manners and customs. They shall at all times be humanely treated, and shall be protected especially against all acts of violence or threats thereof and against insults and public curiosity. Women shall be especially protected against any attack on their honour, in particular against rape, enforced prostitution, or any form of indecent assault.

Common Article 3 to the four Geneva Conventions provides a minimum standard of behaviour that applies to both government and non-government forces in some non-international (internal) conflicts. Prohibited actions include violence to life and person, cruel treatment and torture and humiliating and degrading treatment. It is not made explicitly clear that forms of sexual violence fall within these terms.

The distinction between international and internal conflicts has been highlighted by many legal scholars.[22] Some have argued that it has a gendered dimension in that a much more detailed legal regime protects combatants (mainly men) engaged in international conflicts and considerably weaker legal protection for the civilian population (in which almost all women are located) in times of both internal and international conflict and that the distinction has no basis in the reality of the lives of those caught up in the conflict.[23]

In 1977, Protocols I and II Additional to the Geneva Conventions ("Protocol I" and "Protocol II" respectively) were adopted to update the Geneva Conventions.[24] Protocol I seeks to provide protection for victims of *international*

---

[19] See 75 UNTS 31, 75 UNTS 85, 75 UNTS 135, 75 UNTS 287.

[20] See KD Askin, 1997, p 248.

[21] Article 2 of all 4 Geneva Conventions, above note 18.

[22] See, for example, T Meron, 1993; J Gardam and M Jarvis, 2001; and J Gardam, 1992 and 1997; H Charlesworth and C Chinkin, above note 14.

[23] See H Charlesworth and C Chinkin, 2000, p 317 and J Gardam, as note 21.

[24] "[1977] Protocol Additional to the Geneva Conventions of 12 August 1949, and Relating to the Protection of Victims of International Armed Conflicts" June 8 1977, 1125 UNTS 3 (entered into force 7 Dec 1978), reprinted in 16 ILM 1391 (1977) and "[1977] Protocol

armed conflict while Protocol II relates to protecting victims of *non-international* armed conflicts. They have been described as modernising, strengthening and clarifying humanitarian law.[25]

Article 76 of Protocol I states that:

> Women shall be the object of special respect and shall be protected in particular against rape, forced prostitution and any other form of indecent assault.

Article 2 (e) of Protocol II asserts that the following acts are and shall remain prohibited

> at any time and in any place whatsoever...(e) Outrages upon personal dignity, in particular humiliating and degrading treatment, rape, enforced prostitution and any form of indecent assault.

In these provisions, women are presented as lesser human beings in need of special protection and respect, instead of rape being presented as a violent attack upon the personal integrity of a human being.[26] By designating rape as a crime against honour, rather than one of violence, the provision presents women as the property belonging to men or the family and presents an image of women as needing protection. It also perpetuates the idea that there is a stigma attached to being a rape victim by presenting it as tarnishing women's honour.

Although the idea of rape being a crime against honour derives from the laws of war being based on the laws of chivalry, it is crucial to move away from the categorisation of rape as a crime against women as property or women's honour. The shame of a rape or other sexual assault must be removed from the survivors or their families to rest only with the criminals who perpetrate such crimes.

Other references in the Geneva Conventions emphasise women's reproductive mothering or caring roles. For example, Article 76(2) of Protocol I states that:

> Pregnant women and mothers having dependent infants who are arrested, detained or interned for reasons related to the armed conflict, shall have their cases considered with the utmost priority.

Whilst this is a good thing for pregnant women or women who have dependent infants, it has been argued that such provisions reduce the status of women without children and obscure the fact that girls are especially vulnerable to forms of sexual attack.[27]

---

Additional to the Geneva Conventions of 12 August 1949, and Relating to the Protection of Victims of Non-International Armed Conflicts" June 8 1977 1124 UNTS 609 (entered into force 7 Dec 1978) reprinted in 16 ILM 182 (1977).

[25] See KD Askin, 1997, p 246.

[26] See H Charlesworth and C Chinkin, 2000, p 315.

[27] See H Charlesworth and C Chinkin, 2000.

Under International law, Conventions would normally require a state to be party to them in order for those States to be legally bound. However, it is generally accepted that the 1949 Geneva Conventions, and some parts of Protocols I and II, have become part of customary international law.[28] All nation states are bound by universal, peremptory norms or *jus cogens* and can be held accountable for their breach. As already mentioned, it has been argued that the characterisation of certain gender abuses as constituting violations of *jus cogens* would provide greatly enhanced protections for women. As there is general consensus that prohibitions against genocide, slavery, torture, war crimes and crimes against humanity have attained the status of *jus cogens*, at the very least, rapes classified as crimes against humanity have attained that status. It has been noted that there is evidence of a universal trend toward *jus cogens* status for gender based abuses, particularly violence.[29]

Further relevant provisions on this aspect of the law include the 1974 Declaration on the Protection of Women During Armed Conflict. This mandates that all forms of repression and cruel and inhuman treatment of women and children committed by belligerents in the course of military operations or in occupied territories shall be considered criminal. However, this document is non-binding.

Finally, the Preamble to Hague Convention IV, repeated virtually verbatim in the 1977 Additional Protocol II, contains what is known as the "Martens Clause" which is an established principle of international humanitarian law.[30] This clause envisages that acts committed in wartime fall under the umbrella of protection of rights embodied in the universal concepts of common decency and public morality. The clause applies to belligerents and civilians, affording protection against gross abuses not explicitly prohibited including surely certain sexual assault crimes such as forced pregnancy.

Prior to most of the decisions of the ICTY, hopes were voiced that the court would decide that every instance of sexual assault committed during the course of the war is a violation of the laws or customs of war.[31] If such decisions were taken, they would make a tremendous impact in extending, through international jurisprudence, protection to women both as combatants and as civilians. This is what the ICTY has done.

Given that rape is only explicitly mentioned in Article 5 of the tribunal's Statute, it was commented that the form of the Indictments would be critical to the evolution of normative principles on rape and sexual violence.[32]

In *Gagovic and others (Foca)*, a case involving gross sexual violence, on facts involving rapes and sexual assaults, the accused were indicted pursuant to Articles 2, 3 and 4, as well as Article 5, by referring to those crimes as torture and inhuman treatment; wilfully causing great suffering; outrages upon personal

---

[28] See KD Askin, 1997, p 249; C Chinkin, 1994.
[29] KD Askin, above note 10at p 242.
[30] KD Askin, above note 10.
[31] KD Askin, above note 10 at p 337.
[32] H Charlesworth and C Chinkin, 2000.

dignity; torture as a crime against humanity; persecution on political, racial and religious grounds; enslavement, and rape as explicitly provided for under Article 5(g).[33]

This Indictment sets out the crime of *"forced sexual penetration of a person"* by the accused or by a third person under the control of the accused. This formulation has been praised as allowing consideration of the elements of the offence without importing understandings of rape from any particular municipal legal system and for emphasising the elements of violence and force. The terminology is broad enough to cover any form of penetration and to include male victims by focusing on the conduct of the accused. Arguably, this form of wording removes fixation on rape by replacing it with a recognition of sexually violent conduct.[34]

In *Prosecutor v Furundzija*, 10 December 1998,[35] the issue of rape as a distinct crime was dealt with in the tribunal's judgement. In explicitly setting out the history of rape as specifically prohibited by treaty and in armed conflict under customary international law, the court presented its jurisprudence in a way which seriously took women as human beings. Further, the definition of rape for the purposes of Articles 2 to 5 was developed.[36] The court emphasised that the

> prohibition embraces all serious abuses of a sexual nature inflicted upon the physical and moral integrity of a person by means of coercion, threat of force or intimidation in a way that is degrading and humiliating for the victim's dignity.[37]

The tribunal affirmed that rape can be a crime distinct from torture in that rape may *"amount to a grave breach of the Geneva Conventions"*, a violation of the laws or customs of war and is contrary to customary international law.

Through this process, it has been commented that an international legal understanding of the meaning and jurisdictional basis for rape and sexual assault has been emerging.[38] Such meaning and basis that has been emerging accords women dignity and respect and recognition as humans with their own agency, rather than as passive helpless victims, or as tarnished "goods" with shame.

---

[33] *Gagovic and Others (Foca) Indictment,* 26 June 1996, IT-96-23-I.
[34] See P Viseur-Sellers (adviser to the prosecutor's office of the ICTY on gender issues) in: P Viseur Sellers "The ad hoc tribunals' response to gender based crimes" paper prepared for UN Expert Group meeting on Gender-based Persecution, Toronto Canada Nov 1997 cited in H Charlesworth and C Chinkin, 2000.
[35] *Prosecutor v Anton Furundzija* 10 December 1998, ICTY-95-17/1-T 10.
[36] Ibid., para 165–9.
[37] Ibid., para 174 to 186.
[38] H Charlesworth and C Chinkin, 2000, p 324.

*Grave Breaches*

Further illustration of this developing jurisprudence can be seen in the way that the ICTY has interpreted grave breaches.

Prior to the establishment and judgments of the tribunal, the position as to whether rape constituted a grave breach of the Geneva Conventions was unclear. The resolution of this question is important because grave breaches are subject to universal jurisdiction exercisable in national courts and are regarded as the most significant violations of international humanitarian law.

Under the fourth Geneva Convention, the only persons against whom a grave breach can be committed are those who are *"in the hands of a Party to the conflict or Occupying Power of which they are not nationals"* (Article 4). For grave breaches to exist, the conflict must therefore be international in nature.[39] Grave breaches must be perpetrated against persons or property defined as "protected" by any of the four Geneva Conventions.

Grave breaches are defined in Art 147 of the Geneva Convention (of which Article 2 of the ICTY is a replica). They are defined to include, amongst other things, torture; inhuman treatment; wilfully causing great suffering or serious injury to body or health. It has been argued persuasively that rape and sexual violence falls within the definition without needing to reach the higher standard required to show it was a crime against humanity which explicitly includes rape in its various definitions.[40] Further support for the argument that rape is a grave breach is given by the UN's description of rape as an extremely grave violation of international humanitarian law.[41] However, failure to specify rape explicitly within the definition has been described in critical terms as *"illuminating"*.[42]

The point has also been made that although the 1977 Additional Protocol I to the Geneva Conventions includes amongst its list of grave breaches *"degrading practices involving outrages on personal dignity based on racial discrimination"*, it fails to refer to sex discrimination.[43]

Article 2 (b) of the ICTY's Statute lists "inhuman treatment" as a grave breach. Article 5 (g) and (i) of the Statute lists rape and *"other* inhumane acts" as crimes against humanity.[44] By implication, it is argued that the drafters considered rape to be inhuman or inhumane treatment.[45]

---

[39] Common Art 3 of the four Geneva Conventions applies to situations involving internal armed conflicts – see T Meron, 1993, for a discussion on its applicability.

[40] See T Meron, 1993, p 426–7; C Chinkin, 1994, and KD Askin, 1997, p 310ff; H Charlesworth and C Chinkin, 2000, p 335–6.

[41] UN Doc E/CN.4/1994/5 paras 16–17 of 30 June 1993 "Rape and abuse of women in the territory of the former Yugoslavia: Report of the Secretary-General".

[42] CN Niarchos, 1995, page 675.

[43] See H Charlesworth and C Chinkin, 2000, reference to Art 85(3) of Protocol I 1977.

[44] Emphasis added.

[45] For further analysis of this point and any possible arguments trying to distinguish inhuman treatment and inhumane acts, see KD Askin, 1997, p 313 ff.

Another way to include rape within the definition of a grave breach is by interpreting rape as torture. Torture is defined in Article 1 of the Convention Against Torture as:

> ...any act by which severe pain or suffering, whether physical or mental, is intentionally inflicted on a person for such purposes as...intimidating or coercing him or a third person, or for any reason based on discrimination of any kind, when such pain or suffering is inflicted by or at the instigation of or with the consent or acquiescence of a public official or other person acting in an official capacity.[46]

No exceptions are allowed (for example, because of the extremities of war or orders from superiors). Rape often meets these required elements of torture and international humanitarian law arguably recognises custodial rape as torture and inhuman treatment. As the following argument shows, there can be little doubt that, as a matter of logic, rape can constitute torture:

> It would be considered torturous to beat a confession out of a person. It would be considered torturous to break a person's fingers to extract information. It would be considered torturous to force a person to go without food or sleep for extended periods of time in order to interrogate them. It would be considered torturous to squeeze a man's testicles with pliers in order to terrify him. It would be considered torturous to apply electric shock to a man's genitals in order to obtain information. It should be considered torturous to sexually assault a person for any reason, including in order to intimidate or humiliate them.[47]

Prior to the relevant ICTY cases, The Inter-American Commission of Human Rights in *Mejia Egocheaga* v *Peru* (1996) and the European Court of Human Rights in *Aydin v Turkey* (1997) confirmed that rape can constitute torture.[48]

As shown in the case law analysis which follows, the ICTY has positively developed the jurisprudence in this area and rape is clearly now a grave breach constituting torture, inhuman treatment and wilfully causing great suffering or serious injury to body or health.

In *Prosecutor v Delalic* 16 November 1998, the tribunal extensively examined whether rape could constitute a grave breach of the Geneva Convention.[49] It confirmed that for rape to be torture, it must meet each of the elements of the offence as set out in the Torture Convention.[50] Those elements

---

[46] "Convention Against Torture and Other Cruel, Inhuman or Degrading Treatment or Punishment" 23 ILM 1027 (Dec 10 1984 as modified 24 ILM 535 (1985). Yugoslavia was a party to the Convention and torture is in any event a crime under customary international law.

[47] KD Askin, 1997, p 318.

[48] (1996) 1 Butterworths Human Rights Cases 229 and (1997) 3 Butterworths Human Rights Cases 300 respectively, both cited in *Prosecutor v Delalic and others* 16 November 1998 (see discussion and analysis below). See also analysis by H Charlesworth and C Chinkin, 2000, p 330–1.

[49] *Prosecutor v Delalic and Others*, Judgment 16 November 1998, IT-96-21-T.

[50] Ibid., para 480.

were stated to be broader than, and to include, the definition in the 1975 Declaration of the UN General Assembly and in the 1985 Inter-American Convention and thus reflects a consensus representative of customary international law. The tribunal cited the cases of *Mejia* and *Aydin*.[51] The UN Special Rapporteur on Torture was also cited. In an oral introduction to the 1992 Report to the Commission on Human Rights, the Special Rapporteur stated that:

> Since it was clear that rape or other forms of sexual assault against women in detention were a particularly ignominious violation of the inherent dignity and the right to physical integrity of the human being, they accordingly constituted an act of torture.[52]

The tribunal set out the elements of torture required for the purposes of applying Articles 2 and 3 of its Statute as follows:

(i)  there must be an act or omission that causes severe pain or suffering, whether mental or physical,

(ii)  which is inflicted intentionally,

(iii)  and for such purposes as obtaining information or a confession from the victim, or a third person, punishing the victim for an act he or she or a third person has committed or is suspected of having committed, intimidating or coercing the victim or a third person, or for any reason based on discrimination of any kind,

(iv)  and such act or omission being committed by, or at the instigation of, or with the consent or acquiescence of, an official or other person acting in an official capacity.[53]

Rape was described as "*a despicable act which strikes at the very core of human dignity and physical integrity*".[54] The tribunal further elaborated that it would be difficult to envisage circumstances where rape falling within the fourth element could be considered occurring for a purpose that does not in some way involve the third element. Therefore whenever rape and other forms of sexual violence meet these criteria, they are classified as torture.[55]

This case and test was followed in *Prosecutor v Furundzija* 10 December 1998. The tribunal expressed the view that international case law and various UN and European bodies' declarations, statements and reports:

---

[51] See above note 47.

[52] Cited in the *Delalic* judgment, as note 48 at para 491.

[53] Ibid., para 494.

[54] Ibid., para 495.

[55] Ibid., para 496.

...evince a momentum towards addressing, through legal process, the use of rape in the course of detention and interrogation as a means of torture and, therefore, as a violation of international law.[56]

The tribunal was subsequently clarified that, although the fourth element required for torture, including rape as torture, of *official* involvement, is a requirement under the Convention Against Torture, it is not an element of the crime for the purposes of international criminal law.[57]

Further, as described above in the context of war crimes, wording used in the Indictments shows that the fear of only considering rape as a crime against humanity under Article 5 (g) of the Yugoslav Tribunal's Statute (which requires a higher standard) has not been realised.[58]

In addition to these judgments dealing explicitly with rape as torture, or other grave breaches of international law, the tribunal has also developed jurisprudence on what constitutes an international conflict: which is a necessary component for a grave breach to be committed.

In the 7 May 1997 judgment in *Prosecutor v Tadic*, the tribunal held that because the forces of the Federal Republic of Yugoslavia (FRY) army had withdrawn from Bosnia-Herzegovina after 19 May 1992, the conflict thereafter was not international in character and therefore victims could not be protected under the grave breach protection but were instead covered by Article 3 of the Geneva Conventions (which relates to internal conflicts).[59]

In an appeal in July 1999, this decision was reversed. The issue was said to turn on whether the Bosnian Serbs were considered to be organs of FRY who had to have some measure of control over the Bosnian Serbs.[60] The tribunal applied the "overall control" test where the state (here the FRY) wields overall control over the group, equipping, financing, co-ordinating, providing assistance in planning operations (although not necessarily issuing instructions). On the facts, the tribunal therefore decided on appeal that there was such overall control by the FRY army of the Bosnian Serb army, meaning the conflict was international in character and therefore benefited from the grave breach provisions of Article 2 of its Statute.

*Genocide*

Rape and sexual assault crimes deliberately inflicted upon an ethnic group in an effort to cause that group's destruction, wholly or partially, physically or non-

---

[56] Ibid., para 163.
[57] *Prosecutor v Kunarac et al*, Judgment 22 February 2001, IT-96-23-T and IT-96-23/1-T; *Prosecutor v Krocka et al*, Judgment 2 November 2001, IT-98-30/1-T; *Prosecutor v Broanin*, Judgment 1 September 2004, IT-99-36-T.
[58] Concerns raised by CN Niarchos, 1995; KD Askin, 1994; C Chinkin, and H Charlesworth and C Chinkin, 2000.
[59] *Prosecutor v Dusko Tadic*, Judgment 7 May 1997, IT-94-IT.
[60] *Prosecutor v Dusko Tadic* July 1999 http//www.un.org/icty at para 96.

physically, establish genocidal rape. It has been argued that where rape is carried out on a massive and systematic basis with the intent of destroying the victims' family and community life, of cleansing an area of all other ethnicities by causing mass flight and the birth of children with the rapists' blood, it becomes genocidal.

In reviewing the indictments against Radovan Karadzic, the Bosnian Serb Political leader, and Ratko Mladic, the leader of the Bosnian Serb army, the ICTY itself invited the prosecution to broaden the scope of its characterisation to genocide suggesting that the

> ...systematic rape of women...is in some cases intended to transmit a new ethnic identity to the child. In other cases, humiliation and terror serve to dismember the group.[61]

This characterisation is further supported by the phenomenon in the conflict in the former Yugoslavia of forced detention of women first for impregnation and subsequently to prevent abortion.

*Rape as a Crime Against Humanity*

The term "crime against humanity" has been described in many statutes and documents including the Nuremberg Charter; the Tokyo Charter; Control Council Law no 10; the Secretary-General's ICTY Report; the ICTY's and the ICTR's statutes; the ILC Draft Code of Crimes Against the Peace and Security of Mankind 1996 and the International Criminal Court Statute.[62]

The exact elements of the crime vary in different Treaties and documents with the term being used inconsistently. Although there is no universal consensus of the elements required for constituting crimes against humanity, a common interpretation is in the Secretary-General's Report which states that crimes against humanity:

> refer to inhumane acts of a very serious nature...committed as part of a widespread or systematic attack against any civilian population on national, political, ethnic, racial or religious grounds.[63]

There has been a historic association between crimes against humanity and armed conflict which is continued by the ICTY Statute. However, the tribunal has now clarified that there is no need for the connection.

---

[61] Trial Chamber I Review of Indictment pursuant to Rule 61 K and M cases 11 July 1996 It-95-5-R61 and IT-95-18-R61, paras 94 and 95. The ICTR case of *Prosecutor v Akayesu*, Judgment 2 September 1998, ICTR-96-4-T found acts of sexual violence to be acts of genocide.
[62] See KD Askin, 1997, p 345 ff.
[63] Report of the Secretary-General Pursuant to Para 2 of the Security Council Resolution 808 1993 in 32 ILM at 1159.

Crimes against humanity as commonly interpreted require the offence to be committed as a *systematic* attack, against a *large number* of a particularly *protected group* of persons, who are members of the *civilian population*, and the attack must have occurred on *specifically enumerated grounds*. Identifying rape as a member of this category recognises that rape can be one of the most horrific crimes on earth when committed on political, racial or religious or national or ethnical grounds. So, while it is positive that rape was specifically listed as a crime against humanity in the Statute, the problem is that a particularly vicious sexual assault would need to be committed for a particular reason before achieving redress. An extremely arduous standard is involved in prosecuting this crime, since each and every element of the crime must be established for successful prosecution, and its elements can be prohibitive. They require proof of a specific intent based on discrimination or persecution against classes of people.

In the judgment of *Prosecutor v Tadic* 2 October 1995,[64] the tribunal confirmed that it is a settled rule of customary international law that crimes against humanity do not require a connection to international conflicts, and may not require a connection between crimes against humanity and any conflict at all (so its Statute was more limiting than it needed to be in that respect).

In the *Prosecutor v Mrksic and others* (the *Vukovar Hospital Decision*),[65] the tribunal explained that a link was required between widespread or systematic attack against a civilian population for an act to constitute a crime against humanity. However, a single act (so linked) could constitute a crime against humanity:

> Crimes against humanity are to be distinguished from war crimes against individuals. In particular, they must be widespread or demonstrate a systematic character. However, as long as there is a link with the widespread or systematic attack against a civilian population, a single act could qualify as a crime against humanity. As such, an individual committing a crime against a single victim or a limited number of victims might be recognised as guilty of a crime against humanity if his acts were part of the specific context identified above.[66]

This was confirmed in *Tadic* (May 1997) which further held that:

> A single act by a perpetrator taken within the context of a widespread or systematic attack against a civilian population entails individual responsibility and an individual perpetrator need not commit numerous offences to be held liable…The decision …in the Vukovar Hospital Decision is a recent recognition of the fact that a single act by a perpetrator can constitute a crime against humanity.[67]

---

[64] *Prosecutor v Tadic (Jurisdiction)* Trial Chamber 10 August 1995 and Appeals Chamber 2 October 1995 105 ILR 419.
[65] *Prosecutor v Mrksic and others (the Vukovar Hospital Case)* 3 April 1996, IT-95-13-R61.
[66] *Mrksic* Ibid., para 30.
[67] *Tadic* (7 May 1997), at footnote 57 above at para 649.

Thus each perpetrator of rape in the context of a mass attack can be held guilty of a crime against humanity. Further the requirement that the offences be committed in a *"systematic and organised"* fashion can be inferred from the nature of the crimes and can be satisfied by either a state policy or that of non-state forces including terrorist groups or organisations.[68]

In a judgment in Sentencing Appeals of the *Tadic* case of 26 January 2000, the tribunal had to resolve whether a crime against humanity and war crimes were of the same gravity (and consequently whether heavier penalties should apply for one than the other), the tribunal by majority decided that they were of the same gravity, although Judge Cassese dissented; arguing that crimes against humanity are more serious.[69]

## Positively Including Women as Human

Some argue that although the developments in international humanitarian and criminal law have increasingly considered the situation of women in times of conflict, the heads of jurisdiction and the constraining language of the ICTY (and the ICTR) have obscured rape and other violent crimes against women.[70] Although the ICTY has been described as showing considerable sensitivity to the situation of women, the earlier omission of rape from the formal definition of grave breaches of international humanitarian law has arguably allowed the perception that it is only where rape reaches the systematic or widespread level required for a crime against humanity that it becomes punishable as an international crime; the emphasis in genocide is on the group defined in ethnic racial or religious terms.

While these complaints are well-founded and it would have been better if the ICTY Statute had explicitly included rape and sexual violence as a grave breach, genocide and war crime, the tribunal has positively developed the jurisprudence so that rape and sexual violence can clearly now be classified under all of these categories. This has been developed through the wording of the founding Statute to the ICC which is examined later in more detail.

When the ICTY was established in 1993, there appeared to be confusion over whether rape was even a war crime. Now, not only rape but other forms of sexual violence are unequivocally recognised as grave breaches, war crimes, genocide and crimes against humanity.[71] Marginalisation continues but normative international humanitarian and criminal law is affording more attention to prohibiting and redressing gender-based and sex-based crimes than ever before.

One of the reasons given for the increasing recognition of sex crimes is the growing awareness that the harm caused by sexualised violence permeates every

---

[68] H Charlesworth and C Chinkin, 2000, p 320.
[69] *Prosecutor v Tadic* 26 January 2000, 39 ILM 635 (2000).
[70] H Charlesworth and C Chinkin, 2000, p 321.
[71] See D Koenig and KD Askin, Vol 2, 2000, p 22. See also PV Sellers' analysis of superior command responsibility for sexual violence war crimes in PV Sellers' Individual(s') Liability for Collective Sexual Violence in K Knop (ed), 2004.

level of society in that it is not only the victim but also local and global society who suffer. It is more than a little disappointing that harms against individual women, which may not always explicitly affect society around them, are not enough in themselves to cause change.[72]

For the first time, an international legal body is giving serious attention to prosecuting wartime sexual violence. The political will shown by the Yugoslav prosecutors and judges to punish gender crimes is unparalleled, affording a major process towards successful prosecution.[73]

Jurisprudence surrounding rape at international law has positively included women as subjects in their own right in the ICTY's decisions. Although this does not mean that women are treated equally (either at international or at a domestic level), it is undeniable that normative international criminal law is affording more attention to prohibiting and redressing gender-based and sex-based crimes than ever before.[74]

The development of international institutions continues and it remains to be seen how the ICC will use the ICTY judgments. It is hoped that even though the ICC is not legally bound by the ICTY's judgments, they will be taken into consideration as at the very least persuasive authority, and will certainly be taken into account in some respects as setting out customary international law, when similar cases come before the ICC.

Statements seeing rape and sexual violence as torture, inhuman treatment, wilfully causing great suffering, as a crime against humanity (as have been developed in the international legal context and in the ICTY), provide evidence of an understanding of violations of international humanitarian law and human rights that incorporate the experiences of women and try to widen the concept of the human so that it more fully includes all human beings. Further, arguments suggesting that the collapse of the conceptual boundaries between international human rights and international humanitarian law as two categories of law is good for women may be persuasive. This is because this collapse takes account of experiences that do not differentiate between international armed conflict, internal conflict and "normal" conditions and this is to women's benefit.[75]

**The International Criminal Court**[76]

The UN Diplomatic Conference of Plenipotentaries on the Establishment of an International Criminal Court adopted the Rome Statute of the International Criminal Court on 17 July 1998. The jurisdiction of the court is limited to "*the*

[72] See D Koenig and KD Askin, Vol 2, 2000, p 29.
[73] See KD Askin, 1997, p 373.
[74] D Koenig and KD Askin, Vol 2, 2000, p 29.
[75] H Charlesworth and C Chinkin, 2000, p 332.
[76] Special thanks to Professor Charles Garraway of King's College London and Martha Jean Baker, a member of the Women's Caucus, for their discussions and insights on the negotiation process at the UN Diplomatic Conference of Plenipotentaries.

*most serious crimes of concern to the international community as a whole*" and adopts a principle of complementarity requiring the court to defer to national criminal jurisdiction unless the state is unwilling or unable genuinely to carry out the investigation or prosecution.[77]

The Women's Caucus for Gender Justice in the International Criminal Court, an international NGO, was a driving force behind the inclusion of a fairly broad array of sex crimes within the jurisdiction of the court, crimes constituting war crimes and crimes against humanity including rape, sexual slavery, enforced prostitution, forced pregnancy, enforced sterilisation and other forms of sexual violence of "comparable gravity".[78]

Although there is no explicit reference to rape as a grave breach in the ICC statute, and it remains as defined in the Geneva Convention, it has been argued that Article 8(2)(b) of the ICC Statute concerning "*other serious violations of the laws and customs applicable in international armed conflict*" recognises that sexual violence is incorporated within the grave breach provisions and clearly acknowledges that sexual violence is subsumed within the grave breach provisions.[79] Further, the ICC Statute separates and breaks the link between crimes against honour and sexual violence.

For crimes against humanity, it is now explicit that there is no requirement of a link between these and armed conflict.[80] The list of crimes has been expanded to include not only rape but also sexual slavery, enforced prostitution, forced pregnancy, enforced sterilisation and any other forms of sexual violence of comparable gravity.[81]

## Conclusion

These developments suggest that the international legal system has responded well in taking women's lives into account in these areas of law. Limitations which emphasise women's sexual and reproductive identities and harms inflicted by opposing forces need to be changed. Some feminist scholars are critical that neither the law nor practice relating to armed conflict include women as agents of change or survivors, but instead continue to view them as passive victims of international affairs.[82] This is surely changing and should change further to ensure that women as individual persons in their own rights are accorded the human rights safeguards to which they are entitled as humans. Until violations of women's rights are taken as seriously as other human rights problems, they will continue to be viewed as a "social" problem and considered less serious than other human rights violations.[83]

---

[77] ICC Statute Art 17.
[78] D Koenig and KD Askin in KD Askin and D Koenig, Vol 2, 2000, p 12.
[79] D Koenig and KD Askin in KD Askin and D Koenig, Ibid.
[80] ICC Statute Art 7.
[81] ICC Statute Art 7.
[82] H Charlesworth and C Chinkin, 2000, p 334.
[83] N Kim, 1993, p 79.

In addition, the ICC's statute acknowledges the criminality of several gender-based and sex-based crimes and integrates those crimes into the court's jurisdiction.[84] This is surely a positive hope to enable women to obtain justice for crimes perpetrated on them. The ICC has the potential to therefore contribute to the creation of better lives for individual women with the possibility of contributing to freeing women to exist in lives they authentically choose to live.

---

[84] D Koenig and KD Askin in KD Askin and D Koenig, Vol 2, 2000, p 7.

# Concluding Hope

*"I sense...a new awareness afoot...a renewed respect for the moral and political legacy of universalism..."* Seyla Benhabib[1]

Feminist critiques have shed much insight into the male-based conception of the human being that has permeated Western traditional philosophy and on which conceptions of the legal subject and, correspondingly, the subject who is a rights' holder under human rights and international humanitarian law are based.

Those which seek inclusivity are convincing in their arguments, searching for an inclusive conception of all humanity. The need for universal abstraction is shown to be needed in law to enforce rights claims and to provide for universal common standards. While any view of the human being as atomistic, alone and separate from others is a gross mischaracterisation of the human condition, the value of the heuristic device of critical evaluative and imaginative thinking of the common humanity of all needs to be retained.

A social, interconnected, caring, empathetic environment will allow for a fuller realisation of human potential and permit authentic free informed choices to be made without want and preference deformation and resulting ideas of a devaluation of women's personhood. This environment will encourage such subjectivity to develop and be strengthened and then lead to fuller more fulfilled lives for all. This can happen globally.

Some may think this is highly idealistic but I disagree. The only way to change ideas of the possible is to think the impossible, dream and form ideas and mobilise those into concrete changes. This has happened throughout history and will continue to happen.

---

[1] S Benhabib "Sexual Difference and Collective Identities: The New Global Constellation" in S James and S Palmer (eds), 2002, p 156.

# Bibliography

K Abrams "Sex Wars Redux: Agency and Coercion in Feminist Legal Theory" (1995) 95 *Columbia Law Review* 304–376.

K Abrams "Ideology and Women's choices" (1990) 24 *Georgia Law Review* 761.

B Ackerman "Rooted Cosmopolitanism" (1994) 104 *Ethics* 516.

C Fred Alford *The Self in Social Theory* (New Haven and London: Yale University Press 1991).

B Allen *Rape Warfare: The Hidden Genocide in Bosnia-Herzegovina and Croatia* (Minneapolis and London: University of Minnesota Press 1996).

S Alkire "Global Citizenship and Common Values" in N Dower and J Williams *Global Citizenship: A Critical Reader* (Edinburgh: Edinburgh University Press 2002) p 169ff.

P E Andrews "Violence Against Aboriginal Women in Australia" in A K Wing (ed).

M Anthony and C E Witt (eds) *A Mind of One's Own: Feminist Essays on Reason and Objectivity* (2nd Edn, Boulder, Colorado and Oxford: Westview Press 2002).

D Archibugi and D Held (eds) *Cosmopolitan Democracy: An Agenda for a New World Order* (Oxford: Polity Press 1995).

Aristotle *The Nichomachean Ethics* (Oxford: Oxford University Press 1986).

J Arnaud and E Kingdom (eds) *Women's Rights and the Rights of Man* (Aberdeen: Aberdeen University Press 1990).

KD Askin *War Crimes Against Women* (Dordrecht: Kluwer Law International 1997)

KD Askin and D M Koenig (eds) *Women and International Human Rights Law* (Ardsley NY:Transnational Publishers Inc) Vol 1 (1999) Vol 2 (2000) Vol 3 (2001) Vol 4 (2004).

S Avineri *Hegel's Theory of the Modern State* (Cambridge: Cambridge University Press 1972).

S Avineri and A de-Shalit (eds) *Communitarianism and Individualism* (Oxford: Oxford University Press 1992).

HE Baber "Gender Conscious" (2001) 18 *Journal of Applied Philosophy* 53.

A Baier "The Need for More than Justice" in *Canadian Journal of Philosophy Supplementary Vol 13 Science Morality and Feminist Theory* (1987).

A Baier "Hume the Women's Moral Theorist?" in G Lloyd (ed) *Feminism and History of Philosophy* (Oxford: Oxford University Press 2002) p 227ff.

L Bair *The Essential Rousseau* (New York and Scarborough, Ontario: the New American Library Inc 1974).

JM Balkin "Deconstructive Practice and Legal Theory" (1987 96 *Yale Law Journal* 743.

JM Balkin "Transcendent Deconstruction, Transcendent Justice" (1994) 92 *Michigan Law Review* 1131.

JM Balkin "Being Just with Deconstruction" (1994) 3 *Social and Legal Studies* 393.

J Baker *Arguing for Equality* (New York and London: Verso 1987).

J Barnes *Aristotle* (Oxford: Oxford University Press 1982).

M Barrett and A Phillips (eds) *Destabilising Theory* (Cambridge: Polity Press 1992).

H Barnett *Sourcebook on Feminist Jurisprudence* (London: Cavendish Publishing Ltd 1997)

A Barron "Illusions of 'I': Citizenship and the Politics of Identity" in A Norrie (ed) *Closure or Critique* (Edinburgh: Edinburgh University Press 1993) p 80–100.

A Barron "Spectacular Jurisprudence" (2000) 20 *Oxford Journal of Legal Studies* 301–315.
A Barron "Feminism, Aestheticism and the Limits of Law" (2000) 8 *Feminist Legal Studies* 275.
B Barry *The Liberal Theory of Justice* (London: Oxford University Press 1973).
B Barry *Theories of Justice* (London: Harvester Wheatsheaf 1989).
B Barry *Justice As Impartiality* (Oxford: Clarendon Press 1995).
B Barry *Culture and Equality* (Cambridge: Polity Press 2001).
I Barwell "Towards A Defence of Objectivity" in K Lennon and M Whitford (eds) *Knowing the Difference* (New York and London: Routledge 1994).
Z Bauman *Freedom* (Milton Keynes: Open University Press 1988).
U Beck and E Beck-Gernsheim *The Normal Chaos of Love* (Cambridge Polity Press 1995)
H Bedau (ed) *Justice and Equality* (Englewood Cliffs, New Jersey: Prentice-Hall 1971).
R Beiner and W J Booth *Kant and Political Philosophy The Contemporary Legacy* (New Haven and London: Yale University Press 1993).
S Benhabib *Situating the Self* (Cambridge: Polity Press 1992).
S Benhabib "Epistemologies of Postmodernism: A Rejoinder to Jean-Francois Lyotard" in L Nicholson (ed) Feminism/Postmodernism (New York and London: Routledge 1990).
S Benhabib "On Hegel, Women and Irony" in G Lloyd (ed) *Feminism and History of Philosophy* (Oxford: OUP 2002) p 281ff.
S Benhabib "Sexual Difference and Collective Identities: The New Global Constellation" in S James and S Palmer (eds) *Visible Women* (Oxford and Portland Oregon: Hart Publishing 2002).
S Benhabib, J Butler, D Cornell and N Fraser *Feminist Contentions* (New York and London: Routledge 1995).
S Benhabib and D Cornell *Feminism as Critique* (Oxford: Polity Press 1987).
S Benhabib and F Dallmayr (eds) *The Discourse Ethics Controversy* (Cambridge MIT Press 1990).
SI Benn A *Theory of Freedom* (Cambridge: Cambridge University Press 1988).
I Berlin "Two Concepts of Liberty" in *Four Essays on Liberty* (Oxford: Oxford University Press 1969).
A Bernstein "Foreword: Still Unfinished, Ever Unfinished" (2000) 75 *Chicago-Kent Law Review* 641.
B Bettelheim *The Informed Heart: Autonomy in a Mass Age* (Glencoe Ill: Press Press 1960).
B Bix *Jurisprudence Theory and Context* (2nd Edn London: Sweet & Maxwell 1999).
L Blum "Gilligan and Kohlberg: Implications for Moral Theory" (1988) *Ethics* 98.
B Bosanquet *The Philosophical Theory of the State* (London: Macmillan 1965).
D Boucher and P Kelly (eds) *The Social Contract from Hobbes to Rawls* (New York and London: Routledge 1994).
J Bridgeman "Book Review: Nicola Lacey, Unspeakable Subjects" (1999) 62 Modern Law Review 958.
J Bridgeman and S Millns (eds) *Feminist Perspectives on Law: Law's Engagement with the Female Body* (London: Sweet & Maxwell 1998).
L Brill "MacKinnon and Equality: Is Dominance really Different?" (1993) 15 *UALR Law Journal* 261.
W Brown *States of Injury: Power and Freedom in Late Modernity* (Princeton: Princeton University Press 1995).
A Buchanan "Assessing the Communitarian Critique of Liberalism" (1989) 99 *Ethics* 852–882.
C Bunch "Women's Rights As Human Rights: Toward a Re-Vision of Human Rights" (1990) 12 *Human Rights Quarterly* 486.

C Bunch *Passionate Politics* (London: St Martin's Press 1987).

C Bunch "Organizing For Women's Human Rights Globally" in J Kerr (ed) *Ours By Right: Women's Rights as Human Rights* (London: Zed Books Ltd 1993) p 141–149.

N Burrows "International Law and Human Rights: the Case of Women's Rights" in T Campbell et al (eds) *Human Rights: From Rhetoric to Reality* (Oxford: Basil Blackwell 1986) p 80–98.

J Butler *Gender Trouble: feminism and the subversion of identity* (New York and London: Routledge 1990).

J Butler "Gender Trouble, Feminist Theory, and Psychoanalytic Discourse" in L Nicholson (ed) *Feminism/Postmodernism* (New York and London: Routledge 1990).

J Butler and J Scott (eds) *Feminists Theorise the Political* (New York and London: Routledge 1992).

M Butler "Early Liberal Roots of Feminism: John Locke and the Attack on Patriarchy" in ML Shanley and C Pateman (eds) *Feminist Interpretations and Political Theory* (Cambridge: Polity Press 1991).

P A Cain "Feminism and the Limits of Equality" (1990) 24 *Georgia Law Rev* 803.

T Campbell *Justice* (2$^{nd}$ Edn Basingstone: Macmillan 2000).

T Campbell, D Goldberg et al (eds) *Human Rights: From Rhetoric to Reality* (Oxford: Basil Blackwell 1986).

T Campbell "Realizing Human Rights" in T Campbell et al (eds) *Human Rights: From Rhetoric to Reality* (Oxford: Basil Blackwell 1986) p 1–14.

C Card "Review Essay: Women's Voices and Ethical Ideals: Must We Mean What We Say?" (1988) *Ethics* 125.

M Carmody "Sexual Ethics and Violence Protection" (2003) 12 *Social and Legal Studies* 199.

H Charlesworth "What Are "Women's International Human Rights"?" in R J Cook (ed) *Human Rights of Women* (Philadelphia: University of Pennsylvania Press 1994) p 58ff.

H Charlesworth, C Chinkin and S Wright "Feminist Approaches to International Law" (1991) 85 *American Journal of International Law* 613.

H Charlesworth and C Chinkin *The Boundaries of International Law: a feminist analysis* (Manchester: Manchester University Press 2000).

J Charvet *Feminism* (London: Dent 1982).

C Chinkin "Rape and Sexual Abuse of Women in International Law" (1994) 5 *European Journal of International Law* 326.

J Christman (ed) *The Inner Citadel: essays on individual autonomy* (Oxford: Oxford University Press 1989).

N Chodorow *The Reproduction of Mothering: psychoanalysis and the sociology of gender* (Berkeley, Calif: University of California Press 1978).

G Clement *Care, Autonomy and Justice: feminism and the ethic of care* (Oxford: Westview Press 1996).

D Cockburn (ed) *Human Beings* (The Royal Institute of Philosophy supplement; 29: Cambridge University Press 1991).

M Cohen *Ronald Dworkin and Contemporary Jurisprudence* (Totowa, NJ: Rowman and Allanheld 1983).

GA Cohen "Where the Action is: On the Site of Distributive Justice" (1997) 3 *Philosophy and Public Affairs* 26.

P Collins *Black Feminist Thought: Knowledge, Consciousness and the Politics of Empowerment.* (2$^{nd}$ Edn: New York and London: Routledge 1991).

R Colker "Feminism, Sexuality and Authenticity" in M Fineman and N Thomadsen eds *At the Boundaries of Law: Feminism and Legal Theory* (New York and London: Routledge 1991).

J Conaghan " Reassessing the Feminist Theoretical Project in Law" (2000) 27 *Journal of Law and Society* 351.

R J Cook (ed) *Human Rights of Women* (Philadelphia: University of Pennsylvania Press 1994).

R Coomaraswamy "Reinventing International Law: Women's Rights as Human Rights in the International Community" in P Van Ness (ed) *Debating Human Rights: Critical Essays from the United States and Asia* (London: Routledge 1999) 167–183.

R Coomaraswamy "To Bellow Like a Cow: Women, Ethnicity, and the Discourse of Rights" in R J Cook (ed) *Human Rights of Women* (Philadelphia: University of Pennsylvania Press 1994) p 39ff.

D Cooper "And you can't find me nowhere" Relocating Identity and Structure within equality jurisprudence (2000) 27 *Journal of Law and Society* 249.

R Copelan "Intimate Terror: Understanding Domestic Violence as Torture" in R J Cook (ed) *Human Rights of Women* (Philadelphia: University of Pennsylvania Press 1994) p 116ff.

D Cornell "Institutionalization of meaning: Recollective imagination and the potential for transformative legal interpretation" (1988) 136 *University of Pennsylvania Law Review* 1135.

D Cornell "The Doubly Prized World: Myth, Allegory and the Feminine" (1990) 75 *Cornell L Rev* 644.

D Cornell "Sexual Difference, the Feminine, and Equivalency: A Critique of MacKinnon's Towards a Feminist Theory of the State" (1991) 100 *Yale Law Journal* 2247.

D Cornell *Beyond Accommodation: ethical feminism, deconstruction and the law* (New York and London: Routledge 1991).

D Cornell *The Philosophy of the Limit* (New York and London: Routledge 1992).

D Cornell *The Imaginary Domain* (New York and London: Routledge 1995).

D Cornell *At the Heart of Freedom: Feminism Sex and Equality* (Princeton, New Jersey: Princeton University Press 1998).

D Cornell, M Rosenfeld and D Carlson (eds) *Hegel and Legal Theory* (London: Routledge 1991).

R Cotterrell *The Politics of Jurisprudence: A Critical Introduction to Legal Philosophy* (London and Edinburgh: Butterworths 1989).

R Cover "Foreword: Nomos and Narrative" (1983) 97 *Harvard Law Review* 4.

K Crenshaw "Race, Reform and Retrenchment: Transformation and legitimation in Anti-Discrimination law" (1988) 101 *Harvard Law Review* 331.

A Dally *Inventing Motherhood: the consequences of an ideal* (London: Burnett Books Ltd 1982)

C Dalton "Where we stand" (1988) 3 *Berkeley Womans LJ* 1.

N Daniels (ed) *Reading Rawls: Critical Studies on Rawls' "A Theory of Justice"* (Oxford: Basil Blackwell 1975).

M Davies "Feminist Appropriations: Law, Property and Personality" (1994) 3 *Social and Legal Studies* 365–391.

M Davies "Taking the Inside Out: sex and gender in the legal subject" in N Naffine and R Owens (eds) *Sexing the Subject of Law* (London: Sweet & Maxwell 1997).

S de Beauvoir *The Second Sex* (London: Jonathan Cape 1953, Vintage 1997).

C Delphy "Feminism at a Standstill?" (2000) 4 *New Left Review* .

M Desai "From Vienna to Beijing: Women's Human Rights Activism and the Human Rights Community" in P Van Ness (ed) *Debating Human Rights: Critical Essays from the United States and Asia* (London: Routledge 1999) 184–196.

I Dilman "Sartre and Our Identity As Individuals" in D Cockburn (ed) *Human Beings* (The Royal Institute of Philosophy supplement; 29: Cambridge University Press 1991).

Y Dinstein "International Criminal Law" (1975) 5 *Israel Y B Hum Rts* 55.

C Di Stefano "Dilemmas of Difference: Feminism, Modernity, and Postmodernism" in L Nicholson (ed) *Feminism/Postmodernism* (New York and London: Routledge 1990).

M Dixon and R McCorquodale *Cases and Materials on International Law* (4ᵗʰ Edition, Oxford: Clarendon Press 2003).

C Douzinas on "Identity, Recognition, Rights or What Can Hegel Teach Us About Human Rights" (2002) 29 *Journal of Law and Society* 379–405.

N Dower "Global Citizenship: Yes or No?" in N Dower and J Williams *Global Citizenship: A Critical Reader* (Edinburgh: Edinburgh University Press 2002) p 30ff.

N Dower "Global Ethics and Global Citizenship" in N Dower and J Williams *Global Citizenship: A Critical Reader* (Edinburgh: Edinburgh University Press 2002) p 146ff.

N Dower and J Williams *Global Citizenship: A Critical Reader* (Edinburgh: Edinburgh University Press 2002).

M Drakopoulou "The Ethic of Care, Female Subjectivity and Feminist Legal Scholarship" (2000) 8 *Feminist Legal Studies* 199–226.

E du Bois et al (conversants) "Feminist Discourse, Moral Values, and the Law – A Conversation" (The 1984 James McCormick Mitchell Lecture) (1985) 34 *Buffalo Law Review* 11.

T Dunne and N I Wheeler (eds) *Human Rights in Global Politics* (Cambridge: Cambridge University Press 1999).

A Dworkin *Right Wing Women: The politics of domesticated females* (London: The Women's Press 1983).

G Dworkin *The Theory and Practice of Autonomy* (Cambridge: Cambridge University Press 1988).

R Dworkin *Taking Rights Seriously* (London: Duckworth 1977).

R Dworkin *A Matter of Principle* (Cambridge Mass.: Harvard University Press 1985).

R Dworkin *Law's Empire* (London: Fontana Press 1986).

R Dworkin *Life's Dominion: an argument about abortion, euthanasia, and individual freedom* (New York: Vintage Books 1994).

R Dworkin *Sovereign Virtue* (London: Harvard University Press 2000)

Z Eisenstein *The Radical Future of Liberal Feminism* (New York: Longman 1981).

Z Eisenstein *Feminism and Sexual Equality* (New York: Monthly Review Press 1984).

Z Eisenstein "Elizabeth Cady Stanton: Radical Feminist Analysis and Liberal Feminist Strategy" in A Phillips (ed) *Feminism and Equality* ([Oxford: Basil Blackwell 1987).

J Elshtain (ed) *The Family in Political Thought 1982* (Brighton: Harvester 1982).

K Engle "International Human Rights and Feminism" (1997) 13 *Michigan Journal of International Law* 317.

M Evans *Introducing Contemporary Feminist Thought.* (Cambridge: Polity Press, 1997).

T Evans (ed) *Human Rights: Fifty Years On: A Reappraisal* (Manchester: Manchester University Press 1998).

R Falk *Law In An Emerging Global Village: A Post-Westphalian Perspective* (Ardsley, New York: Transnational Publishers Inc 1998).

R Falk "An Emergent Matrix of Citizenship: Complex, Uneven, and Fluid" in N Dower and J Williams (eds) *Global Citizenship: A Critical Reader* (Edinburgh: Edinburgh University Press 2002) p 15ff.

M Fineman and N Thomadsen (eds) *At the Boundaries of Law: Feminism and Legal Theory* (New York and London: Routledge 1991).

S Firestone *The Dialectic of Sex: the case for feminist revolution* (New York: Bantam Books 1971).

J Fishkin *Justice, Equal Opportunity and the Family* (New Haven and London: Yale University Press 1983).

O Flanagan and K Jackson "Justice, Care and Gender" (1987) 97 *Ethics* 622–37.

J Flax "Postmodernism and Gender Relations in Feminist Theory" in L Nicholson (ed) *Feminism/Postmodernism* (New York and London: Routledge 1990).

M Forsyth and M Keens-Soper *The Political Classics: A Guide to the Essential Texts from Plato to Rousseau* (Oxford: Oxford University Press 1988).

T Franck *Fairness in International Law and Institutions* (Oxford: Clarendon Press 1995).

T Franck *The Empowered Self* (Oxford: Oxford University Press 1999).

E Frazer, J Hornsby and S Lovibond *Ethics: A Feminist Reader* (London: Blackwell 1992).

E Frazer and N Lacey *The Politics of the Community: A feminist critique of the liberal-communitarian debate.* (Hemel Hempstead: Harvester 1993).

S Fredman *Women and the Law* (Oxford: Clarendon Press 1997).

S Fredman in C Gearty and A Tomkins (eds) *Understanding Human Rights* (London: Mansell 1996).

M Freeman "The Philosophical Foundations of Human Rights" (1994) 16 *Human Rights Quarterly* 491.

M Freeman (ed) *Lloyd's Introduction to Jurisprudence* (7th Edn London: Sweet & Maxwell 2001).

M Fricker and J Hornsby (eds) *The Cambridge Companion to Feminism in Philosophy* (Cambridge: Cambridge University Press 2000).

M Fricker "Pluralism without Postmodernism" in M Fricker and J Hornsby (eds) *The Cambridge Companion to Feminism in Philosophy* (Cambridge: Cambridge University Press 2000).

B Friedan *The Feminine Mystique* (London: Penguin 1963).

M Friedman "Beyond Caring: the Demoralisation of Gender" in *Canadian Journal of Philosophy Supplementary Vol 13 Science Morality and Feminist Theory* (1987) p 87ff.

M Friedman "Feminism and Modern Friendship Dislocating the Community" in S Avineri and A de-Shalit (eds) *Communitarianism and Individualism* (Oxford: Oxford University Press 1992).

M Friedman "Feminism in Ethics: Conceptions of Autonomy" in M Fricker and J Hornsby (eds) *The Cambridge Companion to Feminism in Philosophy* (Cambridge: Cambridge University Press 2000) p 205–224.

CJ Friedrich (ed) *Nomos IV Liberty* (New York: Atherton Press 1962).

M J Frug *Postmodern Legal Feminism* (New York and London: Routledge 1992).

F Fukuyama *The End of History and the Last Man* (London: Penguin 1992).

J Gardam "A Feminist Analysis of Certain Aspects of International Humanitarian Law" (1992) 12 *Australian Yearbook of International Law* 265.

J Gardam "Women and the Law of Armed Conflict: Why the Silence?" (1997) 46 *International and Comparative Law Quarterly (ICLQ)* 55.

J Gardam and M Jarvis *Women, Armed Conflict and International Law* (The Hague, London and Boston: Kluwer Law International 2001)

M Gatens *Feminism and Philosophy: perspectives on difference and equality* (Cambridge: Polity Press 1991).

M Gatens "Power, Bodies and Difference" in M Barrett and A Phillips (eds) *Destabilising Theory* (Cambridge: Polity Press 1992).

M Gatens *Imaginary Bodies: Ethics, Power and Corporeality* (New York and London: Routledge 1996).

M Gatens "'The Oppressed State of My Sex' Wollstonecraft on Reason, Feeling and Equality" in M L Shanley and C Pateman (eds) *Feminist Interpretations and Political Theory* (Cambridge: Polity Press 1991).

M Gatens "The Politics of "Presence" and "Difference": Working Through Spinoza and Eliot" in S James and S Palmer (eds) *Visible Women* (Oxford and Portland Oregon: Hart Publishing 2002).

GF Gaus *The Modern Liberal Theory of Man* (London: Croom Helm 1983).

C Gearty and A Tomkins (eds) *Understanding Human Rights* (London: Mansell 1996).

S Gibson "Continental Drift" (1990) 1 *Law and Critique* 173–200.

S Gibson "The Discourse of Sex/War: Thoughts on Catharine MacKinnon's 1993 Oxford Amnesty Lecture" (1993) 3 *Feminist Legal Studies* 179–188.

P Gilbert "New Issues Toleration or Autonomy" (2000) 17 *Journal of Applied Philosophy* 299.

C Gilligan *In a Different Voice: psychological theory and women's development* London: Harvard University Press 1982).

P Goodrich "Barron's Complaint: A Response to "Feminism, Aestheticism and the Limits of Law" (2001) 9 *Feminist Legal Studies* 149–170.

K Graham (ed) *Contemporary Political Philosophy* (Cambridge: Cambridge University Press 1982).

J Gray "On Negative and Positive Liberty" in J Gray *Liberalisms: Essays in Political Philosophy*.

J Gray *Liberalisms: Essays in Political Philosophy* (Milton Keynes: Open University Press 1986).

J E Grbich "Feminist Jurisprudence as Women's Studies in Australian Dialogues" in J Arnaud and E Kingdom (eds) *Women's Rights and the Rights of Man* (Aberdeen: Aberdeen University Press 1990).

J E Grbich "The Body in Legal Theory" in M Fineman and N Thomadsen (eds) *At the Boundaries of Law: Feminism and Legal Theory* (New York and London: Routledge 1991).

T H Green *Lectures on the principles of political obligation* (London: Longmans, Green 1941).

D Greenberg and T Tobiason "The New Legal Puritanism of Catharine MacKinnon" (1993) 54 *Ohio State Law Journal* 1375.

M Griffiths *Feminisms and the Self: the web of identity* (New York and London: Routledge 1995).

E Gross "What is Feminist Theory" in C Pateman and E Gross (eds) *Feminist Challenges: social and political theory* (London: Allen and Unwin 1986).

S Guest *Ronald Dworkin* (2nd Edn Edinburgh: Edinburgh University Press 1997)

A Gutmann *Multiculturalism and the Politics of Recognition* (Princeton, NJ: Princeton University Press 1992).

A Gutmann *Liberal Equality* (Cambridge: Cambridge University Press 1980).

A Harris "Race and Essentialism in Feminist Legal Theory (1990) 42 *Stanford Law Review* 581.

A Harris "Building Theory, Building Community" (1999) 8 *Social and Legal Studies* 313.

JW Harris "Who Owns My Body?" (1996) 16 *Oxford Journal of Legal Studies* 55.

N Hartsock "Rethinking Modernism, Minorty vs Majority theories" (1987) *Cultural Critique* 187–206.

S Haseler *The Super Rich: The Unjust new world of global capitalism* (Hampshire: Macmillan 2000).

GW Hegel *Phenomenology of Spirit* (A V Miller trans Oxford: Oxford University Press 1977).

D Held "The Changing Contours of Political Community: Rethinking Democracy in the Context of Globalisation" in B Holden (ed) *Global Democracy: Key Debates* (New York and London: Routledge 2000) p 18 ff.

V Held *Feminist Morality* (Chicago: University of Chicago Press 1993).

T Heller, M Sosna and DE Wllberg (eds) *Reconstructing Individualism : autonomy, individuality, and the self in Western Thought* (Stanford, Calif: Stanford University Press 1986).

B Herman "Could it be worth thinking about Kant on Sex and Marriage?" in L Anthony and C Witt (eds) *A Mind of One's Own: Feminist Essays on Reason and Objectivity* (2nd Edn, Boulder, Colorado and Oxford: Westview Press 2002).

T Hobbes *Leviathan* (1651, reprint of original, M Oakeshott edn Oxford: Basil Blackwell 1960).

LT Hobhouse *Liberalism* (New York and Oxford: Oxford University Press 1964).

B Holden (ed) *Global Democracy: Key Debates* (New York and London: Routledge 2000).

T Honderich (ed) *The Oxford Companion to Philosophy* (Oxford: Oxford University Press 1995) (extracts).

b hooks "Theory as Liberatory Practice" (1991) 4 *Yale Journal of Law and Feminism* 1.

J Horder (ed) *Oxford Essays in Jurisprudence* (Oxford: Oxford University Press 4th Edn 2000).

A Hunt (ed) *Reading Dworkin Critically* (New York: Oxford, Berg 1992).

K Hutchings "Feminism and Global Citizenship" in N Dower and J Williams *Global Citizenship: A Critical Reader* (Edinburgh: Edinburgh University Press 2002).

K Hutchings *Hegel and Feminist Theory* (Cambridge: Polity Press 2003).

E Jackson "Catharine MacKinnon and Feminist Jurisprudence A Critical Appraisal" (1992) 19 *Journal of Law and Society* 195.

E Jackson "Abortion, Autonomy and Prenatal Diagnosis" (2000) 9 *Social and Legal Studies* 467–494.

E Jackson and N Lacey "Introducing Feminist Legal Theory" in J Penner, D Schiff and R Nobles *Jurisprudence and Legal Theory: Commentary and Materials* (London: Butterworths LexisNexis 2002).

A Jaggar *Feminist Politics and Human Nature.* (Totowa, New Jersey: Rowman and Allanheld, 1983).

A Jaggar "Feminist Ethics" in H LaFolette (ed) *The Blackwell Guide to Ethical Theory* (Oxford: Blackwell 2000).

A Jaggar "Moral Justification" in M Fricker and J Hornsby (eds) *The Cambridge Companion to Feminism in Philosophy* (Cambridge: Cambridge University Press 2000) at 225–244.

A Jaggar "Sexual Difference and Sexual Equality" in D Rhode (ed) *Theoretical Perspectives on Sexual Difference* (New Haven and London: Yale University Press 1990).

S James "Freedom and the Imaginary" in S James and S Palmer (eds) *Visible Women* (Oxford and Portland Oregon: Hart Publishing 2002).

S James and S Palmer (eds) *Visible Women* (Oxford and Portland Oregon: Hart Publishing 2002).

I Kant *Fundamental Principles of the Metaphysic of Morals* (New York: Prometheus Books 1988).

R Kapur "The Tragedy of Victimization Rhetoric: Resurrecting the 'Native' Subject in International/Post-Colonial Feminist Legal Politics" (2002) 5 *Harvard Human Rights Journal* 1.

K Keywood "My Body and Other Stories" (2000) 9 *Social and Legal Studies* 295.

G Kinsman, Jeffrey Weeks "Review: The Lesser evil and the greater good" (1996) 5 *Social and Legal Studies* 123–127.

E Feder Kittay and D Meyers (eds) *Women and Moral Theory* (Totowa, NJ: Rowman and Littlefield 1987).

F Kerr "Getting the Subject back into the World: Heidegger's Version" in D Cockburn (ed) *Human Beings* (The Royal Institute of Philosophy supplement; 29: Cambridge University Press 1991).

J Kerr (ed) *Ours By Right: Women's Rights as Human Rights* (London: Zed Books Ltd 1993).

V Kerruish "Dworkin's Dutiful Daughter" in A Hunt (ed) *Reading Dworkin Critically* (New York: Oxford, Berg 1992).

N Kim "Toward a Feminist Theory of Human Rights: Straddling The Fence Between Western Imperialism and Uncritical Absolutism" (1993) 25 *Columbia Human Rights Law Review* 49.

DL Kirp, MG Yudof and MS Franks *Gender and Justice* (Chicago: University of Chicago Press 1985).

K Knop "Why Rethinking the Sovereign State is important for Women's Human Rights Law" in R J Cook (ed) *Human Rights of Women* (Philadelphia: University of Pennsylvania Press 1994) p 153ff.

K Knop (ed) *Gender and Human Rights* (Oxford: Oxford University Press 2004)

D Koenig and KD Askin "International Criminal Law and the International Criminal Court Statute: Crimes Against Women" in KD Askin and D M Koenig (eds) *Women and International Human Rights Law* (Ardsley NY:Transnational Publishers Inc) Vol 2 (2000).

M Kramer *The Quality of Freedom* (Oxford: Oxford University Press 2003)

H Kung "A Global Ethic for a new Global Order" in N Dower and J Williams *Global Citizenship: A Critical Reader* (Edinburgh: Edinburgh University Press 2002) p 133ff.

W Kymlicka *Liberalism Community and Culture* (Oxford: Clarendon Press 1989).

W Kymlicka "Rethinking the Family" (1991) *Philosophy and Public Affairs* 20.

W Kymlicka (ed) *Justice in Political Philosophy* (Aldershot: Elgar 1992).

W Kymlicka *Contemporary Political Philosophy* (Oxford: Oxford University Press 1990).

W Kymlicka (ed) *The Rights of Minority Cultures.* (Oxford: Oxford University Press 1995).

W Kymlicka *Multicultural Citizenship* (Oxford: Clarendon Press 1995).

N Lacey "Normative Reconstruction in Socio-Legal Theory" (1996) 5 *Social and Legal Studies* 131.

N Lacey *Unspeakable Subjects: feminist essays in legal and social theory.* (Oxford: Hart Publishing 1998).

N Lacey and C Wells *Reconstructing Criminal Law: Text and Materials* (London: Butterworths 2nd Edn 1998).

N Lacey "Violence, Ethics and Law: Feminist Reflections on a Familiar Dilemma" in S James and S Palmer (eds) *Visible Women* (Oxford and Portland Oregon: Hart Publishing 2002) p 117ff.

N Lacey "Feminist Legal Theory and the Rights of Women in K Knop *Gender and Human Rights* (Oxford: Oxford University Press 2004) p 13ff.

H LaFollette (ed) *The Blackwell Guide to Ethical Theory* (Oxford: Blackwell 2000).

R Langton "Whose Right? Ronald Dworkin, Women and Pornographers" (1990) 19 *Philosophy and Public Affairs* 311.

R Langton "Feminism in Epistemology: Exclusion and Objectification" in M Fricker and J Hornsby (eds) *The Cambridge Companion to Feminism in Philosophy* (Cambridge: Cambridge University Press 2000) p 127–145.

G LaFrance (ed) *Ethics and Basic Rights* (Ottawa and London: Les Presses de Universite D'Ottawa 1989).

K Lennon and M Whitford (eds) *Knowing the Difference* (New York and London: Routledge 1994).

C Littleton "Reconstructing Sexual Equality" (1987) *75 California Law Review* 1279.

G Lloyd *The Man of Reason: Male and Female in Western Philosophy* (London: Methuen 1984).

G Lloyd (ed) *Feminism and History of Philosophy* (Oxford: Oxford University Press 2002).

J Locke *Two Treatises of Government* (Cambridge: Cambridge University Press 1988).

A Loux "Idols and Icons: Catharine MacKinnon and Freedom of Expression in North America" (1998) 6 *Feminist Legal Studies* 85.

J Lucas "Against Equality Again" in W Letwin (ed) *Against Equality: Readings on Economic and Social Policy* (London: Macmillan 1983).

J Lucas *On Justice* (Oxford: Clarendon Press 1980).

F Lucash (ed) *Justice and Equality Here and Now* (Ithaca and London: Cornell University Press 1986).

A MacIntyre *After Virtue* (London: Duckworth 1981).

A MacIntyre *Whose Justice? Which Rationality?* (London: Duckworth 1988).

C Mackenzie "Simone de Beauvoir: philosophy and/or the female body" in C Pateman and E Gross (eds) *Feminist Challenges: social and political theory* (London: Allen and Unwin 1986).

C Mackenzie and N Stoljar (eds) *Relational Autonomy: Feminist Perspectives on Autonomy, Agency and the Social Self* (Oxford: Oxford University Press 2000).

CA MacKinnon "Feminism Marxism Method and the State: Toward Feminist Jurisprudence" (1983) 8 *Signs Journal of Women in Culture and Society* 635.

CA MacKinnon "Reflections on Sex Equality Under Law" (1991) *100 Yale Law Journal* 1281–328.

CA MacKinnon *Feminism Unmodified: discourses on life and law* (Cambridge, Mass. and London: Harvard University Press 1987).

CA MacKinnon *Toward a Feminist Theory of the State* (Cambridge Mass. and London: Harvard University Press 1989).

CA MacKinnon *Only Words* (Cambridge Mass. and London: Harvard University Press 1993).

CA MacKinnon "Crimes of War, Crimes of Peace" in S Shute and S Hurley (eds) *On Human Rights: The Oxford Amnesty Lectures* (New York: Basic Books 1993).

CA MacKinnon "Legal Perspectives on Sexual Difference" in D Rhode (ed) *Theoretical Perspectives on Sexual Difference* (New Haven and London: Yale University Press 1990).

CA MacKinnon "Rape, Genocide and Women's Human Rights" (1994) 17 *Harvard Women's Law Journal* 5.

CA MacKinnon "Points Against Postmodernism" (2000) 75 *Chicago-Kent Law Review* 687.

CA MacKinnon "From Practice to Theory or What is a white woman anyway?" (1991) 4 *Yale Journal of Law and Feminism* 13.

CB Macpherson *Democratic Theory: Essays in Retrieval* (Oxford: Clarendon Press 1973).

G Madell "Personal Identity and the idea of a Human Being" in D Cockburn (ed) *Human Beings* (The Royal Institute of Philosophy supplement; 29: Cambridge University Press 1991) p 127–142.

M Mahoney "Women and Whiteness in Practice" (1993) 5 *Yale Journal of Law and Feminism* 217.

E Marks and de Courtivron (eds) *New French Feminisms* (Brighton: Harvester 1981).

B Marshall *Engendering Modernity: Feminism, Social Theory and Social Change* (Cambridge Polity Press 1994).

A Mason "Equality Personal Responsibility and Gender Socialisation" (2000) 100 *Proceedings in the Aristotelian Society* 227–246.

A McColgan *Women under the Law: the false promise of human rights* (Harlow: Pearson Education Ltd 2000).

D McNaughton "The Importance of Being Human" in D Cockburn (ed) *Human Beings* (The Royal Institute of Philosophy supplement; 29: Cambridge University Press 1991) p 63–81.

L McNay *Feminism and Foucault: power, gender and the self* (Cambridge: Polity Press 1992).

L McNay *Gender and Agency: reconfiguring the subject in feminist and social theory* (Cambridge: Polity Press 2000).

C Menkel-Meadow "Portia in a Different Voice" (1985) *Berkeley Women's Law Journal* 1.

T Meron "Rape as a Crime under International Humanitarian Law" (1993) 87 *American Journal of International Law* 424.

T Meron "International Crminalization of Internal Atrocities" (1995) 89 *American Journal of International Law* 554.

T Meron "War Crimes Law Comes of Age" (1998) 92 *American Journal of International Law* 462.

SE Merry "Rights Talk and the Experience of Law: Implementing Women's Human Rights to Protection from Violence" (2003) 25 *Human Rights Quarterly* 343–381.

D Meyers *Subjection and Subjectivity* (New York and London: Routledge 1994).

M Midgeley "Towards an ethic of Global Responsibility" in T Dunne and NJ Wheeler (eds) *Human Rights in Global Politics* (Cambridge: Cambridge University Press 1999) Chapter 5.

J S Mill *On Liberty and Other Essays* (New York and Oxford: Oxford University Press 1991).

K Millett *Sexual Politics* (London: Virago Press 1969).

K Millett "What is to be Done?" (2000) 75 *Chicago-Kent Law Review* 659.

J Mitchell and A Oakley *What is Feminism?* (Oxford: Basil Blackwell 1986)

J Mitchell and A Oakley *The Rights and Wrongs of Women* (Harmondsworth: Penguin 1976).

M Minow, S Kuehl ,W Murphy, D Chin-Brandt, A Scales "Perspectives on our Progress: Twenty Years of Feminist Thought" (1997) *Harvard Women's Law Journal* 1.

A Morris *Women, Crime and Criminal Justice* (Oxford: Basil Blackwell 1987).

W Morrison *Jurisprudence: from the Greeks to post-modernism* (London: Cavendish Publishing Ltd 1997).

S Motha and T Zartaloudis "Review Article: Law, Ethics and the Utopian End of Human Rights" (2003) 12 *Social and Legal Studies* 243.

S Mulhall and A Swift *Liberals and Communitarians* (2nd edn Oxford Blackwells 1992, 1996).

S Mulhall *Heidegger and Being and Time* (New York and London: Routledge 1996).

LA Mulholland "The Innate Right to be a Person" in G LaFrance (ed) *Ethics and Basic Rights* (Ottawa and London: Les Presses de l'universite d'Ottawa 1989).

VE Munro "Square Pegs in Round Holes: The Dilemma of Conjoined Twins and Individual Rights" (2001) 10 *Social and Legal Studies* 459–482.

T Murphy "Feminism on Flesh" (1997) 8 *Law and Critique* 53.

N Naffine *Female Crime: The Construction of Women in Criminology* (London: Allen and Unwin 1987).

N Naffine *Law and the Sexes: Explorations of Feminist Jurisprudence* (London: Allen and Unwin 1990).

N Naffine "The Legal Structure of Self-Ownership: Or the Self-Possessed Man and the Woman Possessed (1998) 25 *Journal of Law and Society* 193.

N Naffine (ed) *Gender and Justice* (Aldershot: Ashgate Publishing Ltd 2002).

N Naffine "Can Women be Legal Persons" in S James and S Palmer (eds) *Visible Women* (Oxford and Portland Oregon: Hart Publishing 2002).

N Naffine "Who are Law's Persons? From Cheshire Cats to Responsible Subjects" (2003) 66 *Modern Law Review* 346.

N Naffine and R Owens (eds) *Sexing the Subject of Law* (London: Sweet & Maxwell 1997).

T Nagel *The View from Nowhere* (1979) (Cambridge University Press).

J Nedelsky "Reconceiving Autonomy: Sources, Thoughts and Possibilities" (1989) 1 *Yale Journal of Law and Feminism* 7.

C N Niarchos "Women, War and Rape: Challenges Facing the International Tribunal for the Former Yugoslavia (1995) 17 *Human Rights Quarterly* 649.

L Nicholson *The Play of Reason: from the modern to the postmodern* (Buckingham: Open University Press 1999).

L Nicholson (ed) *Feminism/Postmodernism* (New York and London: Routledge 1990).

C S Nino *The Ethics of Human Rights* (Oxford: Clarendon Press 1991).

R Norman "Does Equality destroy liberty" in K Graham (ed) *Contemporary Political Philosophy* (Cambridge: Cambridge University Press 1982).

A Norrie (ed) *Closure or Critique: new directions in legal theory* (Edinburgh: Edinburgh University Press 1993).

M C Nussbaum "Objectication" (1995) 24 *Philosophy and Public Affairs* 249.

M C Nussbaum "The Sleep of Reason..." *The Tones Higher* 2 Feb 1996.

M C Nussbaum *Sex and Social Justice*. Oxford: Oxford University Press 1999).

M C Nussbaum *Women and Human Development* (Cambridge: Cambridge University Press 2000).

M C Nussbaum "The Professor of Parody" (1999) *New Republic* 22 Feb 1999 at 37.

M C Nussbaum *Sex, Preference and Family: essays on law and nature* (New York and Oxford: Oxford University Press 1997).

M C Nussbaum and A Sen (eds) *The Quality of Life* (Oxford: Oxford University Press 1993).

J O'Brien "The International Tribunal for Violations of International Humanitarian Law in the Former Yugoslavia" (1993) 87 *American Journal of International Law* 639.

M O'Brien *The Politics of Reproduction* (London: Routledge 1981)

K O'Donovan *Sexual Divisions in the Law* (London: Weidenfeld & Nicholson 1985).

K O'Donovan "Engendering Justice: Women's Perspectives and the Rule of Law" (1989) 39 *University of Toronto Law Journal* 127.

K O'Donovan "With sense, consent, or just a con? Legal subjects in the discourse of autonomy" in N Naffine and R Owens (eds) *Sexing the Subject of Law* (London: Sweet & Maxwell 1997).

S M Okin *Women in Western Political Thought* (Princeton, NJ: Princeton University Press 1979).

S M Okin *Justice, Gender and the Family*. (New York: Basic Books 1989).

S M Okin "Reason and Feeling in Thinking about Justice" (1989) 99 *Ethics* 229.

S M Okin "Gilligan's work: Thinking like a Woman" in D Rhode (ed) *Theoretical Perspectives on Sexual Difference* (New Haven and London: Yale University Press 1990).

S M Okin "Is Multiculturism Bad for Women?" in J Cohen, M Howard and MC Nussbaum (eds) *Is Multiculturalism Bad for Women? Susan Moller Okin with respondents* (Princeton, NJ: Princeton University Press 1999).

J Oloka-Onyango and S Tamale "'The Personal is Political' or Why Women's Rights are Indeed Human Rights: An African Perspective on International Feminism" (1995) 17 *Human Rights Quarterly* 691–731.

F Olsen (ed) *Feminist Legal Theory* (Vols 1 and 2) (London: Dartmouth 1995).

F Olsen "The Family and the Market" in F Olsen (ed) *Feminist Legal Theory* (Vols 1 and 2) (London: Dartmouth 1995).

F Olsen "Feminist Theory in Grand Style" (1989) 89 *Columbia Law Review* 1147.

O O'Neill *Bounds of Justice* (Cambridge: Cambridge University Press 2000).

O O'Neill *Autonomy and Trust in Bioethics* (Cambridge: Cambridge University Press 2002).

N Owen (ed) *Human Rights: Human Wrongs: The Oxford Amnesty Lectures 2001* (Oxford: Oxford University Press 2002).

S Palmer "Feminism and the Promise of Human Rights, Possibilities and Paradoxes" in S James and S Palmer (eds) *Visible Women* (Oxford and Portland Oregon: Hart Publishing 2002) p 91ff.

S Parsons "Feminism and the Logic of Morality: A Conclusion of Alternatives" in E Frazer et al (eds) *Ethics, A Feminist Reader* (London: Blackwell 1992).

C Pateman *The Sexual Contract* (Cambridge: Polity Press 1988).

C Pateman and E Gross (eds) *Feminist Challenges: social and political theory* (London: Allen and Unwin 1986).

C Pateman "Feminist Critiques of the Public/Private Dichotomy" in A Phillips (ed) *Feminism and Equality* (Oxford: Basil Blackwell 1987).

A Patten *Hegel's Idea of Freedom* (Oxford: Oxford University Press 1999).

J Penner, D Schiff and R Nobles (eds) Jurisprudence and Legal Theory: Commentary and Materials (London: Butterworths LexisNexis 2002).

J Peters and A Wolper (eds) *Women's Rights Human Rights: International Perspectives* (New York and London: Routledge 1995).

A Phillips (ed) *Feminism and Equality* (Oxford: Basil Blackwell 1987).

A Phillips *Democracy and Difference* (Cambridge Polity Press 1993).

A Phillips *Which Equalities Matter*? (Cambridge: Polity Press 1999).

A Phillips "Feminism and the Politics of Difference. Or, Where Have All the Women Gone?" in S James and S Palmer (eds) *Visible Women* (Oxford and Portland Oregon: Hart Publishing 2002) p 11ff.

J Pietarinen "Early Liberalism and Women's Liberty" in AJ Arnaud and E Kingdom (eds) *Women's Rights and the Rights of Man* (Aberdeen: Aberdeen University Press 1990) ch 12.

R Plant *Modern Political Thought* (Oxford: Blackwell 1991).

Plato *The Laws* (Loeb Classical Library 1968).

Plato *The Republic* (Harmondsworth: Penguin Books 1987).

T Pogge *Realizing Rawls* (Ithaca and London: Cornell University Press 1989).

J Radcliffe Richards *The Sceptical Feminist: a philosophical enquiry* (Harmonsworth: Penguin Books 1982).

M Ramsay *What's Wrong with Liberalism* (London: Leicester University Press 1997).

A Rao "The Politics of Gender and Culture in International Human Rights Discourse" in J Peters and A Wolper *Women's Rights Human Rights: International Feminist Perspectives* (New York and London: Routledge 1995) at 167–75.

J Rawls J *A Theory of Justice*. (Oxford: Oxford University Press 1971).

J Rawls *Political Liberalism* (New York: Columbia University Press 1993).

J Rawls "Fairness to Goodness" (1975) 84 *Philosophical Review* 537.

J Raz *The Morality of Freedom* (Oxford: Clarendon Press 1986).

B Redhead (ed) *Plato to Nato: Studies in Political Thought* (London: Penguin Books 1995).

H Reece *Divorcing Responsibly* (Oxford: Hart 2003)

D Rhode *Justice and Gender* (Cambridge Mass. and London: Harvard University Press 1989).

D Rhode (ed) *Theoretical Perspectives on Sexual Difference* (New Haven and London: Yale University Press 1990).

A Rich *Of Woman Born* (London: Virago 1976).

P Riley "How Coherent is the Social Contract Tradition?" *Journal of the History of Ideas* 34 (1973) 543–562.

P Riley *Will and Political Legitimacy: A Critical Exposition of Social Contract Theory in Hobbes, Locke, Rousseau, Kant and Hegel* (London: Harvard University Press 1982).

C Romany "Themes for a Conversation on Race and Gender in International Human Rights Law" in A K Wing (ed) *Global Critical Race Feminism* (London: NY University Press 2000) at 57.

C Romany "State Responsibility Goes Private: A Feminist Critique of the Public/Private Distinction in International Human Rights Law" in R J Cook (ed) *Human Rights of Women* (Philadelphia: University of Pennsylvania Press 1994) p 85ff.

R Rorty "Feminism and Pragmatism" (1991) 30 *Mich Q Rev* 231.

R Rorty "Human Rights Rationality and Sentimentality" in S Shute and S Hurley (eds) *On Human Rights: the Oxford Amnesty Lectures* (New York: Basic Books 1993).

J J Rousseau *The Essential Rousseau* (L Bair trans. New York and Scarborough Ontario: The New American Library Inc. 1974).

J J Rousseau The Social Contract (Harmonsworth: Penguin Books 1968).

A Ryan (ed) *Justice* (Oxford: Oxford University Press 1993).

A Ryan (ed) *The Idea of Freedom: Essays in Honour of Isaiah Berlin* (Oxford: Oxford University Press 1979).

A Sachs and J Hoff Wilson *Sexism and the Law: A Study of Male Beliefs in Britain and the United States* (Oxford: Martin Robertson 1978).

M Sandel *Liberalism and the Limits of Justice* (Cambridge: Cambridge University Press 1982, 2nd Edn 1998).

R Sandland "Seeing Double? Or Why 'To be or not to be' is (not) the question for feminist legal studies" (1998) 7 *Social Legal Studies* 307.

R Sandland "Between Truth and Difference: Poststructuralism, Law and the power of feminism" (1995) 3 *Feminist Legal Studies* 3.

R Sandland "The Mirror and The Veil: Reading the Imaginary Domain" (1998) 6 *Feminist Legal Studies* 33.

B de Santos *Toward a New Common Sense* (New York and London: Routledge 1995).

M Saward "A Critique of Held" in B Holden (ed) *Global Democracy: Key Debates* (New York and London: Routledge 2000).

A Scales "The Emergence of Feminist Jurisprudence: An Essay" (1986) 95 *Yale Law Journal* 1373.

P Schlag "Normative and Nowhere to Go" (1990) 43 *Stanford Law Review* 167.

J Schroeder "Taming the Shrew: the liberal attempt to mainstream radical feminist theory" (1992) 5 *Journal of Law and Feminism* 123.

J Schroeder "Catharine's Wheel MacKinnon's Pornography Analysis" (1993) 38 *New York Law School Law Review* 225.

J Schroeder *The Vestal and the Fasces: Hegel, Lacan, Property and the Feminine* (London: University of California Press 1998).

W Schroeder "Continental Ethics" in H LaFollette *The Blackwell Guide to Ethical Theory* (Oxford: Blackwell 2000).

S Schulhofer "Taking Sexual Autonomy Seriously" (1992) 1 *Law and Philosophy* 35.

JW Scott "Deconstructing Equality-versus-Difference: Or the uses of Poststructural Theory for feminism" in F Olsen (ed) *Feminist Legal Theory Vol I* (London: Dartmouth 1995).

L Seidentop "Two Traditions" in A Ryan (ed) *The Idea of Freedom: Essays in Honour of Isaiah Berlin* (Oxford: Oxford University Press 1979).

P Selznick "Dworkin's Unfinished Task" (1989) 77 *California Law Review* 505.

S Sevenhuijsen *Citizenship and the Ethics of Care: Feminist Considerations on Justice, Morality and Politics* (New York and London: Routledge 1998).

M L Shanley and C Pateman (eds) *Feminist Interpretations and Political Theory* (Cambridge: Polity Press 1991).

S Shute and S Hurley (eds) *On Human Rights The Oxford Amnesty Lectures* (New York: Basic Books 1993).

NE Simmonds *Central Issues in Jurisprudence: Justice, Law and Rights* (2nd Edn London: Sweet and Maxwell 2002).

P Singer *Ethics* (Oxford: Oxford University Press 1994).

R Singh *Gender Autonomy in Western Europe: An imprecise revolution* (Hampshire and London Macmillan Press Ltd 1989).

Q Skinner "The Idea of Negative Liberty: Philosophical and Historical Perspective" in R Rorty et al (eds) *Philosophy in History* (Cambridge: Cambridge University Press 1984).

C Smart "The Woman of Legal Discourse" (1992) 1 *Social and Legal Studies* 29.

C Smart *Feminism and the Power of Law* (New York and London:Routledge 1989).

C Smart Law "Feminism and Sexuality" (1994) 9 *Canadian Journal of Law and Society* 15.

RKM Smith *Textbook on International Human Rights* (2nd Edn Oxford: Oxford University Press 2005)

J Sohrab "Avoiding the Exquisite Trap: A Critical Look at the Equal Treatment/Special Treatment Debate in Law" (1993) 1 *Feminist Legal Studies* 141.

E Spelman "How Do they See Me? (Review of Sex and Social Justice and Women and Human Development by Martha Nussbaum.)" *London Review of Books* 16 November 2000 (11).

V Spike Peterson and L Parisi "Are women human? It's not an academic question." in T Evans (ed) *HR Fifty Years on 1998* 132 (Manchester: Manchester University Press 1998).

L Strauss and J Cropsey (ed) *History of Political Philosophy* (3rd Edn Chicago and London: University of Chicago Press 1987).

C Sunstein "Feminism and Legal Theory" (1988) 101 *Harvard Law Review* 826.

R H Tawney *Equality* (London: Unwin Books 1964).

C Taylor "Atomism" in S Avineri and A De-Shalit (ed) *Communitarianism and Individualism* (Oxford: Oxford University Press 1992).

C Taylor "What's Wrong with negative liberty" in A Ryan (ed) *The Idea of Freedom: Essays in Honour of Isaiah Berlin* (Oxford: Oxford University Press 1979).

C Taylor "The Politics of Recognition" in A Gutmann ((ed) *Multiculturism and the Politics of Recognition* (Princeton NJ: Princeton University Press 1994).

C Taylor *Sources of the Self* (Cambridge: Cambridge University Press 1989).

C Taylor *Hegel* (Cambridge: Cambridge University Press 1975).

J Tempkin *Rape and the Legal Process* (Oxford: Oxford University Press 2nd Edn 2002).

K Tomasevski *Women and Human Rights* (London: Zed Books UN N-G Liaison Service 1993).

J Tronto *Caring for Democracy: A Feminist Vision* (Utrecht 1995).

W Twining *Globalisation and Legal Theory* London: Butterworths 2000).

United Nations *The World's Women 1995 Trends and Statistics* (New York: United Nations 1995).

P Van Ness (ed) *Debating Human Rights: Critical Essays From the United States and Asia* (New York and London: Routledge 1999).

P Viseur Sellers "The Context of Sexual Violence: Sexual Violence as Violations of International Humanitarian Law" in G McDonald and O Swak-Goldman (eds) *Substantive and Procedural Aspects of International Criminal Law* (2000) at 263ff.

P Viseur Sellers "Individual(s') Liability for Collective Sexual Violence" in K Knop (ed) *Gender and Human Rights* (Oxford: Oxford University Press 2004)

M Walzer *Spheres of Justice* (New York: Basic Books 1983).

P Ward Scaltsas "Women as ends – Women as means" in AJ Arnaud and E Kingdom *Women's Rights and the Rights of Man* (Aberdeen: Aberdeen University Press 1990).

I Ward *Law and Literature: Possibilities and Perspectives* (Cambridge: Cambridge University Press 1995).

M Warnock *Existentialist Ethics* (London: Macmillan 1967).

K Weeks *Constituting Feminist Subjects* (Ithaca and London: Cornell University Press 1998).

R West "The Difference in Women's Hedonic Lives: A Phenomenological Critique of Feminist Legal Theory" (1987) 3 *Wisconsin Women's Law Journal* 81–145.

R West "Jurisprudence and Gender" (1988) 55 *Univ of Chicago Law Rev* 1.

R West "Love, Rage and Legal Theory" (1989) 1 *Yale Journal of Law and Feminism* 101.

R West *Law, Narrative and Authority* (Ann Arbor: University of Michigan Press 1993).

R West *Caring for Justice* (New York: New York University Press 1997).

R West (ed) *Rights: 2$^{nd}$ Series the International Library of Essays in Law and Legal Theory* (Hants: Dartmouth 2001).

R West *Re-Imagining Justice* (Aldershot: Ashgate 2003)

I Whelehan *Modern Feminist Thought.* (Englewood Cliffs, NJ: Edinburgh Hall 1995).

JB White *Heracles' Bow: essays on the rhetoric and poetics of law* (Madison Wis.: University of Wisconsin Press 1985).

JB White *Justice As Translation: An Essay in Cultural and Legal Criticism* (Chicago: University of Chicago 1990).

JB White "What's Wrong with out Talk about Race" (2002) 100 *Michigan Law Review* 1927.

JB White *Acts of Hope: Creating Authority in Literature Law and Politics* (Chicago and London: University of Chicago Press 1994).

M Whitford *The Irigaray Reader* (Oxford: Basil Blackwell 1991).

B Williams "The Idea of Equality" in H Bedau (ed) *Justice and Equality.* (Englewood Cliffs, New Jersey: Prentice-Hall 1971).

J Williams "Deconstructing Gender" (1987) 87 *Michigan Law Review* 797.

J Williams "Good International Citizenship" in N Dower and J Williams (eds) *Global Citizenship: A Critical Reader* (Edinburgh: Edinburgh University Press 2002) p 41ff.

P Williams *The Alchemy of Race and Rights* (Cambridge Mass.: Harvard University Press 1991).

P Williams *Seeing A Color-Blind Future: the paradox of race: the 1997 Reith Lectures* (London Virago 1997).

A K Wing (ed) *Global Critical Race Feminism* (London: NY University Press 2000).

M Wittig *The Straight Mind and other essays* (New York: Harvester Wheatsheaf 1992).

J Wolff *An Introduction to Political Philosophy* (Oxford: Oxford University Press 1996).

S Wolfram "Husband and Wife are one person: the husband (Nineteenth-century English aphorism)" in AJ Arnaud and E Kingdom (eds) *Women's Rights and the Rights of Man* (Aberdeen: Aberdeen University Press 1990).

M Wollstonecraft *The Vindication of the Rights of Women* (1792: London: Dent 1990).

E Wright *Lacan and Postfeminism* (Cambridge: Icon Books Ltd 2000).

B Yack "The Problem with Kantian Liberalism" in R Beiner and W J Booth *Kant and Political Philosophy The Contemporary Legacy* (New Haven and London: Yale University Press 1993).

I Young *Justice and the Politics of Difference* (Princeton, NJ: Princeton University Press 1990).

R Young *Personal Autonomy Beyond Negative and Positive Liberty* (London: Croom Helm 1986).

# Appendix I

Relevant Extracts from: the Statute of the International Criminal Tribunal for the Former Yugoslavia 32 ILM (1993) 1203

## Article 2 – Grave breaches of the Geneva Conventions of 1949
The International Tribunal shall have the power to prosecute persons committing or ordering to be committed grave breaches of the Geneva Conventions of 12 August 1949, namely the following acts against persons or property protected under the provisions of the relevant Geneva Convention:
(a)  wilful killing;
(b)  torture or inhuman treatment, including biological experiments;
(c)  wilfully causing great suffering or serious injury to body or health;
(d)  extensive destruction and appropriation of property, not justified by military necessity and carried out unlawfully and wantonly;
(e)  compelling a prisoner of war or a civilian to serve in the forces of a hostile power;
(f)  wilfully depriving a prisoner of war or a civilian of the rights of fair and regular trial;
(g)  unlawful deportation or transfer or unlawful confinement of a civilian;
(h)  taking civilians as hostages.

## Article 3 – Violations of the laws or customs of war
The International Tribunal shall have the power to prosecute persons violating the laws or customs of war. Such violations shall include, but not be limited to:
(a)  employment of poisonous weapons or other weapons calculated to cause unnecessary suffering;
(b)  wanton destruction of cities, towns or villages, or devastation not justified by military necessity;
(c)  attack, or bombardment, by whatever means, of undefended towns, villages, dwellings, or buildings;
(d)  seizure of, destruction or wilful damage done to institutions dedicated to religion, charity and education, the arts and sciences, historic monuments and works of art and science;
(e)  plunder of public or private property.

## Article 4 – Genocide
1.  The International Tribunal shall have the power to prosecute persons committing genocide as defined in paragraph 2 of this article or of committing any of the other acts enumerated in paragraph 3 of this article.
2.  Genocide means any of the following acts committed with intent to destroy, in whole or in part, a national, ethical, racial or religious group, as such:

(a)  killing members of the group;
(b)  causing serious bodily or mental harm to members of the group;
(c)  deliberately inflicting on the group conditions of life calculated to bring about its physical destruction in whole or in part;
(d)  imposing measures intended to prevent births within the group;
(e)  forcibly transferring children of the group to another group;
3.  The following acts shall be punishable:
(a)  genocide;
(b)  conspiracy to commit genocide;
(c)  direct and public incitement to commit genocide;
(d)  attempt to commit genocide;
(e)  complicity in genocide.

**Article 5 – Crimes against humanity**
      The International Tribunal shall have the power to prosecute persons responsible for the following crimes when committed in armed conflict, whether international or internal in character, and directed against any civilian population:
(a)  murder;
(b)  extermination;
(c)  enslavement;
(d)  deportation;
(e)  imprisonment;
(f)  torture;
(g)  rape;
(h)  persecutions on political, racial and religious grounds;
(i)  other inhumane acts.

# Appendix II

Relevant Extracts from: the Rome Statute for an International Criminal Court 1998.

The Statute of the International Criminal Court entered into force on 1 July 2002 and from that date the International Criminal Court was in existence.

## Article 5 – Crimes within the jurisdiction of the Court
1.  The jurisdiction of the Court shall be limited to the most serious crimes of concern to the international community as a whole. The Court has jurisdiction in accordance with this Statute with respect to the following crimes:
(a)  The crime of genocide;
(b)  Crimes against humanity;
(c)  War crimes;
(d)  The crime of aggression.

## Article 7 – Crimes against humanity
1.  For the purposes of this Statute "crime against humanity" means any of the following acts when committed as part of a widespread or systematic attack directed against any civilian population, with knowledge of the attack.
...
(g) Rape, sexual slavery, enforced prostitution, forced pregnancy, enforced sterilization, or any other form of sexual violence of comparable gravity;
...

## Article 8 – War crimes
1.  The Court shall have jurisdiction in respect of war crimes in particular when committed as part of a plan or policy or as part of a large-scale commission of such crimes.
2.  [paragraph 2 (b) contains a compilation of norms from precedents other than the grave breaches provisions of the Geneva Conventions.
(b) (xxii) Committing rape, sexual slavery, enforced prostitution, forced pregnancy, ...enforced sterilization, or any other form of sexual violence also constituting a grave breach of the Geneva Conventions;
...

# Table of Cases

# Table of Treaties, Legislation and International Instruments

# Index

*see also* self-reflection
critical theory 8
cultural feminism 14, 57, 61, 62
cultural rights 140–1

de Beauvoir, Simone 34, 36n100
deconstruction 8, 16, 73–4, 77–9, 83,
    88–90
  feminist projects of reconstruction 75
  rights discourse 80–1, 82
  "utopian moment within" 120
Derrida, Jacques 78n27
Descartes, René 17, 22–3
desires 96, 103, 109–10, 111, 112, 118
despotism 101
determinism 64–5
difference feminism 30, 57
"difference/sameness" debate 7, 57–8
discrimination
  international law 135, 138, 142
  Universal Declaration of Human
    Rights 140
Douzinas, C 104n23, 107n39
Drakopoulou, M. 55n74
Dworkin, Andrea 113, 149
Dworkin, Ronald 51–2, 67, 80

Eastern Europe 7
"economic man" 68n137, n138
egalitarian feminism 57
egoism 42
Eisenstein, Zillah 50–1
Elshtain, Jean Bethke 31n75
emotions 33, 40, 112, 118
empathy 55, 65, 69, 116
empowerment 123, 135, 144, 147
  agency 93, 96
  narrative method 122
epistemology 63n115
equality 29, 37, 38, 43, 60, 112
  claims for legal rights 131
  confusion with uniformity 57
  global citizenship 134
  jurisprudence 138
  liberalism 6, 34, 51–2, 80
  Mill 17
  as moral value 50
  power relations 111
  pre-social ideal 70
  reconstruction of 121
  "sameness/difference" debate 58

social deformation of 54
state of nature 20–1, 40
unity of subject and community 122
Universal Declaration of Human
    Rights 140
essentialism 8, 15, 16, 81, 86, 94
  anti-essentialism 75, 83–4
  Cornell 62n111
  denial of 73
  fixed identity 146
  "human core" 111
  liberal individual 46
  MacKinnon 113, 114
  Mill 24–5
  postmodern rejection of 76–7, 82, 90
  the self 28, 35
ethic of care 7, 14, 44, 52–71, 116–17
  creative ways of thinking 68–71
  critiques of 65
  global world order 132
  interconnection and relational ways of
    being 60–8
  moral consciousness of humanity 135
  reasoning process 55–60
ethics
  global 129
  Hegelian 8, 95, 97, 116
  normative 1–2
  *see also* morality
ethnicity 78
European Court of Human Rights 158
existentialism 34, 123

fairness 53, 54, 56
family
  feminist critique of liberalism 119
  Mill 24
  public-private distinction 27–8, 30
  Rawls 25–6
  social construction of family role 30,
    31
femininity
  moral thinking 53
  passions 33, 103
  social reality of 66
  stereotypes of 81
  subordination 116
  transcendence 31–2, 33n86, 34, 35,
    36, 39
  *see also* women
feminism